THE OX

The Ox

The Last of the Great Rock Stars

The Authorised Biography of
The Who's John Entwistle

Paul Rees

CONSTABLE

CONSTABLE

First published in Great Britain in 2020 by Constable

13 5 7 9 10 8 6 4 2

Copyright © Paul Rees, 2020

A CIP catalogue record for this book
is available from the British Library.

ISBN: 978-1-47212-938-3 (hardback)
ISBN: 978-1-47212-939-0 (trade paperback)

Typeset in Palatino LT Std by SX Composing DTP, Rayleigh, Essex
Printed and bound in Great Britain by Clays Ltd, Elcograf S.P.A.

Papers used by Constable are from well-managed forests
and other responsible sources.

Constable
An imprint of
Little, Brown Book Group
Carmelite House
50 Victoria Embankment
London EC4Y 0DZ

An Hachette UK Company
www.hachette.co.uk

www.littlebrown.co.uk

This one's for Chris and Alison – for their trust and
so much more

Contents

Contents

Prologue

Lord of the Manor

Quarwood was resplendent on summer's afternoons such as this in June 2002. With its Gothic edifices of Cotswold stone and its many windows cast in an amber sunlight, the grand old Victorian rectory house appeared truly baronial, regal even. The impression was strengthened by the immediate surroundings. Laid out in front of the house was a sweeping, immaculate croquet lawn of vivid, dappled green. Off to the rear was a verdant expanse of woodland and, beyond that, a vista of dimpled hills that rolled gently to the horizon. All of this was so wondrous that one might overlook the tell-tale signs of decay that were dotted about the fifty-five-room house and its forty acres of land. Chipped masonry, flaked paintwork, or even the dilapidated pool house, the pool itself cracked and drained of water.

On this particular day, the self-styled lord of the manor these past twenty-six years rose from his bed around noon. He was still recovering from a recent bout of 'flu, which had laid him up for several days. Also, he was likely bleary-eyed and thick-headed from indulging too much the night before, which these days

1

was all too often the case. Lisa Pritchett-Johnson, his American girlfriend, might have invited a gaggle of folk up to the house from their local pub in the nearby town of Stow-on-the-Wold. He would have hardly even known most of their names, but all of them would have raided the fully-stocked bar he kept downstairs and helped themselves to his drugs. Like pigs at a trough, they might have gone on gorging till dawn with Lisa cajoling them, always one drink and a line ahead of everyone else. He could not have cared less for any of them, but he would have joined in regardless. It never was his style to be a bystander at a party and especially not one of his own.

Lisa would be left to sleep off her own hangover. He knew full well that if she was not, she would be in a foul mood all the rest of the day and be itching to pick a fight. Not that there had to be a reason any more for the two of them to start with each other. These bouts would escalate until they became vicious, spiteful and destructive, their raised voices and the bangs and crashes that resulted echoing around the halls and staircases.

Once he was up, he followed a well-established routine; he dressed in a crisp cowboy shirt, fresh-pressed jeans and a pair of moccasins, which would be changed for Cuban-heel boots whenever he left the house. Not a crease in sight, or a hair out of place. Hung around his neck on a silver chain was a jewelled spider, gleaming with ruby-red eyes.

From his bedroom suite on the first floor, he walked down the cantilevered staircase and the length of the ground floor to the vast kitchen. Sat there, alone at a long, wooden table, a television silently flickering in one corner, he drank tea from a double-sized mug emblazoned with the image of a medieval knight and into which he dunked one, two, three chocolate biscuits. In between, he smoked a couple of cigarettes and otherwise passed the time poring over the crossword in his daily newspaper.

It was according to this precise order of things that John Entwistle began virtually every day at Quarwood. There was, though, a variation in the usual routine today, brought about by a more eccentric aspect of his nature. He was prone to have whimsical, and usually grandiose, notions pop into his head and would then be compelled to act upon them. On this occasion, he had on impulse thought about planting a Chilean monkey puzzle tree in front of the house. With him being so wilfully extravagant, a potted sapling, such as one that could be picked up from the local garden centre, simply would not do. No, he had determined instead to plant a mighty specimen on his land, one three feet wide at its base and that towered fifteen, sixteen . . . hell, maybe even *twenty* feet tall. The kind of tree, in fact, that would have to be transported by a team of workmen, a flat-bed truck and a crane.

As just this combination rumbled up the half-mile driveway that wound towards the main house, Entwistle sprang into action. Bounding outdoors, he made clear his intention to assist with the planting and this was entirely out of character. At fifty-seven, besides walking his Irish Wolfhound and Rottweiler dogs, he had not undertaken any kind of strenuous physical exercise since running the hundred-yard dash at Acton County Grammar School in the distant 1950s. Even when he was onstage with his band, The Who, where singer Roger Daltrey, guitarist Pete Townshend and former drummer Keith Moon had jumped, lurched, windmilled and generally thrown themselves about, he stood stock still as their statuesque bassist. What's more, long after the others had sworn off – or, in the case of Moon, succumbed to – excesses of booze and drugs, he roistered on. Nightly, he drank copious quantities of fine brandies and vintage red wines and he was systematically blowing his way through thousands of pounds a month on cocaine. Added to that, he chain-smoked and had a terrible diet, principally made up of red meat and deep-fried food.

Doubtless, the workmen that early afternoon could sense that he was vulnerable. When the time came for the tree to be lowered into the ground and Entwistle moved to steady it in place, in unison they exhorted him to step out of the way. He paid them no mind, or actually didn't hear them, since years of playing extremely loud rock music had rendered him all but deaf. Either way, he still stood there, legs splayed, when the crane jerked and pitched. The tree went with it, and a single great branch, leaf spikes as sharp as needle points, was sent jack-knifing up into his crotch, near enough lifting him off his feet. Looking on was Entwistle's grown-up, first-born and only son, Christopher, who had also been commandeered to help with the task. 'Dad swore, threw a couple of things and then stomped back into the house,' he recalls. 'The rest of us carried on and finished the job off without him.'

The planting of the monkey puzzle tree is one of the final memories that Christopher has of his father. It was, too, the last of Entwistle's grand gestures at Quarwood and an altogether fitting one. In all of its over-reaching and haphazardness, it was entirely reflective of how the twilight years of his rollercoaster life had panned out.

■ ■ ■

Entwistle's contemporary and fellow bassist, the former Rolling Stone, Bill Wyman, once dubbed him 'the Jimi Hendrix of the bass guitar'. This was meant as the highest compliment but, with it, Wyman also inadvertently conjured the very demon that would haunt Entwistle throughout his professional life. Indisputably, he was a virtuoso musician, easily the most accomplished player in The Who. He was also a trailblazer on the bass, playing it with a kind of boundless invention that no one else had done before, and precious few have managed since. The problem for him was that his chosen instrument *was* the bass guitar.

In both the popular perception and actual hierarchy of almost every band, the singer is seen to be front and centre of attention, the standard-bearer; the lead guitarist is the creative lynchpin, the driving force and General; and the bassist and drummer, respectively set to one side and the rear, are dutiful infantrymen. This was almost as true of The Who as any other group, save for the fact that Moon, when he was alive, was able through the wild, kinetic abandon of his playing and the careering craziness of his personality, to force himself between Daltrey and Townshend and into the spotlight. That left solid, steadfast-seeming Entwistle to fill the part of anchor, and makeweight. Next to strutting Daltrey, mercurial Townshend and nutcase Moon, it was his lot to be seen as the straight man; by comparison, he appeared sensible, reliable and, as such, dully conservative.

No matter that on The Who's 1965 signature single, 'My Generation', and ever after, Entwistle's bass was just as much the lead instrument as Townshend's guitar. Together, indeed, they were the two primary sources of the band's primal, inexorable power. Nor that Entwistle, proficient, too, on numerous brass instruments, came to assume the role of arranger-in-chief, most notably on Townshend's two magnum opuses, *Tommy* from 1969, and 1973's *Quadrophenia*. Or even that he was the only band member other than Townshend to write consistently for the band, and enduring standards, too: witness 'My Wife'; 'Fiddle About'; 'Cousin Kevin'; and 'Boris the Spider', which for years was their most requested song on tour.

The first nickname that Entwistle had bestowed upon him was indicative of this view of him in the band. Not for him the swagger of Daltrey's 'Rock God', the mystique of Townshend's 'Mad Genius', or the buccaneering extremes of Moon's 'The

Loon'. He became 'The Quiet One'. He grew to disdain this handle so much that he even wrote a song about it for The Who's 1981 album, *Face Dances*. On 'The Quiet One', he sang, 'Still waters run deep, so be careful I don't drown you,' adding, for good measure, 'I ain't quiet . . . everybody else is too loud.'

Continuously, he was nagged and pained by feelings of being misconstrued and underappreciated, by the others in The Who just as much as by the public in general. Though he rarely articulated it to anyone else, the injustice of it festered and burned deep down in his gut, like acid indigestion. Over time, he found ways to compensate. Onstage, he made sure to set his bass at a louder volume than anyone else in the band. Eventually, the backline wall of amplifiers that he played through grew to be so high and imposing that it was christened 'Little Manhattan' by The Who's crew. The unholy racket drove Daltrey in particular to apoplectic rages, and which only made him turn it up even more. It ruined his hearing as a consequence, but it was almost worth it to goad the preening singer to such an extent.

Among those who knew and worked with The Who, Entwistle was the best liked out of the band. Whereas Daltrey could be sullen, Townshend brooding and Moon unhinged, he comported himself with a measure of dignity, like a proper English gentleman, as many would observe. Somehow, this was even the case when he was carousing with Moon, who was the closest Entwistle had to a best friend and ally. Often as not, the bassist would be the instigator of their high jinks but, unlike Moon, who would barrel on regardless of any hurt or damage he was liable to cause, he retained an air of detached decency.

Offstage, he nevertheless resolved to live the devil-may-care life of a rock star to the absolute full. To such an end, he spent money like there was no tomorrow, as if it were sand slipping through his fingers. He bought a fleet of cars – Rollers, Bentleys and Cadillacs – even though he never bothered to learn to drive; he acquired the biggest private collection of bass guitars in the world, hundreds of them, worth a fortune; he accumulated wardrobes full of clothes, boots and jewellery; he stuffed drawers, cupboards and whole rooms with other precious 'treasure' such as antique weaponry, assorted gadgets and plaster-cast fish. His other appetites were just as voracious and unquenchable – for women, booze, cocaine, pills, fags and food.

Even though he carried on in this bacchanalian manner for more than a quarter of a century, it didn't appear to have any debilitating effect upon him whatsoever. For the longest time, no one close to The Who could recall him ever being fall-down drunk or otherwise indisposed. Playing live or in the recording studio, his brilliance was undimmed whatever he might have imbibed or put up his nose. Always, his playing would be so fluid, so daring and so outrageous that it would take one's breath away.

In due course, his iron constitution earned him a second nickname within the camp – 'The Ox'. In this instance, he liked it enough to use it as the name for his first solo band. It became a badge of honour, an acknowledgement that he was one of the last standing of a breed of reckless souls now tamed, wrecked or dead. And therein was the trouble – he grew to trust that he really must be unbreakable, indestructible. Whereas Moon killed himself and Townshend had to dry out, Entwistle believed that he knew his own limits and it emboldened him to go on living at a relentless pace, as if, for him, there could not possibly be a reckoning. About that much, he was to be proved sadly, utterly wrong. To begin with, he just became careless. There would be the odd night when he would have to be helped home to his bed, or the rare show where he couldn't quite scale his usual heights. Then, things became more serious.

By that summer of 2002, the toll on him from every goblet of brandy, line of coke, fish-and-chip supper, pack of cigarettes and long, long night had become all too evident. Much earlier, he had stopped dyeing his hair so it had been left to grey naturally, but now his pallor was just as ashen. He was overweight, often out of breath. Like his mother, he had for years been afflicted with high blood pressure and rampant levels of cholesterol. And he was depressed at the poisonous state of his relationship with Lisa. All things considered, he was a ticking time bomb.

That same month of June, The Who, disbanded by Townshend in 1982 and reformed by him seven years later having been elevated to rock icon status, were about to embark on their latest tour of North America. In spite of his various ailments, Entwistle was passed fit to go back out on the road and he was relishing the prospect. After all, ever since The Who had started to have hit records, when he was still living at home in west London with his domineering mother and despised stepfather, he had wanted nothing more than to be off with the band. Once in the unreal, dream-like state of being on tour, he received the attention and adulation he craved, balms for all of his insecurities and self-doubts and granted a licence to indulge his whims and vices. As it happened, Entwistle flew out to Las Vegas for the first date of the tour, but never again made it so far as the stage. Some time in the morning of Thursday, 27 June 2002, his broken, exhausted heart finally gave out on him.

The circumstances of his passing made headlines around the world, involving as it did both casual sex and illicit drugs. In these respects, he seemed to the end to be the archetypal rock-'n'-roller. Yet the truth of the matter is that much more than that – The Ox's is a complicated, heroic, funny, dark, glorious, tragic and very human tale.

■ ■ ■

In 1990, flush from his share of the profits from The Who's first major reunion tour which had gone ahead the previous year, Entwistle rented a stately pile in Connemara, on the west coast of Ireland. There, he meant to settle to the task of writing up his own story. He jotted down his first rush of reminiscences in books of lined A4 notepaper, his handwriting in pencil and biro neat and ordered. After that, he started to type up the actual book. He was a one-fingered typist, so the work was slow and painstaking.

Ultimately, like so many other courses of action that he embarked upon during his life, he never did get around to completing the book. Even in rural Ireland, there were just too many other distractions. Perhaps he reasoned that life was meant for living and too short to be wasted on looking back; maybe he tired of being engaged in something that didn't bring him instant gratification, or for which at that precise moment in time he was not being well paid. In any event, he left behind just four finished chapters and a sprawl of notes. Among the latter is a brief, elliptical draft of what he meant to be his own author's biography which illuminates the arch, sardonic side of his personality.

'John Entwistle was born a long time ago,' he began. 'He spent his early years dodging dinosaurs and searching for a cave with just the right amount of echo . . . He chose the bass because, longer than the guitar, it was a much larger phallic symbol . . . When asked to sum The Who up in one sentence, he said, "The Who are to the rock industry what French films are to the movie industry: deep and full of messages. But what the fuck are they about?" John is currently sitting with his arse on the coffin lid, although occasionally when he gets up to go to the bathroom, another Who album is released . . . 'n bloody good luck to him!!!'

Also included within the random jumble of his notes is a section that he meant to use as a prologue. It never was to serve that function in his book, but now, it is as good a way as any of diving into this one:

> Don't read this first line and then flip through to Chapter One. If you do, you'll get a completely wrong perspective of this book and what it's really about. After reading all the other Who books, I was left with an overwhelming frustration and anger at what I'd read. This stuff belonged on the Fiction shelves in a library in the middle of nowhere; in a ghost town with tumbleweed scattering the pages to the four corners of a desert – in Hell. Boy, was I angry. I was left with the feeling that I'd never existed . . . that it had all been a dream. I'd never played in a band called The Who. That everything as I remembered it had never really happened. The realisation came over me that if I didn't do something about it, the world would remember me as 'The Quiet One'; the strong, silent, morbid bass player with a string of black humour songs behind him. Only my fellow musicians would have any idea of my contribution to the music and to The Who.
>
> I had two choices: I could die in some real bizarre, mysterious way and become 'a Dead Legend' – the patron saint of bass guitarists. The bass guitarist that was better than every bass guitarist that survived him, because I was dead and they couldn't prove otherwise. Aha, that would fuck 'em. Moony did it. Hendrix did it. I didn't. It passed through my mind – very quickly.
>
> Or . . . I could write a book; a book that would tell the story through my eyes. It was the only way I could think of to lay the spectre of The Who that had been haunting me, clouding my mind, throwing me into fits of depression for days on end, affecting my music. The Who was never The Who that these other books had been presenting, analysing, dissecting.

The Who was fucking FUN. It was the best, loudest, most innovative rock band in the fucking world. We were arrogant, anarchistic arseholes and we loved it! We didn't give a shit about anything else other than playing our music to as many people as possible. We changed the face of rock and everybody else took the credit.

Now, I'm taking it back.

PART I

The Quiet One

17 January 2002 – Entwistle flies to Los Angeles to attend the National Association of Music Merchants' (NAMM) International Music Market, which is to be held over four days at the Anaheim Convention Centre. At the event, he meets up with his old friend, Joe Walsh, who remembers:

I spent a while with John in his dressing room and then we went out to eat . . . I noticed that he was having trouble hearing. Also, he was not making sense like the John that I had known. I didn't know if he was just too drunk, or whatever. At one time, that's how all of us rockers would get to be late, late at night. Personally, I went on in that same way until 1994 and, by then, I had turned into a full-blown alcoholic and cocaine-crazy person. But I hit bottom before I OD'd and died. A lot of my brothers went the other way. Once I had got sober, John and I were living in totally different worlds. I went to see him a couple of times, but I didn't hang out all night and into the next morning like I used to – and as he was still doing. So, we had got to be a little distant from each other.

Over time, I became disturbed by how John was getting to be. But I didn't know what to do about it. I wasn't sure whether I should, or even could, confront him. Ultimately, I was never able to sit down with John and say to him, 'Hey, man, you're fucking up.' Back in those days, I was still trying to figure out my own sobriety. Now, all these years later, I feel quite comfortable in telling someone I care about, 'Listen up, because I know what I'm talking about.'

Those times that I did see John, I would notice a decline in his physical condition, most of all with his hearing, but also in his mental state. He would slur his words and not be as concise with his thought processes. From my perspective, Keith Moon had made up his mind that he was going to take everything as far as it would go, period. Maybe there was a bit of that in John, too. When I first met those guys in The Who back in the sixties in Philadelphia, we had all thought that we were immortal. Over the years, you get to realise that you're not. Always with John, though, across the board, if he wanted to do something, he went right ahead and did it.

Of course, after we'd had dinner that night, he invited me back with him to his hotel, which was the Continental Hyatt House. I didn't stay too long. I left him thinking, 'Jesus, what has happened to my brother?' I also left him with a very bad feeling.

1

Southfield Road

John Alec Entwistle came into a world of chaos and carnage. A war baby, he was born on 9 October 1944 at Hammersmith Hospital as Adolf Hitler was orchestrating a last, desperate bombing campaign on London. The Third Reich's newest weapon of terror was the V-2 long-range missile, and the very first of these to be launched on the city had struck Chiswick the previous month, claiming thirteen victims on the evening of 8 September. The day after Entwistle's birth, the hospital building had shuddered at a second V-2 strike that hit just down the road. In later life, he would point out the birthmark on his leg, which was unmistakably and fittingly shaped like a bomb, fins and all.

He was to grow up at 81a Southfield Road, South Acton, the home of his maternal grandparents and where his mother, Queenie, was also living. His father, Herbert, was away in the Royal Navy, doing his bit for the Allied war effort as Chief Stoker on the HMS *Renown*. A Lancastrian by birth, Herbert Entwistle had in 1930 gone to sea straight out of school. War had broken out by the time he met Queenie Maude Lee. Like so many other young couples at the time, their futures unimaginable, they had rushed into marriage in 1941. Herbert was twenty-five by then and Queenie eighteen. By nature, Herbert was bluff, good-humoured and kindly, his new bride a pretty, gregarious and fun-loving party girl. The thing that they had most in common was a love of music; Herbert played trumpet in the Navy band and Queenie honky-tonk piano in the pubs and clubs around west London.

Their union didn't survive the end of the war. Inevitably, Herbert returned home a changed man. His elder brother, who had travelled with him to Liverpool to enlist, was on the HMS *Hood* when it was sunk by the German battleship *Bismarck* in May 1941, killing all but three hands. On *Renown* in the South Atlantic, the crew had endured months on an enforced starvation diet which left Herbert requiring long-term hospital treatment. Apart for almost all of their first four years of marriage, when Herbert and Queenie came back together, they found that they hardly even knew each other. Their only child was eighteen months old when they separated; Herbert moved into a lodging house and would visit his son at Southfield Road every Friday night.

John and Daisy Lee's terraced maisonette at 81a was right across the street from the Wilkinson Sword factory. In this particular part of industrial west London, the factory was a local landmark. As a whole, the sprawl of Acton was commonly known as 'Soap Suds Island' on account of the 600 or so laundries that operated in the area, a result of its abundant soft water resource. The Lees were a tight, close-knit family; Daisy's two sisters, Edith and Flo, both lived within a mile radius and the young John grew up surrounded by great-aunts and -uncles. 'We lived upstairs at 81a and another couple, Jock and Florrie Leslie, downstairs,' he wrote of his childhood home.

Jock was an angry little Scottish bloke, on the short side with wild eyes that blazed continuously as though he was always about to hit somebody; it was usually Florrie. Ours was a three-bedroom house: two singles and a double. I slept in the single at the front of the house. Unfortunately, my very earliest memory of the room was of my great-grandmother dying in there. She was laid out with pennies on her eyes and I was made to kiss her goodbye. The bed faced the window under which sat my gran's Singer treadle sewing machine. Behind the bed was a curtain which concealed a hanging area for clothes. I spent many sleepless nights waiting for my dead great-grandmother to crash through the curtains and leer over the headboard with those pennies on her eyes. Though in fact what scared me more was being woken by gran peddling that damned sewing machine in the morning.

The whole interior of the house was painted brown and cream, as were most houses after the war. Back then, the limited choice of paint extended only as far as either good old camouflage green and brown, underbelly of Spitfire cream, or battleship grey. Drainpipes and fences were always green. Our kitchen was split into three rooms: there was an eating area, which overlooked our opposite neighbours' kitchen, four feet away; the scullery contained a gas cooker on which we heated our hot water. In the corner, between the cooker and sink, was the coal hole. A short corridor led to the toilet; opposite that, in pride of place, was our aluminium bath. Our back yard was a concrete path with two feet of soil on either side, leading to a wooden gate that opened on to a communal alley – my playground.

Grandad John was a gambling man till the end of his life. He was half-Irish on his father's side and had a pretty volatile Irish temper, especially when the dog or horse that he'd backed lost. He wasn't a tall man, about 5ft 8in, very gaunt and with a distinct Roman nose, part of which I inherited. His left eye, which he refused to have removed, was glazed with glaucoma. The old photographs of my gran as a young woman show her as tall, thin and dark-haired, but I remember her as being little, portly and grey. Her cooking was always delicious. Gran's greatest pleasure in life was 'nossin''. This was the expression we used for whenever she was sat looking out of the front room window. The front room was sacred. The best furniture in the house was there. It was used for birthdays, weddings, funerals, Christmas, and Gran's nossin'. She would sit hidden behind the lace curtains, a discreet corner moved to one side, and could tell you what the neighbours were up to at any time of day.

Gran was partially deaf and, being something of a seam-stress, made herself special aprons to carry around the huge hearing-aid equipment of those days. Grandad would tease her mercilessly by cutting his voice mid-sentence and carrying on merely mouthing the words. Gran would turn up her hearing aid, thinking it was shorting out, and he would suddenly scream into the microphone. On the other hand, whenever she was annoyed with him, she would switch it off.

Each Saturday morning, Queenie would take young John shopping with her up the Chiswick High Road. On these excursions, she would allow him a weekly treat, which was to pick out a single, lead model soldier and so began the first of what was to be her son's many collections. Being an only child, Entwistle was self-contained, something of a loner, and got used to living inside his own head. He would play out by himself in the back alley, sneaking off as he got older to enact war games in the rubble of the scores of burned and bombed-out buildings that littered the neighbourhood. Food rationing was still in effect and he was a sickly infant. By the time he was five years old, he had contracted mumps, chickenpox, whooping cough and measles, had numerous bouts of 'flu, countless colds, and suffered with catarrh which, he wrote, 'blocked up my nose and caused strange noises in my head and a peculiar numb feeling in my body'.

According to his mother's recollection, he showed an interest in music from the age of two. In the front room at Southfield Road, next to Queenie's piano, was a Victor Talking Machine record player. Settling her toddler in front of the old wind-up machine, Queenie would spin for him selections from her collection of 78s, which ranged from military marches to Glenn Miller. Also by five, he had memorised the words to the Andrews Sisters' swing staple 'Boogie Woogie Bugle Boy of Company B' and was adept at performing two of Al Jolson's vaudeville standards, 'Sonny Boy' and 'My Mammy'. Not that these mother-and-son sessions passed by uninterrupted; grumbling one afternoon at being unable to hear the football results on his radio, Grandad John took revenge by fetching an old bird's nest from under the eaves and secreting it down the horn of the machine. Thereafter, the Victor was mysteriously muffled.

Grandad John did, though, see value in his grandson's pre-cociousness. He started to take Entwistle along with him to his working men's club, the Napier Sports Club. There, the old man would encourage the boy to stand up on a table or chair and sing his two Al Jolson numbers for the other patrons. As his grandson went through his act, Grandad John would have a cap passed around the room for loose change, using the proceeds to fetch lemonade and crisps for the budding singer. This routine of theirs went on for weeks until the youngster grew over-zealous during one performance, tumbling off a table and gashing his forehead. After that, Queenie put a stop to them going out together to the Napier.

■ ■ ■

In the summer of his fifth year, Entwistle was packed off to Southfield Road Primary. The school was a five-minute walk from his grandparents' house, but to such a singular boy it must have seemed like an entry into another, more forbidding world. The old, red-brick Victorian building was imposing with its looming bell tower and iron railings; similarly intimidating was the school's headmaster, Mr Healey, a stickler for discipline who wielded a wicked birch cane.

At home, there came about an even more jarring and unwanted interruption to what until then had been the gentle ebb and flow of life. On Saturdays, Queenie would go out dancing at the Hammersmith Palais. One night there, she was whisked on to the floor by a tall, rail-thin suitor who bore a passing resemblance to the American movie star, Clark Gable; this was apt, since Gordon Johns was working at that time as a cinema projectionist. To Queenie, the good-looking, fleet-footed Johns seemed quite the catch and, in time, she agreed to let him walk her home one night from the dance. These trysts soon became a regular event and, on the occasions that he missed his last bus home, Johns would stay the night at 81a, where he slept under Queenie's piano. Eventually, he moved in completely.

To Entwistle, Johns was 'Gordon the Lodger' and an instant adversary. 'Like most kids separated from their father, I resented Gordon,' he wrote. 'He wasn't my real dad and he had no authority over me. That was my opinion and I bloody stuck to it – for years. Every Friday, two buckets of water went on to the gas stove and the bath was ceremoniously carried into the scullery. Being the member of the family that needed the most cleaning, I had the first bath. Two people had to bathe in one load of water and Gordon usually followed me.' Knowing as much, before he got out of the bath, Entwistle would never fail to take a pee in the water.

With Johns' arrival on the scene, the young Entwistle grew more reserved, as if he were seeking to escape into the background. For companionship, he had his grandparents' dog, an ugly little Yorkshire terrier with a sour temperament and few teeth that the old folks had named Scruffy. Grandad John also began to take him out to the pictures twice weekly, and he would sit rapt in the dark of the Acton Odeon or the Gaumont cinemas. 'Films affected me in a huge way,' he wrote. 'After seeing *Ivanhoe* and *Knights of the Round Table*, I developed a passion for armour and weapons that is still with me to this day. Though I also lost count of the times my Grandad and I were thrown out of the cinema. He had a nasty habit of shouting out during the films. "Look out behind you!" was his favourite, or else grabbing someone in front of him during the scary bits. The inevitable would then happen, a torch shone in our eyes and, "Excuse me, sir . . . we'd like you to leave."'

From the age of seven, a less welcome distraction was introduced by Queenie who decreed that he should take piano lessons. Each Tuesday evening after school, she would drag him a mile down Acton Lane for tutoring by Mrs Jones, a severe, round-shouldered lady in her seventies whose house was overrun with cats. At their first meeting, the formidable Mrs Jones informed Queenie that she didn't teach lazy little boys, and Entwistle was set the additional task of practising the piano for a minimum of one hour every night. 'I remember thinking, "My mum's giving me a witch,"' he recalled of the old piano teacher. 'I have been suspicious of the motives of old ladies owning cats ever since and Tuesdays became the blight of my life. I hated the piano. I had begun to hate music. It had come to mean practising boring pieces, the freezing cold of Mrs Jones's house and, above all, the smell of cat's piss.'

However, this weekly dose of unpleasantness was nothing next to the outrage he felt when Queenie and Johns' relationship progressed in 1953 to marriage. Gordon the Lodger was now Gordon the Stepdad and, from that moment on, the extent of their mutual antipathy only ever deepened. In so far as he could, Johns shunned his stepson. But also, he would never miss an opportunity to carp and gripe to Queenie about the boy's idleness and general no-goodness. For his part, Entwistle went right on peeing in the interloper's bathwater.

Herbert Entwistle, too, was remarried that same year, taking for a bride his landlady, Dora. A widower, Dora had two children of her own from her previous marriage, Bernard and Linda, and so the now nine-year-old John gained a stepbrother and stepsister who were respectively three years and a month his seniors. Herbert had got himself a good engineering job, and continued to call at 81a every Friday night, roaring up on his Norton motorbike. Now, though, he would often bring Bernard along with him. Entwistle looked forward to Herbert's visits as the highlight of each week. When, later in 1953, Herbert was able to move his new family out of London and into the Buckinghamshire countryside, he sorted out visiting rights to have his young son come and stay over with them at appointed weekends.

'John would visit us every couple of months,' remembers Bernard. 'Things would get a bit fractious sometimes between Bert and Queenie. If Bert was late arriving at Acton, Queenie would have a go at him. For his part, Gordon didn't seem to like or want anything to do with anyone. Gordon would pass me on the stairs without so much as uttering a word. Most often, though, if they knew Bert was coming to pick John up, Gordon and Queenie would make sure to be out.

'John and I bonded quite well. He was such a thin, straggly thing . . . all fingers. It's funny, but his fingers made you think of nothing so much as spider's legs. I used to breed budgerigars

22

in my bedroom. Up to then, I don't think John had ever seen a budgie. He would put his hand in the nest box and pick up these tiny hatchlings. They would only have been hatched about a week and he would bring them out on the end of a finger. Most of us would have cupped them in our hands.'

Across the country, the pall of post-war austerity was being lifted from over Britain. A million new homes had been built since 1945, and the average national wage rose as the moribund British economy at last started to soar. By the end of the decade, 75 per cent of households would have a television set and Prime Minister Harold Macmillan was emboldened enough to tell the British people that they had never had it so good. Within the confines of 81a Southfield Road, the knock-on effect of these good times was two-fold. First, Johns was able to get a better-paid job as an estate agent. Second, like millions of their fellow Brits, as a family they found themselves able to take an annual summer's holiday. In their case, this was a two-week jaunt out to the Coronation Holiday Camp on Hayling Island, a twelve-square-mile blob of land off the south coast from Portsmouth.

As Entwistle wrote thirty-five years later, it was at the Coronation Holiday Camp in August of 1955 that 'something happened to rekindle my love for music. Because the camp was so self-contained, I was left to my own devices and, when I wasn't emptying my favourite penny machine, I'd hang out by the ballroom, sucking on a banana milkshake, and listen to the resident dance band. The normal foxtrots and waltzes the band did hadn't interested me much but, one night, they played something that made my ears prick up. It was a trumpet solo titled 'In a Persian Market'. The piercing sound of the trumpet impressed me so much I just had to learn how to play it.'

With the trumpet being Herbert's instrument, this discovery also allowed him to forge another strong bond with his dad and, by extension, to make a symbolic and defiant stand against Gordon the Stepfather. Once they were home in Acton, Entwistle badgered his mother to let him take up the trumpet. Queenie finally relented, but on the condition that he continue with his piano lessons. In the event, Queenie's resolve in this matter held up for just two months. By then, Herbert had loaned the boy his old silver trumpet and, in the course of his once-weekly visits, coached him to blow a full, though somewhat shaky, scale C.

Required to practise out of his disapproving stepfather's sight, Entwistle alighted upon the toilet as his makeshift music room. Upon entering the loo one day, he discovered his own particular reason to trust that things would get better – the belated arrival at 81a of toilet paper. 'I found the usual knotted squares of newspaper to be missing,' he wrote. 'Anxiously, I shouted out, "Where's the paper, Gran?" "It's the white stuff on the roll," she replied. No more newsprint on my bum. We were on our way up!'

2

The Hockey Misfits

The divided state of things carried on at 81a Southfield Road. In equal measure, Queenie fussed about and nagged at both her husband and son. Whenever he was in the house, Gordon would be in a scowling mood, although he increasingly absented himself down the pub. Entwistle, meanwhile, went right on blowing his dad's old silver trumpet in the loo. Come the following summer of 1956, he also started at a new school. Against his own expectations, he passed the eleven-plus examination which, rather like the Hogwarts' Sorting Hat, was the means by which the British education system separated out supposedly more academically-gifted children. Entwistle's success in this regard meant that he escaped the stigma of being seen to go to either of Acton's two comprehensive schools and, instead, was elevated to the giddy heights of the local grammar.

Opened in 1906, Acton County was the first purpose-built grammar school in the county of Middlesex. As was the nature of such institutions at the time, it operated to rigid strictures and conservative tradition. In 1956, it was still an all-boys school, although a new headmaster, Mr Kibblewhite, had just recently been appointed to prepare Acton County for the shock of admitting its first intake of girls the very next year. The masters, male for the greater part, almost exclusively middle-aged or older, would sweep about the place in their billowing black gowns, like great bats, administering discipline to unruly pupils with a sharp clip around the ear, or else a well-aimed board rubber.

To go along with their navy-blue caps, blazers and jumpers, and red-and-black striped ties, first-year boys were required to wear short trousers. Entwistle's mother had already graduated him to long trousers the previous year, so this last imposition was a blow to his self-esteem. In total, the first year at Acton County seemed to him a slow and joyless grind. The formalities of the school were unbending; each day would begin at 9.00am precisely with the whole school gathered in the hall for a morning assembly of hymns and a Bible reading. In one class after another, masters would direct the boys to work from the blackboard in strict silence, sat side by side at their fold-up wooden desks.

'I had the new problem of homework to suffer with, and also the never-ending harassment of the older boys,' Entwistle later wrote. 'This latter happening was called fag-baiting – "fag" being the term given to boys just starting at the school and which dated from the previous century. Still, I earned myself a reputation for being difficult to harass as I got into the habit of fighting back. At that time, I was the second biggest kid in my year, and taller than all but two of the second-year boys.'

However, one particular morning his attention was roused by a new initiative at the school. In assembly that day, the music teacher, Mrs Holman, stood and announced the formation of a school orchestra, encouraging budding applicants to report to the music room at the end of the day for try-outs. At final bell, Entwistle rushed to the designated venue, but not quickly enough. He arrived to be told that the brass section was over-subscribed with aspirants. Unbowed, he protested to the officious brass teacher, Mr Barnes, that he was already proficient on the trumpet. This was not entirely true, but it got him an audition. Mr Barnes, he wrote, 'beckoned me past eight pupils gathered round an ancient tenor horn wrapped in Sellotape to seal the leaks in the pipe work. I smiled as the first four produced deafening silence, whilst going red in the face. "Fuckin' thing don't work," number four said under his breath as he headed past me to the door. I knew something he didn't. You don't just blow into the mouthpiece; you have to produce a raspberry and vibrate the lips. Thank God my father had given me those lessons. I produced the first note of the evening and was told to stand to one side. I was feeling very smug and pleased with myself, but my thunder was immediately stolen by another late arrival, Middleton. He brought the house down by playing of all things a whole piece of music on his very own trumpet. Anyway, three of us were chosen: Middleton, Merriweather (the only boy in my year taller than me) and me. Middleton, of course, was delegated first trumpet, while Merriweather and I were given two ancient tenor saxhorns.'

In spite of their being a semi-tone lower, out of necessity the saxhorns had to fill the role of French horns in the orchestra. By the time the parts meant for French horn had been transposed to take into account the key difference, they were all but impossible to render on such archaic instruments. The gangling Merriweather quit the orchestra in frustration; Entwistle stuck to the task and was rewarded when the school eventually coughed up for an actual French horn – matt, silver-plated and procured from a brass band.

His dedicated approach to the trumpet also reaped dividends at home. Soon after the acquisition of his French horn, his mother and Aunt Flo clubbed together to buy him his first trumpet, a

Boosey & Hawkes Model 78 coated in gold lacquer. Entwistle recalled: 'The shop assistant remarked in passing, "The first valve needs a bit of oil." Lying bastard – that first valve had a mind of its own and the Entwistle temper caused it to fly across the room.'

The troublesome valve was replaced soon enough and, in the first report that Entwistle received from Acton County, he was awarded an 'A' grade for music, Mrs Holman remarking that he was 'most enthusiastic' and 'making splendid progress on trumpet'. The rest of the report was not quite so glowing. He got a 'C' in English and a 'D' for both Mathematics and PE. Even still, his form tutor, Mr Paulin concluded, 'He is a good pupil and has done a good year's work.'

■ ■ ■

At the outset of Entwistle's second year, girls arrived at Acton County. The 'cruds', as they were referred to by the senior boys, initially made up just one half of the new first-year intake. However, the total numbers of boys and girls was intended to balance out exponentially over the ensuing three years. This was a prospect that delighted Entwistle, as he later recorded: 'I had already worked out that by the time I was sixteen there would be two-hundred little cuties looking goo-goo-eyed at us older boys. The string section of the orchestra would also finally be up to strength – none of us boys would dream of learning to play the sissy violin.'

In fact, he might well have thought that things in general were looking up. Around this time he made his first public appearances as a jobbing musician at a series of Saturday night dances in Acton. A local big-bandleader, one Teddy Fullager, lived a couple of doors down from 81a on Southfield Road. The carrot-haired Fullager was a drummer and unfortunately afflicted with a nervous twitch. Before the war, he had played in a trio with Entwistle's mother. Queenie took it upon herself to persuade him to take her son on as second trumpeter in the Teddy Fullager Band. For these occasions, Entwistle was attired in an old tuxedo that was donated to him by Fullager's father, who so happened to be squat in stature and to have a tin leg.

'Fortunately, the audiences were there to dance and not to listen,' Entwistle recalled. 'The singer would announce: "Ladies and gentlemen, kindly take the floor for a foxtrot," and a few bars into every song, the guitarist would break another string. For a long time, I thought this was just a natural occurrence, one of the things guitarists had to put up with, like my sticky valve. Later, I realised he had been using cheap, shitty strings. He would even try tying knots on some of the broken ones.

'I would spend the whole Saturday dance looking down the front of my oversized dress trousers at my underpants, praying that no one else could see. I learned two things from the experience. If you're underage, you're underpaid . . . and how to drink rum and blackcurrant.'

Being a second-year at Acton County, Entwistle was now permitted to wear long trousers to school and able to 'carry a briefcase instead of the stupid little shoulder satchel that first-years had'. He also struck up the first binding friendship of his young life with the lad he was sat next to in their new form class. Mick Brown had been born just a day apart from him and also at Hammersmith Hospital. The two boys quickly found that they shared a mutual love for horror movies and the American comic, *Mad*. For his part, Entwistle was also admiring of Brown's flat-top haircut.

'We laughed a lot together,' recalls Brown. 'It was all terribly innocent fun. He would scrunch his features up into a funny face, which cracked me up every time he did it, and he would occasionally talk in that same deep voice that he later on used for "Boris the Spider". I always called him "Ent", never John. Whenever he came round to my house, my parents would remark on how Ent was a very nice and polite young man. Interestingly, though, I don't remember ever going back to *his* house.'

One of the principal attributes upon which Acton County prided itself as an institution was its excellence at sport. In this arena, Entwistle proved himself to be a capable sprinter. That year, he went on to compete at athletics events for the school over both 100 and 200 yards and equalled the county record at the shorter distance. He stood out, too, on account of the bright-red running shoes that he wore. By disposition, though, he was not a natural athlete and this commitment to running soon petered out.

At most other sports, Entwistle was either disinterested or else plain hopeless. Along with ten other boys, he found himself banished from football and cricket sessions by the PE master, Mr Yates, and instead 'stuck in our very own game – hockey. Mr Yates called us his "Hockey Misfits" and, after teaching us the fundamentals, left us to kill each other. Not a month went by without one of us being carried unconscious to Acton Hospital, conveniently sited next door to Acton County. The rest of the school came to regard us as a bunch of violent crazies and we developed a kind of macho pride at being members of the Hockey Misfits.'

Also included in the Hockey Misfits was Brown, even more ungainly than his new friend; a Welsh lad named Gannon; the three smallest boys in the year, Bird, Godsmark and Carr; and a rather withdrawn character with piercing blue eyes and a large nose, Pete Townshend. A late arrival to the school, Townshend was born into a family of musicians and entertainers. His father, Cliff, was a professional on the saxophone and clarinet, and mum

Betty a singer. Entwistle's first recollection of Townshend was of him being '6in shorter than me. Then, suddenly, during a matter of months, he shot up the extra inches, causing him to stoop as if he didn't know where to put the additional half foot.'

In due course, Townshend, by dint of his own regard for *Mad* magazine and compatibly sly sense of humour, was welcomed into the Entwistle–Brown clique. After school, the three of them would now gather in Brown's bedroom, where their attentions were chiefly occupied with the new reel-to-reel tape recorder that Brown had been bought by his parents. Inspired by the two principal forces in British comedy of the time – Tony Hancock and radio's *The Goon Show* – they began to make their own loosely scripted comic recordings, the ripeness of their satire perhaps suggested by Brown's and Entwistle's teaming up in one sketch to play the superhero characters 'Fatman and Robert the Boy Blunder'. A keen drawer from an early age, Entwistle was also becoming adept at sketching out caricatures, signing off one pen-and-ink rendering of Brown as a trench-coated, trilby hat-sporting spiv as 'Jet Entwistle'.

The other passion that united them was for music and particularly the new and eruptive sounds that roared into and reverberated around Britain at that moment in time. From across the Atlantic had come rock-'n'-roll, a frenetic bastardisation of three strands of American folk music – blues, R&B and country – given voice and cocksureness by such rebellious-seeming practitioners as Elvis Presley, Jerry Lee Lewis, Chuck Berry, Little Richard, Eddie Cochran, Gene Vincent and Bill Haley. At thirty-three, hangdog-eyed and overweight, Haley in reality was hardly a vision of renegade youth. Yet the first UK tour that he undertook with his band, The Comets, in February of 1957, had nonetheless prompted scenes of unrestrained bedlam at town halls and ballrooms across the land. A home-grown upsurge was under way, too, and this brought about by a revival of yet another form of American folk music, the so-called 'jug band' sound of the pre-war years. Re-branded as 'skiffle', it was pioneered by a wiry, unprepossessing-looking Scotsman named Lonnie Donegan, who went to Number One that same year with his version of a traditional Appalachian folk tune, 'Cumberland Gap'.

The effect of all this was to open up a yawning generation gap between, on the one hand, grandparents and parents who had lived through two world wars and, on the other, their off-spring, for whom a new, collective noun could now be applied – teenagers. It was now possible to choose between the more genteel, inoffensive world of big bands, trad jazz, easy-listening crooners and Vera Lynn; or opt for the leering, swaggering tilt at convention represented by Presley's swivelling hips, the inherent menace of the self-styled 'Killer', Jerry Lee Lewis, and a predatory black man, Berry. At thirteen, Entwistle and his two cohorts happened to straddle both sides of this ever-widening divide.

Brown it was who bought a 78 of Lewis' exultant 'Great Balls of Fire' from Ewin's music store on Acton High Street. Afterwards, the three of them gathered around the record player in Brown's bedroom to marvel at its sheer impudence. Entwistle adopted a slightly longer version of Brown's crew-cut, and got himself kitted out with a pair of luminous, odd-coloured socks, then the rage among Britain's nascent Teddy Boys, a vivid red on one peg, lurid yellow on the other. Every Sunday evening, each of them would tune into the *Top Twenty* countdown show on Radio Luxembourg. Yet, in spite of the invasion of the British charts by this rock-'n'-roll advance guard, the two biggest selling singles of that year in the UK were much milder confections: Paul Anka's saccharine 'Diana' and 'Mary's Boy Child' by Harry Belafonte.

The first, hesitant musical steps that Entwistle took together with Townshend were just as wedded to the conventions of their parents. Towards the end of 1957, and with Entwistle on trumpet and Townshend having taught himself the rudiments of the banjo, they cobbled together a shaky-sounding trad-jazz band with a pair of other Acton County boys, Phil Rhodes on clarinet, and a drummer, Chris Sherwin. Weekly on Thursday evenings and Saturday afternoons, this four-piece practised together at the so-called Congo Club, which was the youth club run out of the Acton Congregational Church. In time, they worked up a set that included selections by such British traditionalists as Acker Bilk, Kenny Ball, the Chris Barber Band and Ken Colyer. Billing themselves 'The Confederates', they even managed a solitary public performance. An inauspicious event, this was at the annual staff dance at the local Corgi Books factory. Entwistle wrote of it: 'We played the interval in between the audience dancing to records and we were awful.

This was even with the help of another, older lad, Rodney Griffith, who had an old tuba. Griffith wasn't able to actually play it, but he could hum very loudly through it. Sherwin had fixed the date up for us and had been very evasive when asked how much we were getting paid. Rightly so, as after the dance had finished, the organiser pointed to a huge pile of books stacked against a wall and told us, 'All right, lads, take as many as you can carry.' We threw Sherwin out of the band.

Phil Rhodes and me were into real jazz – Bix Beiderbecke and Jelly Roll Morton – and gradually became proficient enough to play it . . . or at least a semblance of it. Rodney the humming tuba player had a couple of banjo-playing friends who attended the local technical college and, after jamming with them a few times, and as it was Christmas, we decided to go busking round the pubs. Pete asked if he could come along for the ride. We hoped to take advantage of the Christmas drunks, and we did, passing round the hat. We had done three of the best pubs in Hammersmith and were having a well-deserved drink using our ill-gotten gains when Pete nudged me: 'Isn't that your mother and stepfather over there?' he asked. I jumped. Oh fuck, they were coming over. I shrank down in my chair. They had witnessed our whole performance. My stepfather proceeded to reel off a list of the pubs we weren't to go to. 'That's where I drink and I don't want any bloody noise while I'm doing it,' he instructed.

We made about a fiver each that night, with Pete receiving a quid as he was a late-comer. Walking home with him afterwards, he told me that he was giving up the banjo. 'There's too fucking many of them,' he said and, from that point on, he switched to the guitar.

By the end of that school year, The Confederates were no longer a going concern. Briefly and without much enthusiasm, Entwistle, along with Rhodes and the errant Sherwin, threw in his lot with another neighbourhood collective being run by one of the technical college banjoists and inaccurately named Alf Maynard's New Orleans Jazzmen. Increasingly, trad jazz seemed old hat to him and, in any case, he had a troubling issue to contend with at home. Herbert had been offered a promotion at work, but it would necessitate him relocating again, this time to south Wales. To Entwistle's dismay, his father decided to take the job and moved his second family to Newport. The Welsh town was 140 miles to the west of London, which, in 1958, may as well have been on a far-off continent. Effectively, Herbert at a stroke had all but vanished from his life. With Gordon barely acknowledging him, his father's absence scarred Entwistle and in ways that would never fully heal.

A sense of Entwistle's turbulent mind can be gleaned from his school report for that year. Once again, he was deemed to have excelled at music, having scored 83 per cent in the second-year exam, and he was awarded another 'A' for the subject. This was, though, an isolated instance. He scraped a further 'C' in English, but had managed just 28 per cent in his Geography exam and, worse still, 24 in German, bad enough for him to be graded 'D' in both subjects. His form teacher, Mr Lyons summed it up: '[His] exam results confirm the impression I have received that he is making very little effort.'

Going into his third year, Entwistle did at least find a new, albeit still very regimented outlet for his music. At the urging of 'Rodney the humming tuba player', he was enlisted in the Acton Congregational Boys' Brigade and joined its band. From its inception in 1883, the Brigade had sought to instil in boys 'habits of obedience, reverence, discipline, self-respect and all that tends towards a true Christian manliness'. Entwistle's thoughts on the matter were rather less pious. He wrote: 'The church that the company was affiliated to had twelve of the most beautiful girls I had seen up to that point in my life. They were all in the Girl Guides and two years older than us, but that didn't matter.'

The tantalising presence of these Girl Guides was reason enough for him to troop dutifully along to the church for band practice every Tuesday evening and drill parade on Fridays, kitted out in his navy-blue uniform. The Brigade's resolute marching repertoire was hardly a challenge for him and he caught the ear of the company captain, a certain 'Horsey' Hughes who elevated him to lead bugler. As such, he was the focal point for the Brigade parades, which were undertaken one Sunday a month and with the whole company marching through the streets of Acton, all of them lined up behind the band and their star soloist. Overall, this was, he considered, 'the first time that I had used my musical ability to attract the opposite sex'.

As it happened, his first serious girlfriend did end up being a Girl Guide, but one of the younger members. He was fourteen and Alison Wise thirteen when he took her out on their first date, which was to a national Boys' Brigade concert at the Royal Albert Hall on 28 January 1959. A fellow Acton County pupil, Alison had been among the 1957 intake of girls to the school and had joined with her twin sister, Christine. The Wise girls were mirror twins, both pretty, vivacious and with mousy-brown hair. About the only appreciable difference between them was that Alison was left-handed and Christine right. Their father had worked in the rag trade and had grafted to make the family comfortably middle-class, but he had suffered a heart-attack and died when the girls were just seven. Their mother, a devout church-goer, was left to bring Alison and Christine up on her own. 'My first impression of John was that he was rather lovely,' Alison says of Entwistle. 'At school, I would go into classes and find that he had left notes for me inside the desks. I used to call him "Twistle". I'd tell him, "Get on with your work, Twistle." Even back then, he had a very black sense of humour. Christine used to think he was hilarious until he did a quite wicked caricature of her for the school magazine. She never forgave him for it.

'We would meet up at lunchtimes and go and sit in the park . . . have a snog and then a master would come along and tell us off. You couldn't get away with anything in those days. If we were going out after school, I'd go down to 81a to meet up with him and sit with his mum and gran and grandad. His grandparents were lovely. John just did everything to appease his mother so that she wouldn't get into trouble with Gordon. Gordon would take everything out on Queenie and that would upset John terribly. Gordon was a horrible man, a pig. I got on well with everyone else in the family. They had a lot of family parties where Queenie would sit playing at that old piano. She was very good, but she wouldn't half vamp a lot.

'John was always very conscious of how he looked. I remember when he wanted to have drainpipe trousers. Queenie refused to take his trousers in for him, so he marched her up the high street to see people with drainpipes on to convince her that they looked better. After that, she did take his trousers in and he wore his new drainpipes to school. That was deemed to be very fashionable.'

This sartorial indiscretion also got him sent home from school. Not so much for the sheer tightness of his newly customised trousers, but that they were light grey in colour as opposed to the prescribed dark. Either way, Entwistle was now engaged upon a mission to make himself the most outlandishly dressed boy at Acton County. Rather than navy-blue, he started to sport a light-blue blazer, attaching the school badge to one of its lapels with a paper clip, making it easier to remove once outside the school gates. In place of the uniform black casual shoes, he peacocked in one morning in a pair of brown brogues that tapered to a winkle-picker point. This also got him sent home for the day. However, he was in the process of establishing a look for himself that immediately made him feel as though he stood apart and comfortable in his own skin. Next, he needed a musical instrument that would serve the exact same purpose.

3

Detours

The entertainment options open to teenagers around Acton in the late 1950s were strictly limited. There was the Congo Club, the two cinemas and, round the corner from Southfield Road, a recreation ground. Or else, most Saturday nights, a dance would be held at one of the several halls in the area. Next to the other offerings, these dances must have seemed thrilling enticements – ripe with the promise of stolen kisses or, better still, a quick grope in the dark of the cloakroom. And they promised even more excitement as the musical backdrop to all of this awkward fumbling shifted inexorably from big bands towards rock-'n'-roll. Certainly, for the fourteen-year-old Entwistle, the weekly dance was 'always the highlight of my world. I was becoming a pretty efficient jiver,' he recorded, 'and found that girls were actually asking me to dance for a change.'

Even more intoxicating to him was the sound of a living, breathing rock-'n'-roll band, despite the gaucheness of most of the local combos. Where trad jazz was refined and practised, this was simplistic, primal; the crash of an electric guitar, the tribal pulse of double-bass and drums and, carried right along with them, the whiff of subversion. Being a horn player, the saxophone seemed to offer Entwistle the most likely route into rock-'n'-roll as a musician. Occasionally, a band would turn up to a dance with a saxophonist in their ranks. In the loo at home, he tried to make his trumpet sound more like a sax by blowing it into an old American football helmet that he had been given so as to make the notes rasp. Clocking the American guitarist Duane Eddy's propulsive 'Ramrod' single on Radio Luxembourg, Entwistle became an instant disciple. By rote, he learned the sax parts to Eddy's 1958 album, *Have Twangy Guitar Will Travel*.

With his spirits lifted by this feat, he sought to form his own rock-'n'-roll band with a new acquaintance, Peter Vernon Kell, who lived in the same block of flats as Phil Rhodes. Kell had an electric guitar, and the two lads would meet up in the evenings to practise together in his bedroom. Before too long, though, Entwistle grew exasperated with being drowned out by Kell and gave up their sessions as a bad job. Reasoning that what was required was a more forceful, unyielding instrument, and one that could be quickly mastered, he alighted next upon the drums. With £3 of saved birthday money, he bought himself a second-hand snare drum, gold-lacquered and sparkling, and a pair of drumsticks. This, though, was yet another fleeting venture. 'Promptly,' he wrote, 'I was asked by my family to choose between the snare and living at home. I chose home, but kept the sticks.'

Entwistle eventually happened across his solution at a dance that was held in the school hall at Acton County. One of the regular local bands was booked to play in the interval and since the last time that he had seen them, there had been a noteworthy change to their rhythm section. Instead of the old, stand-up double bass that he had been using, the lad stationed stage right now brandished an electric bass, which he had slung around his neck on a black leather strap. In popular use in America from the start of the decade, the first electric basses had only just begun to find their way into music stores in Britain. At that point, Entwistle had never before heard, much less seen one being played, but he found himself captivated by the heavy, ominous-sounding clunk-clunk that emanated from the speakers. He moved to stand at the lip of the stage, facing the bass amplifier so that the sound would hit him full in the chest. Right there and then, he determined to take up bass guitar, and it was to Pete Townshend that he now turned.

Townshend had only just returned from a spell of being exiled from their group. During a schoolyard spat, a careless swing of his schoolbag had left his opponent, Chris Sherwin, with a case of concussion. The others had sided with the hapless Sherwin, and Townshend had used his period of isolation to accelerate his transition to guitar. He had picked up a second-hand Czech guitar for the same princely £3 sum that Entwistle had paid for his snare drum and had had it electrified. When Entwistle told him of his intention to learn bass, Townshend offered to lend him the guitar that he had been using up to that point, an old acoustic that had been bought for him by his grandmother. By taking off the top two strings, Entwistle manufactured a makeshift bass and once more applied himself to the task of studying Duane Eddy's instrumentals. Now, he navigated their driving rhythms, spending hours listening and then playing along to Eddy's album 'until it was worn out. I was getting good at being Duane Eddy, but the cello guitar wasn't the same as having a real bass,' he wrote.

> I began saving and eventually made a pilgrimage to Harry's music shop in Hammersmith, where I'd bought my latest trumpet. Harry was a nice old bloke with milk bottle-bottom glasses and

an old cardigan that had more holes than wool. A cigarette hung permanently from a corner of his mouth and, somehow, the falling ash would always land on the counter next to the ashtray. Harry had been very helpful to me in the past. In fact, after repairing my old trumpet's sticky valve for the umpteenth time, he had kindly advised me to 'sling this fucker'. I now informed him of my new love for the bass guitar. 'Well, mate, you've got three alternatives,' he said. 'There's the Hofner violin bass, fifty quid; a Framus Star bass, at sixty; or a Tuxedo, thirty quid and a piece of shit.' I moaned that these were all too expensive for me. "Then there's only one thing you can do, son," Harry said, picking up a little blue box from under the counter.

He opened the box and inside was a small, chromed pick-up, which reminded me of a sardine tin. Hanging from it was a short, white lead with a jack plug. 'Buy a lump of wood,' Harry continued. 'I'll fret the fingerboard for you and stick this on – £2 10s! There's a timber yard on the corner. Tell the geezer there it's for a guitar; he's done it before.'

Clutching the pick-up in a sweaty palm, I rushed off to the timber yard. Tony the owner was also very helpful with his tips on how to construct a guitar. Pointing to a piece of mahogany that was leant against a wall, he said, 'Take this home and draw the shape on it. I'll cut it out for you on my jig and then put a nice bit of Rosewood on as a fingerboard. The Rosewood's free and three quid for the cutting.'

I knew exactly what shape it was going to be. Just like one of those Fender basses I had seen in photographs with a long, long neck and an evil-looking headstock. The next day, a Saturday, I was back on the bus and half-an-hour later Tony was cutting out my creation on his jig. Ten bus stops and about two hundred 'Excuse me, I'm sorry's' later, I staggered back up the stairs of our maisonette. 'What the bleeding hell is that?' said my grandfather, fixing me with his one good eye. 'It's my new bass guitar,' I replied proudly. 'Well, don't let your grandmother see it; she'll have one of her funny turns.'

The next Monday afternoon, he bunked off the last lesson of the school day, which was his hated PE, and returned once more to Harry's to have his bass finished. The proprietor added to it a Hofner scale, a tailpiece, a bridge purloined from a spare Tuxedo and, just for show, three control knobs from an old radio. For the scratch plate, Entwistle picked out a black pearl number, a foot square. The completed instrument had a neck that extended ten inches longer than the fretboard, was heavy, unwieldy, looked like nothing so much as a giant football boot, and about which Entwistle was wholly pragmatic. 'I could forgive all its faults,' he wrote. 'It was a bass guitar, and mine, all mine. By ten o'clock that night, the glue on the scratch plate and the varnish on the bass had dried, and I was playing it. I had only forgotten one detail – an amplifier!'

Despite this new-found obsession, Entwistle persevered with the more formal side of music. He remained an active member of both the school orchestra and the Boys' Brigade band. In the summer of 1960, he also passed an audition to join the Middlesex Youth Orchestra on the French horn. Founded two years earlier, the orchestra was made up of ninety of the outstanding young musicians drawn from schools across the county. These recruits were required to attend rehearsals once a month and also a week's residential course over the Easter holidays, which climaxed with a concert at the Royal Academy of Music to which parents and schoolfriends were invited.

It wasn't until the following year that he performed with the orchestra at the Royal Academy. The occasion was marked by a piece in the 13 April 1961 edition of the local newspaper, the *Acton Gazette and Post*. This was accompanied by a photograph of Entwistle, in jacket, shirt and tie, cheeks puffed in the act of blowing his horn and captioned: 'A deep breath and sixteen-year-old John Entwistle of Southfield Road, Acton, resumes practice on the French horn.' In the piece itself, the director of the course, Mr Roy Slack, opined: 'These children have tremendous enthusiasm for music . . . Don't get the idea these are the long-haired musician types. They are just ordinary children – but we don't have any teenage trouble.'

Entwistle's elevation to the orchestra earned him the rare approbation of his stepfather. Says Alison, 'That was the only time that Gordon was ever proud of him. He even gave him some money to take me out for a drink, which was unprecedented because he was so tight.'

However, Entwistle's commitment to the bass guitar was not to waver. He corrected his amplifier oversight, purchasing a Goodman's 18in speaker, taking his total outlay to just over £10. With no decorum to adhere to in the pursuit of rock-'n'-roll, he convinced his grandmother to re-fashion an old curtain into a speaker cover of vivid red, yellow and turquoise. Mindful of the tumult provoked at home by his snare drum, on week nights he would lug bass and multicoloured amplifier the two miles to the Townshend home, a flat on Uxbridge Road, where the two of them would practise knee to knee in Townshend's bedroom. Soon, too, there was a band – Townshend on guitar, Entwistle on bass, the faithful Mick Brown on drums and a fourth Acton County boy, Pete Wilson, on rhythm guitar. They called themselves 'The Scorpions'.

'We used to go round to Pete's flat and listen to Cliff and the Shadows,' recalls Brown. 'Both John and Pete could more or less pick up a tune and chords within minutes, which I thought was very clever, because all that I did was hit something with sticks. We would also practise in the garage of Pete Wilson's house in West Acton, or else there was a pub near to where I lived in Ealing where we were able to use a room on a Sunday morning. It was just schoolkids making a noise; there were no paid gigs or anything like that, though I do remember us getting up and doing The Shadows' "Man of Mystery" at the youth club. Unlike John and Pete, I didn't have a burning ambition to be in a band.'

The Scorpions never were destined for life beyond their final summer term together at Acton County, but their end was hastened by a serendipitous event. Walking home one night from a rehearsal in the Wilsons' garage, Entwistle happened upon Roger Daltrey coming the other way. Daltrey had been in the year above Entwistle and Townshend at Acton County and where he was generally known as 'Perce', on account of his parental home being at Percy Road, Shepherd's Bush. In common with most other pupils, Entwistle and Townshend had given him a wide berth at school, since in spite of the fact that he stood at just 5ft 7in, Daltrey was also referred to as 'Big Bad Rog', such was his predilection for fighting and all-round mayhem.

Daltrey's reputation had been sealed by his expulsion from the school before he could sit his final exams. He had gone on to start an apprenticeship at a local sheet-metal factory. Skiffle had inspired him to pick up the guitar and now he had a band of his own – The Detours. Like The Scorpions, they were in thrall to Cliff and the Shadows and not that much more advanced. Coincidentally, The Detours were in need of a bassist, the previous incumbent, a Vic Arnold, having just walked out on them. As their paths crossed, Daltrey couldn't fail to see that Entwistle was hefting a bass and seized his opportunity. Writing of this meeting in 2018, Daltrey remembered: 'I hadn't really known John at school, but I'd spotted him. You couldn't help it . . . he was big and tall. He had a strange gait. He walked like John Wayne. I hadn't seen him since I'd left school, but now here he was . . . and I lied to him. "We're getting real bookings and going to start making real money."[1]

In truth, The Detours were earning pocket money playing works' outings, weddings and bar mitzvahs, but this was enough for Entwistle to see them as a step up from The Scorpions. Daltrey invited him along to a rehearsal at their drummer Harry Wilson's house in Shepherd's Bush the following week, after which Entwistle accepted an offer to join the band. He was also swayed by the fact that The Detours had the use of a Vox amplifier, which was altogether more potent than his Goodman and he would be able to share.

That July, Entwistle and his cohorts left Acton County. He had managed a handful of O-level passes, Music, Art and English among them and, like Townshend did, might have gone on to Ealing Art College. He was, though, expected by his stepfather now at least to contribute to the household costs at 81a Southfield Road. He took a junior civil servant's position in the Ministry of Pensions department at the Inland Revenue offices on Bromyard Avenue, where his mother was also employed. The role required him to wear a suit and tie, although the work was otherwise undemanding. Just as Queenie had counselled, as long as he walked around all day with reams of paper stuffed under his arms, he would look busily occupied.

Outside his nine-to-five job, Entwistle continued for a time to see Mick Brown, the two of them meeting up on Saturday afternoons to go to the pictures. One night, they went together to see the hallowed Cliff and the Shadows at the Dominion Theatre

---

[1]   Taken from *Thanks a Lot, Mr Kibblewhite: My Life* by Roger Daltrey, Blink (2018)

in nearby Southall. Brown remembers that Entwistle stood rigid and silent all through that show, fixated on the bass playing of Jet Harris. Once weekly, he also went back to Acton County to partner Alison at a ballroom dance class. 'John was a very good dancer,' she says. 'Partners were made to dance in class holding up a 78 record between them, so you would have to be pretty close. I didn't mind that one bit.'

To begin with, his other means of escape with The Detours proved to be more testing. The band as it was just didn't feel right to him; for one thing, their singer, Colin Dawson, was an acolyte of the squeaky-clean Cliff Richard and so, Entwistle considered, 'just a bit too dapper'; for another, in his opinion neither Harry Wilson nor rhythm guitarist Reg Bowen was up to much. He started a campaign of carefully badgering the volatile Daltrey, their self-appointed leader, with a ready-made fix for one of these handicaps at least. In the event, it took him months to convince Daltrey to make an overture to Townshend. Even then, Townshend was only persuaded on board by Entwistle dangling the carrot of the self-same Vox amplifier.

■ ■ ■

By the summer of 1962 and with Townshend now in their ranks, The Detours had started to gig more earnestly around London. Among the earliest recorded dates by the new line-up was an engagement at Boseley's Dance Hall in Shepherd's Bush that June and a brace of shows at the Paradise Club, Peckham, on 1 July and 2 August. On 1 September, they played Acton Town Hall and, in between these shows, did one-night stands at the Jewish Club in Ealing and at a company do at the engineering firm where Alison went to work as a secretary upon leaving Acton County.

Prior to that Shepherd's Bush booking, Harry Wilson took off on a fortnight's holiday with his family and thereby sealed his own fate. The drummer brought in that night by Daltrey as an intended fill-in turned out to be a much more able player and, upon his return, Wilson was let go without ceremony. Doug Sandom had been a jobbing musician for five years by that point and struck up an immediate rapport with Entwistle. Sandom also informed his new, teenage band-mates that he was twenty-four, when in reality he was thirty-two.

'Irish' Jack Lyons had moved from his native Cork a couple of years earlier to live with his uncle and aunt in Shepherd's Bush. Nineteen years old and working in the post room of the local London Electricity Board office, he was among the thirty-three souls to pay 3s 6d admission to witness the Detours' performance at Boseley's Dance Hall. 'They elected to play on the dance floor because the stage was so big and it seemed about a mile away,' he recounts. 'There were five of them in the band. The first thing that struck me was their funeral suits – with white shirts and ties and three-pointed cardboard handkerchiefs in the top pockets of the jackets. The drummer had the letters 'DS' emblazoned on his bass drum and looked to be at least ten years older than the others. The singer looked like Cliff Richard and sang several Cliff hits such as 'Move It' and 'The Young Ones'. They did some trad jazz numbers by Acker Bilk and a lot of Shadows material. They even did the dance steps whilst playing. The bass player was obviously the one with the most talent.'

At this formative stage, The Detours' one and only fanatical supporter was Townshend's mother. The assiduous Betty Townshend hustled them dance hall bookings and then drove them to these dates in a rented Ford van. Crucially, she also called in a favour from a contact she had made during her time as a big-band singer when she had gone by the stage name of Betty Dennis. Through his company Commercial Entertainments, Bob Druce was the biggest booking agent in the region, running a circuit of venues that included the White Hart Hotel in Acton, the Goldhawk Social Club in Shepherd's Bush and, further afield, the Florida Rooms at the Brighton Aquarium. Getting on Druce's circuit could keep a band in steady, year-round employ.

Betty cajoled Druce along to the group's Acton Town Hall date in September, but their act that night left him underwhelmed. Mrs Townshend, though, was nothing if not persistent and persuaded Druce to give them a second chance. By way of an audition, Druce booked them as the opening act to his premier band, The Bel Airs, at another of his venues, the Oldfield Hotel in Greenford. The warm reception they subsequently got from the Oldfield regulars convinced Druce to take them on for his standard agent's fee of 10 per cent, plus an additional 10 per cent commission for management duties. Druce also loaned them £40 to buy a van. Daltrey picked out the vehicle – an old Austin Post Office van. They painted it maroon and black, and daubed 'DETOURS' down one side in white. To complete the transformation, Daltrey welded a black pipe to the roof like a chimney.

They had an inauspicious beginning under their new agent. Druce signed them up to a regular gig at his latest venue, a pub in the sleepy Kent seaside town of Broadstairs. Every week there they played to sparse audiences of less than twenty souls, Daltrey now piloting their van across London and out to the Kent coast, despite the fact that he hadn't yet got his driver's licence. However, with their mettle tested, Druce moved them up to his livelier, better-paying venues and soon they were playing four or five nights a week, their sets geared towards songs in the Top Forty hit parade.

One night in October 1962, Daltrey brought along to rehearsals a new single that he had picked up. 'Love Me Do', Daltrey informed the others, was by a band out of Liverpool, The Beatles. Trained by the Middlesex Youth Orchestra in perfect, concert pitch, the song was an affront to Entwistle's exacting standards.

'Roger thought The Beatles were going to be big, so we had to learn it,' he wrote. 'When he played us the record, I was horrified. John Lennon's mouth organ was out of tune. It drove me nuts. I prayed that it wouldn't be a hit, but of course it was and when Roger played the mouth organ part onstage with us, he was even more out of tune than Lennon, if that was possible. It meant that because of that one song, we had to tune all of our instruments to the harmonica. I was in hell.'

Easy enough to maintain for art school student Townshend, the relentlessness of their schedule was exacting on Entwistle and the others who had day jobs. It left none of them time to keep up friendships outside of the band and tensions soon bubbled to the surface. By the end of the year, Colin Dawson had departed. His replacement, Gabby Connolly, was until then serving as bassist in The Bel Airs and his transfer to The Detours was indicative of the younger band's ascendancy. Connolly's tenure lasted just a matter of months, the workload too much for his fiancée who gave him an ultimatum – her or The Detours. As a parting shot, Connolly sold his Fender Precision bass guitar to Entwistle.

By this process of elimination, Daltrey now became their singer. Daltrey was mindful of the fact that Townshend was a much better guitarist than him. Also, at one of their last gigs with Connolly, they had all been impressed with the blazing, four-piece line-up of the band that they were opening up for, Johnny Kidd and the Pirates. That night, frontman Kidd had sported a pantomime eye patch and waved about a plastic cutlass. Daltrey was by no means that kind of colourful character, but he was charismatic and he looked the part. At nineteen, he saw himself as a man of the world. He was soon to be married, too, having got his sixteen-year-old girlfriend pregnant. Sandom was also married and Townshend affected a bohemian lifestyle in his student digs, but the eighteen-year-old Entwistle was still living at home. That same year, he moved with his mother and stepfather out of Southfield Road and a stone's throw away into a terraced house at 18 Lexden Road. There were, too, other reasons for him being regarded as the odd one out in the group.

'John was even more introverted than Pete in the beginning,' says Richard Barnes, Townshend's flatmate at the time. 'We were at art school, smoking pot and had long hair. John worked in the tax office. We were very judgemental; we used to laugh our heads off at him. He was weird, too. There was this one thing that Pete used to point out; sometimes after a gig, we would go to the Wimpy bar in West Ealing, which was a big treat. Pete would sit and watch as John habitually picked the gherkin off his burger and very carefully peeled from it all of the skin. This would take him about ten minutes to do.

'None of them socialised outside of the band. The chemistry between them was really odd. A lot of that was down to Roger, who was difficult to get on with, and John never said very much. He would tend to blend into the background. Back then, he and Alison only had eyes for each other. Whenever she came along for a night, it was like we would have to throw a bucket of cold water over them in the back of the van.'

Around this same time and doubtless to try to appear more enigmatic, Entwistle adopted his girlfriend's forename. For a very brief period, he went by the alias of 'Johnny Allison'. 'He stopped using it because I told him it didn't sound right and that it was daft,' Alison insists. 'But there's love for you.'

■ ■ ■

A turning point for popular culture in Britain came to pass at 6.35pm on the evening of Wednesday, 1 January 1964. It was then that the first episode of the BBC's new music television show, *Top of the Pops*, was broadcast from a disused church in Rusholme in Manchester. Among the acts appearing that night were The

Beatles, performing 'I Want to Hold Your Hand', their third UK Number-One single in a row, and the band that was shaping up to be their closest rivals, The Rolling Stones, with their version of another Lennon-McCartney song, 'I Wanna Be Your Man'.

Ten days earlier, The Detours had encountered The Stones for the first time when they opened up a show for them at St Mary's Hall in Putney. The two bands played together again at the Glenlyn Ballroom, Forest Hill, on 3 January. At the first of these dates, Townshend had spied The Stones' guitarist, Keith Richards, warm up by raising his arm vertically over his guitar and then swinging it down again like a windmill. Soon enough, Townshend would make the windmill part of his own act.

Townshend had also been gifted a collection of R&B and blues records by an American college friend who was being deported. Choice selections from this motherlode, such as James Brown's 'Please, Please, Please' and Howlin' Wolf's 'Smokestack Lightning', were now popping up in The Detours' sets, with the effect of making their sound harder and more urgent. They were getting louder, too, principally Entwistle and Townshend, as a result of their mutual discovery of a music shop in West Ealing. The proprietor of Marshall's Music, Jim Marshall, had begun manufacturing his own signature amplifiers and Entwistle bought himself one of the very first of these, a four-by-twelve bass cabinet. Entwistle was so taken with his new acquisition that he quickly shelled out for another, doubling his volume. Townshend followed his example, kick-starting a battle for supremacy that was to last the better part of forty years.

What The Detours didn't yet have was a name that slipped off the tongue easily, like The Beatles or The Stones did; or the kind of impresario manager that those bands had in the form of Brian Epstein and Andrew Loog Oldham – someone able to launch them up and out of the grinding pub circuit. The fix for the first of these problems was pressed upon them on the evening of 1 February, when they witnessed an Irish band calling themselves Johnny Devlin and the Detours performing on ITV's popular light entertainment show, *Thank Your Lucky Stars*. Assembled at Townshend's flat the very next Friday night to brainstorm alternatives, it was Richard Barnes whose suggestion was the only one to win unanimous support – The Who.

Sandom's sister-in-law, Rose Kume, introduced them to the man who was to be their first manager. Like Epstein, Helmut Gordon was Jewish, but there the similarities between the two men ended. A German refugee, Gordon was forty-nine, short, balding, lived with his mother and owned the doorknob-making factory where Rose worked. Gordon had no experience of the music business, but money to spare and that was enough to lure the newly-christened Who. Immediately, Gordon funded the purchase of a new van, a Commer diesel. Next, he dispatched them to be kitted out with new stage gear – leather waistcoats, and to go along with these, the kind of ankle-length, Cuban heel boots worn by The Beatles and made by Anello & Davide's of Covent Garden. Since they were on Gordon's bill, Daltrey, Townshend and Sandom each picked out two pairs of boots. Entwistle, on the other hand, just had to have a pair in every available colour and got himself fourteen. He also tapped Gordon up for a set of gold doorknobs to go on the chest of drawers in his bedroom at home, but in this instance was made to fork out 6s for the privilege.

The most significant effect that Gordon had was an entirely unintended one but, ultimately, it completed them as The Who. That spring, he arranged for them to audition for Chris Parmenter, an A&R rep and producer for Fontana Records. The audition went ahead on 9 April at a restaurant club on Edgware Road, the Zanzibar, that Gordon had hired for the occasion. That afternoon, they ran through several numbers, impressing the watching Parmenter. However, Parmenter also told them that Sandom's drumming wasn't up to scratch. Straight away, Townshend snapped at Sandom to sort himself out. The humiliated Sandom quit on the spot, although he was talked into staying on just long enough for them to honour their most pressing commitments.

What took place next has been a matter of some conjecture, but most of the principal participants have agreed that Keith Moon entered the picture at the Oldfield Hotel, Greenford, on the night of 30 April 1964. The Who had got hold of a stand-in drummer for this date, Dave Golding, a session player who also worked at Marshall's Music. Golding was behind the kit for their first set that night. During the interval, Moon approached Entwistle, Townshend and Daltrey and asked them if he could sit in for their second set.

Moon was the drummer for another of Bob Druce's acts, The Beachcombers, but had wearied of their more sugar-coated sound. He made a strong enough impression for the three of them to consent to him joining The Who for three songs, using Golding's kit. But then, the puppy-eyed, hyperactive Moon was a born show-off. That particular evening, he also appeared to be even more striking than usual. He had made an ill-conceived attempt to dye his hair blonde so as to look like his hero, Dennis Wilson of The Beach Boys, and turned it instead a carrot-shade of orange. In any event, the effect of Moon hurling himself into the first of his allotted numbers – Bo Diddley's 'Road Runner' – was instantaneous, whiplashing The Who up to full throttle.

Directly after that second set, Daltrey made arrangements with Moon to collect him for their next gig, which took place two nights later at a twenty-first birthday party at a pub on the North Circular Road. Moon brought along his own powder-blue kit to that show, fastening it to the stage with a length of rope in order to stop it from collapsing under the fury of his assault. At seventeen, Moon was appreciably younger than the other three, and different also in the respect that he was from north London and had not gone to grammar school. At once, though, Moon ignited something in each of them that, in turn, fired The Who to a whole new level – Entwistle most of all.

It was the utter abandon of Moon's playing that compelled Entwistle into becoming The Who's anchor, since he had no option but to secure their sound against this new drummer's battering. Clownish, effervescent, Moon was also a foil for the blackly comic side of Entwistle's personality, much more so than Townshend who had always held something in reserve and in ways that were simply alien to Daltrey's nature. In summary, he was to fill a yawning gap in Entwistle's life. 'Moon was,' Entwistle once expressed, 'like a little brother.'

4

Fab Four

Even before Moon appeared on the scene, Helmut Gordon had been enthusing about the boundless potential of his charges to almost everyone he met. This included his barber, Jack Marks. It so happened that another regular at Marks' Soho barbershop was a go-getting young man looking to make a name for himself in the music business. Peter Meaden was a twenty-two-year-old Londoner, an advertising copy-writer by trade, but had parlayed his way into doing freelance publicity for The Rolling Stones. Nothing if not persuasive, Meaden looked the part, since he got himself up in a sharp Italian suit, had his hair clipped into a French-style crew-cut, and spoke with the rat-a-tat intensity of machine-gun fire. A dedicated follower of the aspirational, fashion-conscious youth cult that sprang from Soho coffee shops in the late fifties, Meaden was a Mod – and not just any Mod, but an 'ace face', which is to say that even among his fellow Mods he was viewed as a trend-setter.

Meaden's association with The Stones had tailed off by that spring, so that when he heard of The Who mid-haircut from Marks, he pressed him for an introduction to Gordon.

The obliging barber took Meaden along to a meeting with Gordon and also Bob Druce, still retained as the band's agent. Fuelled by all the amphetamine pills he was taking, Meaden's typically fast-talking pitch won the two older men over and Druce handed him £50 seed money to open his campaign for The Who. Foremost in Meaden's thinking was his intention to mould them into being the first true Mod band. In this respect, he could be forgiven for thinking that he had picked the perfect moment.

The Mod movement had just then gravitated from its traditional central and west London enclaves into the white-hot spotlight of national notoriety. Two months earlier, several hundred Mods had travelled down from London to Clacton for the Easter weekend and had clashed with police along the seafront of the Essex town. Minor skirmishes in reality, they were leapt upon by the English press as a glaring example of depraved youth. This view was to gain traction on the Bank Holiday Monday of 18 May when more gangs of Mods fought with their arch enemies, the Rockers, in three other seaside towns – Brighton, Margate and Bournemouth – prompting newspapers such as the *Daily Mirror* to posit that the very social order of the country was in jeopardy. The Who were actually in Brighton that same Bank Holiday weekend to play a brace of shows at Druce's Florida Rooms on 16 and 17 May.

By that point, the band had done a second audition arranged for Chris Parmenter and his boss at Fontana, Jack Baverstock. This also went ahead at the Zanzibar on Tuesday, 5 May. For safe measure, Gordon covered the expense of having a back-up drummer, Brian Redman, travel down from Liverpool should Moon prove as unpalatable as poor Doug Sandom to the record company executives. In turn, Moon and Redman sat in with the band on one of the songs they performed that afternoon, a wannabe Mod anthem titled 'I'm the Face' written by none other than the scheming Meaden. This audition was a success, Parmenter and Baverstock committing to cut a record with The Who. Redman was returned to Liverpool, having been paid £40 for his troubles.

From 7 May at the Oldfield Hotel, Greenford, to 31 May at the White Hart Hotel, Acton, the band did fifteen more shows with their new drummer. The Entwistle–Moon axis began to be established during this burst of activity, both at the core of the band's sound and on a more personal level. Moon's playing was every bit as wilful and impatient as his character. This presented Entwistle with an opportunity as much as it did a challenge, and the push and pull that went on between the two of them – and Townshend – was the dynamic that ultimately led The Who to forge their own unique identity. For as well as compelling Entwistle into being custodian of the band's tempo, Moon's erratic time-keeping also made elastic the limits of what might be possible for the three of them musically.

Genetically incapable of adhering to basic twelve-bar blues patterns, from these initial gigs onwards, Moon got down to reshaping and hurrying The Who along with his epileptic volleys and fills. Townshend followed suit with terse, slashing chords, doubling up the beat. Just as significantly, it was a fortunate accident for The Who that in Entwistle they had a bass guitarist with the instincts of a horn player and an only child's craving for attention. Rather than settle in the pockets of space vacated for him by Moon and Townshend, as the typical bass player would, and so fasten them to the same moorings as The Beatles and The Stones, Entwistle sought to inhabit every square inch at his disposal.

Like Moon, the way that Entwistle began to play was reflective of facets of his personality. Ordered and dependable on the one hand, he was on the other just as extravagant and unpredictable.

In total, what this made The Who into was a rock band able to play with the dash and flair of a free jazz trio; or, as Townshend wrote: 'We each occupied a specific part of the sonic spectrum. John was always uneasy with being merely a bass player [and] even at this time his playing was expressive and creative, almost a second lead instrument.'[2]

In the more human sense, Moon's presence in the band gave Entwistle someone who he could spark off, an accomplice. When Daltrey and Townshend each started to drive their own cars to shows, Entwistle and Moon became inseparable, travelling together and beginning to form their very own comic double act. United in their outlandish humour, they were soon also maintaining an antipathetic distance from the conflict of will and ego that was to escalate within The Who, and which was to rage between Daltrey and Townshend for the leadership of the band.

■ ■ ■

One afternoon in June, The Who went into the Philips studio at Stanhope Place, Marble Arch, with Parmenter and Baverstock to record their début single. The track chosen was 'Zoot Suit', also nominally written by Meaden, but in effect an almost note-for-note revision of another song, 'Misery', released a year earlier by the Detroit R&B group The Dynamics. The only real changes that Meaden made for his version of the song were to the title and the lyrics, re-fashioning it as a Mod manifesto for the band. That much was blatant from the opening lines that he had Daltrey sing: 'I'm the hippest number in town and I'll tell you why; I'm the snappiest dresser right down to my inch-wide tie.'

At this distance, all that stands out about 'Zoot Suit' and also 'I'm a Face', which was picked to be its flip side, is how subdued each song sounds. There is none of the firepower The Who had

---

[2] Taken from *Who I Am* by Pete Townshend, Harper (2012)

started to be able to conjure; not a trace of Entwistle's vaulting harmonics, much less a hint of the state of near-tumult that he, Moon and Townshend would attain. It is recognisably Daltrey, albeit at a formative moment, but the band behind him might as well have been a conventional beat group.

With the single in the can, Meaden embarked upon the next stages of his grand plan for the band. First, he convinced them that they required a more Mod-friendly name. They also acquiesced to his suggestion – 'The High Numbers', an overt reference to the Mod movement's pill-popping aesthetic. Indicative of hustle on Meaden's part rather than their own status, the 27 June edition of the *Melody Maker* reported the change of name in its news pages. Second, Meaden set about doing all that he could with Druce's £50 to get them to look less like The Beatles, with their Pierre Cardin leather jackets and floppy-fringed haircuts, and more like hip-to-it Mods. In this endeavour, he found a most willing guinea pig in Townshend, while Daltrey and Moon were happy enough to go along with the ruse. Entwistle proved to be tougher to convince and made sure to get something for himself out of the deal.

'Peter took us to his barber's and we had all of our hair cut off,' he recalled in 1986. 'Roger was given decent clothes to wear – a nice seersucker jacket, white Italian shoes with a black surround. The rest of us got taken to a sports store and were bought ice-skating jackets, Levi jeans with half-inch turn-ups and boxing boots. I wanted Roger's clothes instead of the stupid skating jackets. The first puddle I made sure to walk through, the soles of the boxing boots fell off. Eventually, we all got to wear seersucker jackets.'[3]

Sixteen at the time, Ian Gillingham was Entwistle's cousin and had also been brought up in South Acton. 'John was three years

---

[3] Taken from an uncredited interview on YouTube dated 20 March 1986

older than me but, in those days, I was the same size as him,' he says. 'He started to go to Carnaby Street and in one swoop would buy twelve pairs of mohair trousers and the same number of jackets and shirts. He'd wear these clothes once and then wouldn't want them any more. I'd go round to his house and buy armfuls of his cast-offs from his mum at three bob a time; keep what I wanted, sell on the rest and make a tidy profit. John took a smaller shoe than me. There was one occasion when he threw out these lovely, leather stage shoes and I just had to have them. They had to have been a size too small for me, but I wore them for one whole day until my feet bled.'

Credited to The High Numbers, the 'Zoot Suit'/'I'm the Face' single was released by Fontana on Friday, 3 July. Meaden made sure that it was accompanied by a profile piece on the band in the 11 July edition of *Record Mirror*. Hailing the single as 'the first authentic Mod record', the article went on to give pen portraits of the four members. For the purpose of this, the conflicted Entwistle had temporarily reverted back to his alias, but the music paper nonetheless presented him in just one dimension. 'On bass is John Allison,' *Record Mirror* announced. 'He is certainly the most conservative of the group, preferring classical music to most other kinds.'

The single was Meaden's trump card but, in effect, it was hardly given a chance, since Fontana only had a scant 1,000 copies pressed up. Meaden did his best to get it to chart, buying up 250 copies from the record company and paying 'Irish' Jack Lyons in Purple Hearts pills to hawk them at Shepherd's Bush Market that Saturday. 'What a fool I was,' says Lyons. 'I spent three hours baking in the hot July sun, but nobody wanted to know. In the entire time, I sold just three copies. I think John's aunt ended up buying a dozen copies on her own, which dried up the stock of one record shop in Acton.'

It was all for nothing. The single didn't manage even to scrape into the national Top Fifty and sank without trace. This was a mortal blow for Meaden, for with a band that was becoming as ruthlessly determined as this one, failure would simply not be tolerated.

■ ■ ■

In the two weeks leading up to the release of the single, the band had begun a new Tuesday night residency in the dingy basement room of a north-west London hotel, the Railway. The nights were being co-promoted by Richard Barnes who meant to turn the Railway's traditional 'Bluesday R&B Club' into a rallying point for the local Mods. Billed on both occasions as The Who, they débuted on 30 June and, by the next 7 July date, the street outside the Railway had already started to be lined with Lambretta and Vespa scooters.

'It was a packed room, like a dungeon, and they had a tiny stage down there,' remembers Ian Gillingham, who was to become a Railway regular. 'All the local Mods would go there and they loved the band. Two things you were always guaranteed at the Railway – a fight, and that The Who would be brilliant.'

'Those were fucking amazing nights,' adds Barnes. 'We stuck black tape over the windows to make it darker, put in red lightbulbs and had all the radiators turned up so that it would be even hotter down there. The band just got better and better, week by week. The Railway was a shithole, but it very quickly became their Mod club, even though John hated the whole Mod thing. Unlike the others, he just didn't go along with it at all.'

On the night of Tuesday, 14 July, Barnes spied an unfamiliar face lurking at the front desk of the hotel. With his dark-grey suit and immaculately polished shoes, Kit Lambert looked to Barnes to be utterly out of place and like nothing so much as a council official. Fearing that he was about to be inspected for overcrowding the venue, Barnes confronted Lambert who told him that he was, in fact, on the look-out for a band to hire.

At twenty-nine, Lambert was from a privileged background. His late father, Constant Lambert, had been a well-respected composer and had also founded the company of the Royal Ballet. Lambert had progressed from public school to Trinity College, Oxford, where he had studied history. He was also conspicuously gay at a time when homosexuality was still deemed to be a criminal offence in Britain.

After Oxford, Lambert had gone into the film industry at Shepperton Studios, serving as assistant director on *The Guns of Navarone* and, more recently, a James Bond film, *From Russia with Love*. At Shepperton, he had befriended Chris Stamp, seven years his junior, a working-class East End lad by birth and younger brother of the actor Terence Stamp. Lambert and Stamp entered into a production partnership and, for their first project, they had designs to make a documentary film about a young group making its way in the booming London music business. On a tip-off, Lambert had gone along to the Railway to scout the Tuesday night house band. The Railway was to him like a vision of Hades and he was no more than a dilettante where rock-'n'-roll was concerned, but he knew enough to recognise the galvanising effect of this four-piece. After being introduced by Barnes to Meaden, he made arrangements to have Stamp fly over from Ireland, where he was working on another film, to check out the band for himself at their next gig at Watford's Trade Union Hall that coming Saturday.

Stamp, along with another associate, Mike Shaw, only made it to Watford in time to catch the last fifteen minutes of The High Numbers' set, but he was as enthusiastic as his partner about the band. Events proceeded at a pace from this point. Although Lambert shot forty minutes of black-and-white, 16mm footage of the High Numbers' 11 August set at the Railway, the film idea had by then become very much a secondary concern. Uppermost now in Lambert's and Stamp's minds was the notion that they take over the band's management. To that end, they had courted the four principals with the offer of a guaranteed salary of £1,000 a year each. Daltrey – separated from his teenage bride and, by sheer coincidence, dating Constant Lambert's god-daughter, Cleo – emerged as their strongest advocate within the group.

To draw up a formal contract, Lambert and Stamp took on the Beatles' lawyer, David Jacobs, who also advised them on extricating the band from the terms they had signed with both Gordon and Druce. Since Meaden was freelance, Lambert proposed to pay him off with a cursory sum of £500. Entwistle, like the others, had no particular loyalty to either Gordon or Stamp, but felt honour-bound to Meaden. Even still, and again like Daltrey, Townshend and Moon, he wasn't about to let that stand in the way of bettering both the band's and his own lot. By the middle of that August, Lambert and Stamp had seized the reins, Gordon, Druce and Meaden were all out of the frame and, soon enough, the new managers had ditched The High Numbers name and had them revert back to being The Who.

There wasn't time for any of them to stop and take stock. Gordon's last act had been to talk another prominent booking agent, Arthur Howes, into putting the band on as opening act at a series of seaside package concerts that he had set up for that August; the catch being that they were allotted just fifteen minutes for their sets and also had to double up as backing group for another of Howes' acts, a singer named Val McCullam. Intermingled with their own regular dates, the first of these shows had gone ahead on Sunday, 9 August at Brighton Hippodrome with Gerry and the Pacemakers topping the bill. By the next Sunday, Lambert and Stamp had assumed charge of their affairs when they were to journey up to Blackpool. Howes had booked them for matinée and evening shows at the town's Opera House, and where The Beatles would be headlining. 'Blackpool, up north in a converted furniture van (top speed 40mph),' Entwistle recalled, taking up the story in handwritten notes he prepared for his autobiography:

There was no M1 motorway back then, just the good old winding, dangerous A1. Keith and I decided we wouldn't be able to stand the trip, so we hitched a lift in Kit Lambert's Volkswagen – 80mph of unleashed fury, downhill. Pete and Roger were there already when we arrived. They'd left the day before us and stayed the night in Rugby. I was particularly excited to do our sound check as I'd just bought a brand-new Rickenbacker bass, only the second in England, and had developed a twangy, trebly bass sound through my two Marshall amps. We went back to our dressing room and waited excitedly for The Beatles to turn up. 'Hard Day's Night' had just been released and The Beatles were the biggest thing in England since fish and chips.

A sudden commotion signalled their arrival. I poked my head around the dressing room door just as John Lennon rushed by. 'Hey ya!' he shouted into my face. The smell of beer nearly knocked me over. By the time I recovered, the other three Beatles were already in their dressing room.

Coming offstage after our first set, I found myself face to face with Paul McCartney. 'The Rickenbacker sounded pretty good – what's it like?' he asked me. 'It's great, nice trebly strings; you just have to watch the angle of the strings in the nut,' I told him. I guess he must have believed me – he bought one soon after.

We settled down in our own dressing room to listen to The Beatles. The old theatre dressing rooms in those days always had a speaker feed on the wall direct from the stage mics. The noise of little girls screaming was so deafening that all you could hear of The Beatles' instruments was the intros to each of their songs. The direct feed, though, allowed the four of us to hear their words loud and clear. It became apparent that The Beatles had figured that since the screaming couldn't be stopped and no one out front in the audience could possibly hear a thing, then they might as well have some fun. Soon, the four of us were crying with laughter at the words they were singing and which only we were able to pick up on: 'It's been a hard day's cock . . .' 'I wanna hold your cunt . . .' They struck a last chord and they were gone. And we got on with the task of packing our own gear away.

Witnessing The Beatles at such close quarters, Entwistle and his band-mates would barely have been able to contemplate reaching such a rarefied level. In regard to making a career for themselves, they still lagged a way behind another band on that Opera House bill, one that had come together in north London just a matter of months earlier – The Kinks. That much was made glaringly apparent when Lambert and Stamp tried accelerating them into a bigger, south London venue as the main attraction. They booked them to do four shows at Greenwich Town Hall from 23 September and, at each one of these dates, attendances were embarrassingly sparse.

Yet also over the course of those next few weeks, aspects that would define them as a band and as individuals came into sharp focus. At one of their regular Railway Hotel shows that September, Townshend smashed up a guitar onstage for the first time. On that occasion, Townshend did it thoughtlessly, instinctively; he had inadvertently stuck the neck of his guitar through the venue's low ceiling and, enraged by laughter coming from the audience, took out his frustrations on his instrument. Moon aped him at one of their next gigs, leaping up at the end of their set to kick and hurl his drums across the stage. By the time they played the Olympia Ballroom in Reading on 10 October, both destructive acts had become fixtures in their show. At the first of the ill-starred Greenwich shows, meanwhile, an eyewitness reported Townshend to have played with a Union Jack flag draped over his amp.

Entwistle's response to the carnage spiralling onstage was to typify him – he remained apparently impassive, unperturbed, offering up at most a sardonic smirk. In fact, the wantonness of it all appalled him. He regarded musical instruments as being precious, near-sacred objects to the extent that were he ever to scratch a bass or trumpet, it would make him sick to his stomach. He, too, though, was at that very same time changing and evolving. In his case, it was as if through his alliance with Moon he was able to absolve himself from keeping up appearances and freed to unleash his instincts. To begin with at least, this 'coming out' happened in just one area of his life, in small increments, and with nothing but minor collateral damage as a result.

'There was a girl who I fancied rotten, used to travel into work with every day, and John went and nicked her,' remembers Ian Gillingham. 'She had gone to see The Who, met John and he had taken her phone number and called her. She hadn't known he was my cousin. He was with Alison, but he carried on for a little while with this girl, too. That was John. Eventually, he had a girl in every port, I think.'

Townshend once again noted: 'Roger and I got the impression that John and Keith did almost everything together, including having sex with girls.'[4]

---

[4] Taken from *Who I Am* by Pete Townshend, Harper (2012)

5

Maximum R&B

The one major weapon that The Who still now lacked was their own material, and of the kind that Lennon and McCartney gave The Beatles and that Ray Davies had just begun to service The Kinks with, namely hits. Lambert turned to Townshend, encouraging him towards this new form of expression and with almost instant results. 'I Can't Explain' was among the first songs that Townshend put down on tape, working solo at his flat. Musically, he took his cues from 'You Really Got Me', the Ray Davies tune that he had first heard from The Kinks in Blackpool. That summer, it had topped the UK singles chart. Just like it, Townshend's was a frenetic, two-minute eruption with a near-identical thwacking guitar riff. Both songs were also about sexual yearning but, in this regard, they were pitched very differently. Whereas Davies's song was lustful, cocksure, Townshend's was repressed, frustrated.

'You Really Got Me' had been recorded for The Kinks by a twenty-seven-year-old, ex-pat American producer named Shel Talmy. In 1962, Talmy had moved to London from Los Angeles and got himself a job as in-house producer at Decca Records.

Fortuitously, Lambert's and Stamp's secretary, Anya, happened to be friends with Talmy's wife and it was via this circuitous route that Lambert got Townshend's demo into the hands of the producer. Talmy liked what he heard and fixed up with Lambert to have The Who audition for him.

'I went to see them at a church hall,' Talmy recalls. 'It literally took me four bars to say, "Yes, I want to sign them." They were amazingly good from the get-go. When I got to London, all the music in England was what the crib sheets would call "polite". There were no real kick-ass bands around. The Who was the first kick-ass band that I heard in England.'

Talmy offered to fund a recording session, which went ahead one afternoon in early November 1964 at Pye Studios, off Marble Arch. There, over two hours, The Who cut 'I Can't Explain' and an additional track, 'Bald-Headed Woman', written by Talmy and which gave him the prospect of future royalties. Talmy also brought in a vocal trio, The Ivy League, to sing harmonies on 'I Can't Explain' and his regular session guitarist, a certain Jimmy Page, to add a fuzz-boxed rhythm track to 'Bald-Headed Woman'. Chris Stamp would later insist that Talmy had also wanted to substitute a session drummer for Moon, a claim the producer denies. What isn't in doubt is that no one but Entwistle was ever considered to accelerate 'I Can't Explain'. Using his new Rickenbacker and with wire-wound strings, Entwistle brought to Townshend's song an abrasive, toughened-up undercurrent that it would otherwise have lacked.

When he first heard 'I Can't Explain', Andy Fairweather Low was starting out as a musician in his native Cardiff. 'John's bass was not an instrument I'd been exposed to before,' he says. 'But then, nothing like that had ever been done. You can play the same notes, but the sound that John got with those wire strings and his whole personality – that was completely unique.'

Talmy adds, 'Entwistle and Moon were the two best players I've ever had together in one band. Together, they worked brilliantly. All of those guys were good. Hell, I think we got the song done in two, three takes. Everybody in the band I got along with fine, except for Daltrey. He apparently had at least two chips on his shoulders. I mean, great voice, could sing his ass off, but difficult.'

With 'I Can't Explain' in the can and undeterred by the setback in Greenwich, Lambert and Stamp redoubled their efforts to gain The Who a foothold in London beyond the confines of the Railway and their home turf. It was Stamp who orchestrated their next move that same month. The previous March, the Marquee Club had moved from Oxford Street to new Soho premises at 90 Wardour Street. Founded in 1958, the club had established its reputation promoting jazz and blues acts, becoming synonymous with the venerated likes of Chris Barber, Johnny Dankworth and Alexis Korner. Even though The Rolling Stones had débuted at the Marquee as far back as 1962, the club was nonetheless perceived to be in the vanguard of conservatism, or in Mod parlance, 'for squares'. As if to demonstrate the point, Tuesdays were still 'jazz night' at the Marquee, but these were proving the least popular events of the week at the poky new venue. Stamp made an entreaty to the Marquee's manager, Ziggy Jackson, assuring him that if he were to grant The Who a regular Tuesday night slot, it would be filled by the same band of loyal west London Mods that had turned out each week at the Railway.

Jackson took the bait, agreeing to book The Who on Tuesdays for sixteen straight weeks, two sets per night and starting 24 November. The two managers cranked their operation up a gear, enlisting 'Irish' Jack Lyons and another west London Mod, Martin Gaish, to be cheerleaders for the Marquee shows. Lambert had posters and handbills made up to advertise the residency, both bearing the same striking elements: a black-and-white photograph of Townshend in mid-windmill; a new band logo that had an arrow jutting up out of the 'o'; and under the graphic Who, the words 'Maximum R&B'. Lambert's was an adroit piece of image-building, but when the first Marquee night rolled around, neither it, nor the attentions of Lyons and Gaish, appeared to have worked. The club was all but deserted for both of their opening sets. The Who, though, played that night and the ones following as if their lives depended on it and, in due course, word began to spread. By the end of the year, they had broken the house attendance record and Jackson extended their residency for seven more weeks.

■ ■ ■

Lambert was fixated on Townshend, but The Who grew as a band over the entirety of the Marquee run, establishing roles for themselves onstage and within the framework of the group that would endure. In Entwistle's case, this was to be the glue that held a sometimes fragile, always volatile operation together. But also, there was no mistaking the fact that he was the outstanding musician of the four. Working as a correspondent for a teen magazine, *Fabulous*, Keith Altham was dispatched to the Marquee to report on The Who. 'That first time, I caught the end of their set, the last three or four numbers, and I didn't know what to make of them,' he recounts. 'I mean, they were hideously loud for a start. And then, the drummer appeared to be at war with the singer.

> The two of them kept on swearing at each other. Right at the end, there was the explosive business of Townshend ramming the neck of his guitar through his amp and Moon kicking his drum kit over in an apparent frenzy of fury; and John Entwistle looking on in the time-honoured manner of an umpire at a cricket match.

As I was going out the door, I was grabbed by the arm by this gnome-like character with an upper-crust voice – Kit Lambert. I went back into the Marquee bar and the first one of them out of the dressing room was Moon. 'Terribly sorry, dear boy, but I can't stop,' he told me. 'The singer wants to kill me. Might have something to do with the fact I told him he couldn't sing for shit.'

'After that first night, I crossed paths with them quite regularly. John was the hardest to get to know. He was kind of reclusive and very laid back in demeanour. People tended to leave him alone. I thought there was a ventriloquist's act going on between Entwistle and Moon – and with Moon being the dummy. As time went by, I discovered that it was John who put Moon up to a lot of the pranks that made his reputation. All of these outrageous acts would be John's ideas, but Moon got the credit because he was the one putting them into practice. Rather like Bill Wyman and Charlie Watts in The Stones, I think John preserved his sanity by keeping in the background and not getting in the firing line. In point of fact, he was very bright and had quite a lot say for himself once you got to know him.

Certainly musically, John filled in the gaps and kept the band together in many respects. I can't think of another bass player who could have actually played with Moon successfully. I mean, Moon was all over the bloody place. John was disciplined, but he was also dextrous and enormously important to them. Once they got into their stride, you'd watch them onstage and they would just fly. On nights such as those they were extraordinary – the most perfect rock-'n'-roll band I've ever heard.

In the aftermath of the Pye session, Talmy engineered deals for The Who with Decca in the UK and US. Lambert and Stamp leapt at these opportunities. Yet in their haste, the two managers made a series of egregious errors. First, they wrongly presumed that Decca UK and Decca US were one and the same company. They were, in fact, separate entities and the mustier US side of the operation was not functioning all that differently to the way that it had when it first started out in 1934. Second, they committed The Who to a paltry royalty rate of 2.5 per cent, half the industry average. And third, they additionally signed The Who up to Talmy's production company, tying them to the brash American for five years. In total, this would soon enough be to all of their considerable costs. However, it was not apparent to any of them on 15 January 1965 when 'I Can't Explain' was released in the UK through Decca's Brunswick imprint.

The single got off to a slow start, entering the UK chart at a lowly 45. But then it picked up traction, boosted by airplay support from two pirate radio stations, Radio Caroline and Radio London, and, even more so, the exposure afforded by the band's first national TV appearances on *Top of the Pops* and its more youthful, commercial TV equivalent, ITV's *Ready, Steady, Go!* By that April, 'I Can't Explain' had surged into the Top Ten. The immediate effect on The Who was to increase their workload further and they were to play almost 200 shows in 1965 alone. This apparent overnight success also had several more transformative effects on their enigmatic bassist.

The very day that 'I Can't Explain' came out, Entwistle became the last member to commit full-time to the band. His departure from the tax office was months behind Townshend's dropping out of college and even the ever-cautious Daltrey's giving up of his apprenticeship. At a stroke, the move reopened hostilities at home. 'Gordon wasn't at all happy about it,' notes Alison. 'He didn't think John was going to be able to bring in the pennies.' Directly afterwards, Entwistle set about presenting himself in a new light, one that was more befitting the exotic status of a pop star. His hair was naturally a mousy-brown in colour, so he dyed it jet-black. He had been disdainful when art student Townshend had first smoked dope, but that was when he was still an upstanding civil servant. Now, he started to develop the same greedy appetite for pep pills as both Townshend and Moon, and he also took up smoking.

'He never used to smoke until he was twenty,' says Alison. 'His mother smoked, so did his grandad, his gran was never without a fag in her mouth and I had been a smoker from when I was sixteen, but not John. Straight away, he was flashy about it, too. He would smoke these Russian cigarettes – Sobranies – that came in all kinds of different colours.'

From the outset, Entwistle's stepfather was correct to assume that this new career of his would be no guarantee of a steady income. Brunswick sold over 100,000 copies of The Who's single, but thanks to their paltry royalty rate, this yielded the four band members just £250 apiece. Moon's and Townshend's nightly bouts of instrument-trashing quickly ate that up. Since their weekly stipend from Lambert and Stamp also remained fixed at £20, Entwistle's total earnings were effectively more than halved. The spiteful Gordon didn't miss a chance to let his stepson know that he'd told him so, but Entwistle's circumstances were nothing like as stark as Daltrey's. With an estranged wife and child to support, the poverty-stricken singer was reduced to living out of the band's van. Testy at the best of times, Daltrey now seethed with resentment.

He had even been conflicted with the part he had played on 'I Can't Explain', having felt uncomfortable fronting Townshend's self-doubting words. Daltrey made this known to such an extent that Lambert suggested to Townshend that he placate him with a more inclusive role on the next single, which was to be 'Anyway, Anyhow, Anywhere'. Townshend acceded to Lambert and Daltrey was allowed to pitch in with the odd lyric. That subsequently got him a co-writing credit on the song, but it was to be a strictly one-off arrangement and, in any case, Townshend, Entwistle and Moon were also agitating to be rid of their singer. The night after recording a TV spot with Daltrey at the Marquee on 11 May, the three of them performed without him at an unbilled gig at the Top Rank Ballroom in Bury, Lancashire.

Steve Bolton, who would subsequently go on to tour as second guitarist with the band in 1989, was at this show. 'We got word on the Mod grapevine in Manchester that The Who were doing a secret gig three miles away and piled over to Bury in someone's car,' relates Bolton. 'It was actually too much of a secret. The three of them proceeded to do the gig to about forty people in the hall. They started off doing The Beach Boys' "Barbara Ann" with Moon singing and ended the set by completely destroying their gear.

'Before the show, they were all mingling about in the hall and I spoke to John Entwistle. He told me they were playing as a three-piece because Roger had done too much speed and was in hospital. Fast forward to 1989, and I brought up that very Bury gig with John at a party. On that occasion, he admitted that they had done the show just to see how things sounded without Roger.'

As it happened, so underwhelming was the experiment without Daltrey that it was ditched out of hand and he was back on board for their 13 May show in another Lancashire town, Barrow-in-Furness. At that time, the crew surrounding the band was expanding and the four of them would soon become accustomed to having someone to do their bidding. In this respect, Entwistle and Moon were first among equals. That same spring, Mike Shaw, working now as the band's production manager, enlisted a friend of his, Dave Langston, to help out with duties on the road. A capable guitarist, Langston was a larger-than-life character; voluble, uproarious and known to one and all as 'Cyrano', or 'Cy' for short, on account of his enormous nose. As it happened, Langston was only in The Who's employ for four months, but long enough for his eagerness to please to be noted by Entwistle. On account of that, he might, Entwistle considered, be a very useful man to have around and so he kept in touch.

■ ■ ■

Released on 21 May, 'Anyway, Anyhow, Anywhere' followed 'I Can't Explain' into the UK Top Ten. More pointedly, since Talmy had set Townshend's feedbacking guitar at the heart of the track, it sounded like a challenge to convention; so much so that Talmy received a telegram from Decca in America, complaining that he had sent them a faulty recording. This lack of comprehension on the record company's part doubtless contributed to the single's failure to chart in America. Indeed, altogether it was reflective of the generally troubled, dark mood around The Who.

'The members of the band were all very young and under the influence of Lambert, who became more disgusting as we went on together,' opines Talmy. 'Stamp, on the other hand, was a nonentity who never said much of anything. Everybody told me he was always stoned and I could believe it.'

The single also signalled another shift for The Who, and this was away from Mod and towards another, vogueish movement of the time – Pop Art. In The Who's case, their Pop Art period was heralded with an even more blatant appropriation of the Union Jack flag than Townshend's using of it merely as a drape for his amp. At Lambert's direction, Townshend had five Union Jack-emblazoned jackets made up at a Savile Row tailor's and which he and Entwistle routinely began to wear on- and offstage. Entwistle, though, took things further and had jackets made up for himself out of the Royal Standard flag and the Scottish cross of Saint Andrew, and took to parading about done up in waistcoats adorned with military medals and insignia.

'Once we got into the Pop Art clothes, we started to feel good about ourselves,' he said later. 'Performing-wise, it was important to feel in some way superior to the audience, and that we were ahead of them in dress. The Mod thing had made us feel at one with the audience and that hadn't been very good for our egos, and especially mine.' On the same subject, he added, 'My method was: if you're the only member of the band that's standing still, you've got to attract attention somehow. So I dressed like a peacock.'[5]

That summer, the band criss-crossed the country, playing an almost unbroken run of one-night stands. In contrast to their new Pop Art garb, the venues sounded wholly unglamorous – the Rondo, Leicester; the Co-Op Ballroom, Nuneaton; Stourbridge Town Hall; the Floral Hall Ballroom, Morecambe; the Gaiety Ballroom, Ramsey. And with whatever time he could snatch in between these dates, Townshend had started to work up a new song. It began as a slow blues, but one meant to capture something of the trailblazing, live-fast spirit of the speeding times. Entwistle had got to hear of Townshend's latest creation by 16 July when The Who pitched up in Cheltenham to play a local social club.

Attending that night was Entwistle's and Townshend's old schoolfriend and bandmate, Mick Brown, now moved to the area: 'I had lost touch with both of them completely for eighteen months or so, but then I saw a mention of them in the *New Musical Express* and rang John. He told me they were coming to Cheltenham the next week and we arranged to meet up for a

---

[5] Taken from an uncredited interview on YouTube dated 20 March 1986

cup of tea before the show. The first thing that struck me was that his hair didn't used to be black. After he had told me they had got managers and about their record contracts, he said, "Townshend's writing all the songs now . . ." – I thought it odd that it wasn't "Pete" any more – "and the next one's going to be called 'Talkin' 'Bout My Generation'." Then he added, "It's shit, but I suppose we'll have to do it."'

6

Latin Lover

The months either side of the making of 'My Generation' were turbulent even by the standards of a band as inflammatory as The Who. Indeed, just four weeks before they were due to go into the studio, they came as close to breaking up as they ever had done. That September in 1965, they made a quick sortie on to the continent to play five dates in Holland and Denmark. Daltrey's simmering frustrations with the other three's growing intake of amphetamines – the way the little 'French blues' pills made them chatter incessantly and their playing speed up – boiled over right after a chaotic show in the Danish port town of Aarhus. Storming back to the dressing room, Daltrey proceeded to flush Moon's stash of pills down the toilet, whereupon Moon leapt at Daltrey brandishing a tambourine as a weapon and the singer punched the flailing drummer, knocking him out.

There was no question that Entwistle would side with Moon, or that Townshend would back the two of them over Daltrey. The upshot was that Daltrey was effectively cast out from the band, pending the interventions of Lambert and Stamp, and with a recording session to fulfil. It was in this poisonous state that The

Who gathered with Shel Talmy at central London's IBC studios on Portland Place late on the evening of Wednesday, 13 October to cut 'My Generation'. Since the summer, Townshend had made progress with the song, re-demoing it at a faster tempo and with the suggestion of stuttered lead vocal lines, which ironically referenced the fractured speech patterns of pilled-up Mods. According to Townshend, he had also set aside a part in the mid-section of the song for Entwistle to 'do a little Duane Eddy bit'.[6]

Around midnight and on their third pass at the song, Entwistle stepped up to take his lead role. He had bought an American-made Danelectro bass especially for the occasion, believing the extra-thin, wire-wound strings used on the model would allow him best to approximate Eddy's signature twanging sound. For the same reason, he elected just this once to use a plectrum over his preferred finger-picked method of playing. That first go he broke a string. The next, Townshend and the others complained that he'd made the part too fast, or too complicated, or both. Whatever Townshend might have had in mind, it's also likely that it didn't encompass the totality of what Entwistle summoned on the fifth take from 55 seconds into 'My Generation'. At around 30 seconds in duration, Entwistle's wasn't much more than a fleeting instrumental break. But his one-two-three punch of bubbling, rubbery notes gave an already thrilling-sounding song the electric-jolt shock of the new and pioneering.

'There were two standout things about the song, which were Daltrey's stammer and the bass solo,' considers Glyn Johns, Talmy's engineer at the session. 'I do remember thinking at the time that John's part was just fantastic and also a first. As a band, they were all quite original in their approach to what they were doing, but you could say that John was even more so, because he

---

[6] Taken from *Who I Am* by Pete Townshend, Harper (2012)

was so completely different to any other bassist. People were in awe of what he was doing and it *was* pretty jaw-dropping stuff.'

Talmy adds: 'Beforehand, I had spent two, three hours in the studio with just Pete, positioning mics around the recording room so that I could best capture the harmonics and overtones. In the studio at that time, John never said a goddamn word. In all the times that I recorded The Who, I never heard more than a dozen words out of him. He would just nod. At one point, I was concerned that he couldn't speak. But I've got to say that whole bass part was John's idea. Obviously, in the rock business it's become the most iconic bass solo of all time. And it was brilliant – there's nothing else to be said about it.'

'My Generation' was released in the UK a mere sixteen days after the session. Commercially, it performed better than either of its two predecessors, racing to Number Two on the charts. More significantly, in Britain it instantly resounded as an authentic, tremoring moment in pop culture: Daltrey's stammering; the pure brazenness of Townshend's 'hope I die before I get old' exhortation; and the furiousness and innovation of his, Entwistle's and Moon's musicianship. The combination of all of these elements into a three-minute pop single served to set The Who as a band apart. It also propelled them to the vanguard of a stirring in music, art and fashion that within six months would have been given a name by a cover story in American *Time* magazine – 'Swinging London'.

Two days after the 'My Generation' session, the band's internal frictions were put into sharp context. Driving their gear up north, Mike Shaw was involved in a serious road accident that was to leave him paralysed. It would be more than two years before he was able to return to an office job with The Who. Whether or not Shaw's plight focused minds isn't a matter of record, but the latest ruction with Daltrey was resolved soon afterwards.

Lambert and Stamp convened a band meeting; at this summit, Daltrey was told in no uncertain terms that, if he were to remain with the group, he would be required in future to exercise control of his temper. Crucially, Daltrey's acceptance of this condition marked the point at which he fully ceded leadership of the band to Townshend, and neither Entwistle nor Moon was about to let such a tilt pass without comment.

'The others begrudged my return,' Daltrey stated later. 'Keith, now that he was released from the threat of violence, would do everything he could think of to rile me up. If anything, John was worse. John had a spiteful streak. I don't know if it was because he was an only child, but he could be mean and say smart-arse things that deserved a punch in the mouth.'[7]

Apart from the band, Entwistle had other, more personal matters on his mind. Since The Who had been booked to do a show in Carlisle on the date of his twenty-first birthday, 9 October, a party was belatedly held for him the week following at Lexden Road. Moon was the sole other representative of The Who present that night. Herbert gifted his son a set of driving lessons. Entwistle was to take up just one of these lessons, before deciding he would much prefer to be able to drink than drive. That same evening, he also announced his engagement to Alison Wise.

'He had proposed to me when I was sitting on a pommel horse in the Acton Congregational Church hall,' Alison recalls. 'Just before his birthday, he went to see my mother to ask her for my hand in marriage. She listened to him very politely, thanked him very much for coming, but told him no. Then I went storming in and said, "Too bad, and whether you like it or not." My mother was a terrible snob, you see, and she didn't approve of his job.

---

[7] Taken from *Thanks a Lot, Mr Kibblewhite: My Life* by Roger Daltrey, Blink (2018)

'John got me a platinum engagement ring with a solitaire diamond, which he presented me with at the party. By then, my mother had gone into hospital. When she came out, she didn't pass comment on the ring, didn't admire it or anything. I was very upset at the time. Later on, she also tried to persuade my cousin, Ron, who was going to give me away, to talk me out of marrying John. But he refused.'

'It was a fun party,' furthers Ian Gillingham. 'And John was all right until Moon turned up. Moon brought along a bottle of Pernod and the two of them got absolutely slaughtered. We didn't see much of John after that; the two of them went upstairs to John's bedroom. All that was heard of them for the rest of the night was John wailing away on his trumpet.'

■ ■ ■

Such homespun occasions had become momentary interludes in between band business. Four days later, The Who were back out on the road. In quick succession, they ticked off dates in Southampton, Milford Haven, Bishop's Stortford, Slough, Watford and Swindon, rounding out the month playing a Hallowe'en Ball at Manchester University on 30 October and, the next night, The Beatles' old Liverpool stomping ground, the Cavern Club. In November, their schedule of live dates was just as full. That month they also went back into IBC with Talmy and recorded their début album over an intense three-day period.

More than fifty years on, the *My Generation* album still crackles and fizzes with a hit-the-ground-running sense of excitement. Essentially, an unadorned distillation of their live set of the time, it caught the young Who plugging in and letting rip, as callow and hyperactive as they were tenacious and elemental; the archetypal garage-rock band a couple of decades in advance of that term even being coined. Of its twelve songs, eight were Townshend's, three were covers, including tentative passes at a brace of James Brown tunes – 'I Don't Mind' and 'Please, Please, Please' – while the closing instrumental, 'The Ox', was credited to the band and session man Nicky Hopkins, whose piano was the only item of dressing. The title track and a wider-eyed call to arms from Townshend, 'The Kids Are Alright', stand out, but the lasting essence is of sharp, brittle edges, dilated pupils and a racing pulse.

My Generation was released on the same day – 3 December – as the album that signalled The Beatles' great leap forward, *Rubber Soul*. Next to the Fab Four's record, which set out to dazzle, The Who's début seemed snot-nosed, scuff-kneed and the work of a band more likely to pick a fight than pick up a sitar. That impression was reinforced by its cover, the four of them photographed at drab, grey Surrey Docks in the East End of London on a frigid winter's morning, stood there leering up at the camera. The album soon went gold in the UK but, regardless, The Who had to carry on living hand to mouth since the band's coffers remained frozen in a perilous state.

At home at Lexden Road, Entwistle was paying his mother £2 a week for room and board. In his box bedroom, he kept his bass guitars, turntable record player and records, toy soldier collection and the cage in which perched his new pet, a budgie he named Ollie. Removed from simple domesticity, he was ever keen to cultivate for himself a reputation for unrestrained largesse. Clothes and shoes he continued to buy by the armful, everything in every available colour. Along with Moon, he was chauffeured everywhere and back – to the studio, to shows, to Carnaby Street boutiques and to West End clubs. Following Cy Langston's departure earlier that summer, they had got themselves a new driver, Richard Cole, a nineteen-year-old jack-the-lad from Kensal Rise in north London. 'My first job was to drive the two of them up to Scotland,' says Cole. 'We were passing through this little town north of the border when Moon said to me, "Stop the car."

He got out and went into a hardware shop. I looked at Entwistle and asked, 'What's he doing?' He gave me an inscrutable smile – as always, he never said a word. He knew exactly what was going on, but he wasn't about to divulge anything. Moon had gone to fetch weed killer and sugar so they could make a bomb. Moon let the fucking thing off in the Caledonian Hotel in Edinburgh and we all got thrown out.

John and Moon were close, like brothers, and more or less always together. And they liked the idea of being driven around in a car. Moon always sat up front and John was quite happy in the back. The routine would be that I'd pick John up in Acton and then we'd hurry over to Moon's in Wembley. Moon was also still living with his mum, dad and sister. Mr and Mrs Moon would always welcome you into their house. I don't believe I was ever invited into John's house. I always got the feeling that Queenie looked down on us.

'The two of them had no money, but they had an account at a clothing shop. They would talk about how they couldn't believe their luck. It was like the producer Mickie Most once said to me, 'What are all your mates doing – laying bricks?' And more or less, they were. So what did we have to complain about? I don't remember ever having a thought about the future, which was not like John. He would talk about how when The Who made it big he was going to buy himself a Citroën car, which he did, and how he wanted to have a couple of Irish Wolfhounds, which he had. From the start, he had very precise ideas of what he wanted.

John was somewhat mysterious. He was very reserved, but that didn't mean he didn't get up to a lot of mischief. He would just be very discreet about it. Moon was like an ambassador for

English rock. If ever there was a big American band in town, like
The Byrds, or The Beach Boys or The Lovin' Spoonful, he would
always troop along to their hotel and introduce himself, and
John would go along, too. We would have a handful of Purple
Hearts or French Blues and go down to Blaze's in Queensgate
and mix with Ronnie Wood and some of The Pretty Things.
Then round the corner to the Cromwellian and you might see
Georgie Fame or Peter Noone of Herman's Hermits. After that,
straight down the Cromwell Road, through the tunnel, right at
Fortnum & Mason's and left into Mason's Yard for the Scotch of
St James. There you would find a Beatle or two and Eric Burdon
of The Animals. For sure, John liked the girls and a drink. His
tipple of choice was Courvoisier and Coke, but his demeanour
would never change. You would never know if he was drunk or
not. It was me that gave him the name Ox.

I remember Alison being very petite and also quiet. Sometimes
John would bring her along to a Who show, but not very often. If
I took him and Moon out, I typically wouldn't have to get them
home – often as not the girls from the clubs would take care of
them for the rest of the night. There would always be lovely girls
coming up to Lambert's and Stamp's office, too – most of the top
models of the day. Oh yeah, John enjoyed a good time.

■ ■ ■

Following on from 'I Can't Explain', neither 'Anyway, Anyhow,
Anywhere' nor 'My Generation' made more than ripples in
America. The latter had peaked on the *Billboard* chart at a
basement 74. The US release of their début album was also being
delayed by Decca until April 1966 with no indication that it would
be accompanied by any great fanfare. It had been two years now
since The Beatles had blazed a trail across the Atlantic, pulling
along in their slipstream The Stones, The Animals and planeloads

of other British hopefuls. Yet the world's most lucrative market remained all but shut off to The Who. That fact, and the binding of the deals that they had signed with Talmy, obvious to them now, nagged at and exercised Lambert and Stamp.

At the turn of the year, Stamp flew to New York in an attempt to charm and goad Decca US to action. But he took little encouragement from meetings with the label's executives. However, while Stamp was there, he was approached by a second US label, Atlantic Records, a slicker, hungrier operation with a reserve of outstanding black R&B and soul acts, and with a counter-offer that would more than double The Who's royalty rate. Back home, Lambert had also fixed the band up with a new, go-getting booking agent, Robert Stigwood. A thirty-one-year-old Australian, Stigwood was, like Lambert, extravagantly camp, but with a finer-tuned entrepreneurial flair. Stigwood was in the process of setting up his own independent record label, Reaction, and had secured for it major distribution deals with Polydor in the UK and, by coincidence, Atlantic in America. That February, emboldened by these developments, Lambert and Stamp made their move to break The Who out from their contract with Talmy.

First, Lambert took the band into London's Olympic Studios and oversaw the recording of a new Townshend song, 'Substitute'. Stigwood had agreed to release it as a single through Reaction in direct competition with the track Brunswick had lined up as their next Who single, 'Circles', and which Talmy had produced for the band just the previous month. These machinations apart, 'Substitute', musically breezy, lyrically sardonic, indicated a refinement in Townshend's song-writing with the extra ballast of Entwistle's hulking bass parts. On this occasion in the studio, Entwistle took matters into his own hands when it came to making himself heard.

'Pete was always influenced by other artists and "Substitute" was him trying to play a Four Tops song, "I Can't Help Myself",' he told music writer Johnny Black in 1994. 'The way that it turned out, I decided to use my usual sound on it, instead of a Motown sound, and played a Gibson SG bass. I also figured it should be a bass solo, and because we were recording live to tape, when I turned up, there was nothing anyone could do about it.'

For the 'Substitute' flip-side, Lambert had the band re-record 'Circles' and re-title it 'Instant Party'. No sooner had 'Substitute' come out on Reaction that March than Talmy served an injunction on it, just as Lambert and Stamp had anticipated, and the dispute hastened to the High Court. That April, almost on the court steps, the two warring parties reached an agreement. It meant that Lambert and Stamp had succeeded in wrenching the band from Talmy and Brunswick, but at a heavy price – Talmy would keep his percentage of all the records The Who were to release over the next four years, and which would end up including *Tommy*. And although the band was also now free to sign with Polydor in the UK, they would still be wedded to Decca in the US. Talmy was left to claim a victory, albeit one that was bittersweet.

'I sued, I won,' he says. 'But unfortunately, I never got to record with The Who again. I'd never got any sense from the band that they weren't happy. Jesus Christ, why wouldn't they be? All I'd ever had with them was hits. But Kit Lambert was one of the biggest fucking assholes I've ever met in my life.'

■ ■ ■

This repositioning of the band's affairs didn't change the fundamental fact that they had to keep working just to remain solvent. Through to late summer, their live bookings took them up and down the country almost nightly. Occasionally, the odd gig would stand out, such as the 1 May date at the Empire Pool, Wembley, for the *New Musical Express*' Poll Winners Party. That night, they played to an audience of 12,000, sharing a bill with The Beatles, The Stones, Herman's Hermits, The Small Faces, Dusty Springfield, Roy Orbison and, as a vivid reminder of their teenage selves, Cliff and the Shadows. Or else there was their 30 July, bill-topping appearance at the Sixth National Jazz and Blues Festival in Windsor. Earlier on that same Saturday afternoon, England had triumphed over West Germany in football's World Cup Final at Wembley Stadium. Not one of The Who could have cared less for football, but the climax of their forty-minute set – Townshend and Moon unleashing a gleeful, frenzied orgy of destruction as smoke bombs went off around them onstage – suited the general, uproarious national mood.

More typically, they were stuck on a treadmill of town halls, ballrooms and bigger clubs. The routine and scenery was unchanging, incessant, apart from the odd day in a studio, such as 14 June when they put down their next single, 'I'm a Boy', Lambert again producing. Each afternoon, Cole would pick up Entwistle, then Moon in their rental car and proceed to Buxton, Walsall, Blackburn, Lincoln, Hull or wherever was next on the agenda. That March, Moon was married to his pregnant girlfriend, Kim Kerrigan. But just like Entwistle with his engagement to Alison, Moon regarded this new state of affairs as being no impediment to their ribaldry. With the limits of their roistering beginning to seem boundless, Entwistle's and Moon's close proximity could also on occasion spell trouble for The Who as a whole. That May, both of them almost brought about the end of the band.

At the start of the month and exasperated with the drummer's waywardness, Daltrey was considering quitting and absented himself from gigs at Stourbridge Town Hall on 4 May and at Kidderminster Town Hall the next night. Down to being a trio once again, Townshend and Entwistle shared lead vocal duties at each of these shows. After the latter, a young Robert Plant buttonholed Townshend at the stage door and offered his services to The Who. Townshend politely declined the presumptuous teenager and Daltrey reappeared next morning for a three-day jaunt over to Ireland, but a premonition of Plant's future band overshadowed the rest of that month. On 16 May, Moon joined up with Jimmy Page and Jeff Beck of The Yardbirds, Nicky Hopkins and another first-call session player, John Paul Jones, for a late-night, cloak-and-dagger session at IBC Studios. That evening, the five moonlighting musicians cut an instrumental track, later titled 'Beck's Bolero', and Page pitched them the idea of forming a new, virtuoso hard-blues band. In turn, Moon suggested Entwistle as the ideal bassist and singer for just such an outfit.

Four nights later, and with that same notion rumbling around both of their heads, Moon and Entwistle fell to partying with a visiting Beach Boy, Bruce Johnston. The Who had a show to do in Newbury, two-hours' drive from London, but that seemed of minor concern as they set about ingratiating themselves with their new friend. As the drink flowed and pills were popped, Entwistle even posited a name for this new band of theirs – Lead Zeppelin, as he meant for it to be spelled – joking that like the Hindenberg it was destined to go down in flames. Eventually, Entwistle and Moon managed to tear themselves away, but arrived hopelessly late for the band's engagement and to find Daltrey and Townshend already onstage at the Ricky-Tick Club and performing with two pick-up musicians. As the recalcitrant pair moved to reclaim their rightful places stage-right and behind the drum kit, mayhem ensued.

'Keith said sorry to Pete, and Pete turned around and smashed him in the face with his guitar,' Entwistle related in 1974. 'So Keith and I left and went home, took the phone off the hook, and went to see our managers to tell them we were through.

Somehow, we got back together again. In those days, we were breaking up every week.'[8]

Page's vaulting concept also wouldn't begin to be realised for another two years. That same summer of 1966, Richard Cole picked up his umpteenth speeding ticket and lost his driver's licence, which had the immediate effect of making him surplus to Entwistle's and Moon's requirements. As it happened, Cole went directly on to work for The Yardbirds and their manager, Peter Grant. 'I was with The Yardbirds in New York in March 1968 and I mentioned to Jimmy how John had come up with the name Lead Zeppelin,' Cole recounts. 'John never did pull me up on it. More than likely, he had completely forgotten about it. He would come out with these off-the-cuff sorts of things all the time.'

The character recruited in Cole's stead fit the madcap, skewed sides of Entwistle's and Moon's natures to a tee. Following a childhood trauma at nine, John Wolff had been left completely bald and shorn of eyebrows. He had taken to covering up the baldness with a mop-top wig that he believed made him look like John Lennon. Soon enough at The Who's gigs, Wolff would ritually pluck this wig from his head with a flourish, and upend it to pour out rivulets of sweat, making it look as if his brain had leaked. This party trick never failed to provoke appalled screams, which Wolff delighted in almost as much as he did in finding ways to keep his new charges amused.

Alongside Wolff's arrival, Entwistle and Moon had shelled out £400, a small fortune at the time, on their own car, a vintage 1943 Bentley Continental. The practical Wolff rigged the Bentley up with a makeshift PA system and record turntable, ensuring hours of fun for his two passengers. 'It was a big old lump that

---

[8] Taken from 'Madness with Quadrophenia', *Circus Raves* article by John Swenson, March 1974

car, and there was a yawning gap in between the front grille and the radiator,' explains Wolff. 'To the front of the radiator and back of the grille I fitted and wired up the biggest outdoor Tannoy speaker I could find and a separate amplifier to feed it, so it had considerable power.

We would drive up north and cause a riot with this thing. Whenever we got stuck in traffic, I'd turn Moon loose on the microphone. In his finest upper-crust accent, his voice would come booming out of this thing: 'Registration WBC 246, pull over left and stop . . .' just like the Old Bill. You would see the driver in front stiffen, then he'd pull over and we'd belt on by, music blaring out now, one of Moon's surf records. Moon just loved being centre of attention and to have noise going on all around him. The Bentley also had a sun-roof. With loud music playing as we would be racing up the M1 motorway, he would stand up through the sun-roof and give the Nazi salute. 'Oh, he's off,' John would say. John was like the elder statesman, even then.

I thought John was very deep. He was very moral, very upstanding, but really not quiet. He was boiling, seething, very creative and very artistic. He used to love to go out shopping and to show off his latest gear or toys. I used to say to him, 'It'll bankrupt you, John.' That was a saying between us right up until the last time I spoke with him. He would astound you with different things. One time, he went out and bought himself a starting pistol. He brought it along with him when we went up to Morecambe that same year.

After the gig, we got a bit outrageous being by the seaside. We unlatched some kids' boats and had ourselves a whale of time rowing them around the harbour. Back at the hotel, really wound up by now, John whipped this pistol out and announced, 'Right – let's see how loud this thing is!' Our rooms were arranged in a block looking out on to a tight, enclosed square, like a funnel. Now, just like a Tannoy, a funnel amplifies sound. John fired the gun out into the square, once, twice. It was gone midnight. The retorts were deafening and went binging off around the building. Of course, then Moon wanted a go. He fired once, loud enough to bring the Old Bill running from miles around. Before Moon could shoot again, I managed to grab hold of the pistol and discharged the other chambers. John was delighted. He was going, 'This is great! I'm going to get a Gatlin Gun next!' But John was also a stalwart guy. All of this time, he was the only one really who was looking out for Moon. He used to roll his eyes at Keith but, at the same time, he did worry about him getting out of control.

Finally, at the start of that August, Lambert and Stamp allowed their exhausted band two weeks off. It was their first extended break from each other in more than two years, but Entwistle and Moon chose to spend it together on holiday. With Alison and Kim, they jetted off to Torremolinos on Spain's Costa del Sol. There, the two couples whiled away the long, hot days sunbathing by their hotel pool, and playing cards at night. Alison has kept the photographs of that holiday in the same leather-bound album that Entwistle mounted them in, black-and-white and faded now. One picture is of a bikini-clad Alison, stretched out on a patch of grass, and captioned by Entwistle: 'Grazing cow'. Under another, of Alison and Moon reclined on two sun-loungers, he misspelled Moon's forename as 'Kieth', likely deliberately as a private joke. A third is of Entwistle himself, stood out on the hotel steps in an open-necked shirt, the sea behind him still and calm, and to which he added two words: 'Latin lover'.

They are the photographs of ordinary, young, happy couples who have got away from everything – smiling faces, at ease with one another, the promise still of their having all the time and opportunities in the world. 'I loved Keith to start with,' says Alison, regarding the picture of the two of them. 'He was very sweet. But,' she adds sadly, 'he got changed, by the fame and by everything else.'

For all concerned, it was the merest respite. Four days after they flew back to London from Spain, on 18 August, The Who went back to work, travelling south for a date at the Palace Ballroom, Douglas, on the Isle of Man. Entwistle recalled the occasion in a brief, handwritten note for his autobiography: 'Friendly promoter gets me drunk before the show,' he began. 'At the end of the show, I walk down stairs into the audience and they tear my clothes to shreds. I fall face down into a chicken supper and wake up next morning wondering why I'm wearing the rest of the band's clothes.'

Part II

Success Story

January 2002 – the NAMM event in Los Angeles once again. On an afternoon off, Entwistle pays a visit to Peter Noone, the singer with Herman's Hermits and whom he had hardly seen in a quarter of a century. Noone had moved out with his wife to Santa Barbara. 'I had a friend who owned a fish-and-chip restaurant that was out by the beach and we took John there,' says Noone.

John had brought a young girl along with him. We had lunch looking out over the yacht club. A waiter came over and asked what we would like to drink with our food. John ordered a bottle of cognac and a bottle of rosé. Before the food had even come out, John and the girl had polished off most of their bottles.

Afterwards, they came back to my house. A neighbour of ours had a McLaren F1 Roadster and, as soon as he saw it, John wanted to take it out for a ride. We had to talk him out of it. Never mind that he couldn't even drive, the guy said to him, 'Look, I made a promise to my wife and children that I would never get in a car with anyone who'd had a drink.' That closed the matter down.

Of course, John was not the boy that I had first met back in the sixties. My wife thought that he was as pale as a heroin addict. You just can't do as much blow as he was doing by then and stay alive. You can go on drinking for a long time, but doing booze and blow will get you every time.

7

'Otherwise Occupied'

A t the end of that summer of 1966, Lambert and Stamp tried another way to ease the band's seemingly interminable money troubles. The pair negotiated a new publishing deal that guaranteed The Who a welcome cash advance, but which was set against future royalties on songs to be written by Entwistle, Daltrey and Moon. In essence, this required Townshend to collaborate more freely with his band-mates and also committed the three of them to each contributing songs to the band's next album, which they were due to start work on imminently.

They applied themselves to this task with varying degrees of commitment. In late September, the sessions began with Lambert at IBC and Pye Studios, Daltrey having managed just one song, the slight, airy 'See My Way'. Moon's contribution was not much greater, amounting to a throwaway Beatles pastiche, 'I Need You', the lyrics for which he had Entwistle help out on, and a child-like, unhinged marching-band instrumental that wound up being titled 'Cobwebs and Strange'. All that needs be said about how Daltrey and Moon adapted to this new discipline is that neither of them would ever again write a song for the band.

Entwistle, though, was always on the alert for opportunities to stake out his own territories within The Who and grabbed the chance. He went out and bought for himself the exact same set-up of tape machine and microphones that Townshend was using for his home demos, and arranged them in the cramped bedroom at Lexden Road. The initial brace of songs that he knocked off there, perched on the end of his bed, showcased his mordant wit, and also a knack for simple, but appealing melodies. The first, 'Whiskey Man', was an amiable, chugging rocker given a more sinister edge by Entwistle's detached lead vocal. Since he had no confidence in his own singing voice, he double-tracked the vocal to make it sound fuller. And as unsure of himself as he was, he also sought the approval of his mother and Alison before he felt able to share the song with the rest of the band. 'I said to Alison, "What's it like?"' Townshend recalled. 'And she said, "Oh, it's lovely – much better than your songs."'[9]

His second song was just plain macabre about an unfortunate arachnid that got flattened with a book. The title was derived from a drunken conversation Entwistle had had one night at the Scotch of St James with The Rolling Stones' Bill Wyman and Charlie Watts. Late into that evening, the subject of comic names for creatures had come up, and when Wyman posited Bill the Badger, Entwistle shot back with Boris the Spider, thinking of the horror movie actor, Boris Karloff. Backed by a clunking, repeating bass riff, which he had bluffed on the spot when challenged by Townshend at a band rehearsal to share his new tune, 'Boris the Spider' came off as a Brothers Grimm-like fairy story put to music. Completing the effect and aping Spike Milligan's Throat character from his beloved *Goon Show*, Entwistle sang the title chorus in a guttural growl.

---

[9] Taken from the documentary film *An Ox's Tale: the John Entwistle Story* directed by Glenn Aveni and Steve Luongo, Act 1 Entertainment (2006)

As much as anything else that was included on the *A Quick One* album, 'Boris the Spider' was something of a rarity for The Who – it was a record that they had fun making. Putting down 'Cobwebs and Strange', Lambert had them march around the studio in single-file, Entwistle on French horn and trumpet, Townshend on penny whistle, Daltrey blowing a trombone and Moon a tuba. They cut a spirited version of Holland-Dozier-Holland's effervescent Motown hit 'Heatwave', a Number One for Martha and the Vandellas back in 1963. Townshend, meanwhile, served up three snappily insistent songs – 'Run Run Run', 'Don't Look Away' and 'So Sad About Us' – and also the ranging, multi-part near-title track, which over its near-ten-minute course took on board elements as diverse as British music hall and American country and western.

'A Quick One, While He's Away' came about when Townshend complained to Lambert that he didn't have enough material to fill up the album. Lambert's rejoinder to Townshend was that he should write instead a series of shorter pieces, and connect them together into a kind of mini-opera. Amateur dramatic-standard and by no stretch opera, the five pieces that Townshend subsequently wove together, bawdily reciting the tale of an adulterous wife, were nonetheless representative of a brand new, forward-thinking concept for rock music. Not that The Who took the idea overly seriously just yet – witness Entwistle's scenery-chewing vocal on 'Ivor the Engine Driver', sung with the relish of a moustache-twirling villain. And when, on grounds of cost, Lambert refused the band's request to add a string section to the piece, the four of them went into the studio and harmonised the words 'cello, cello, cello' in the appropriate parts.

Released on Reaction that December, *A Quick One* replicated the success of their début in the UK, reaching Number Four on the album chart and going gold. By then, Lambert and Stamp had followed the lead of Robert Stigwood and were in the process of setting up their own record label. Henceforth, all future Who records would come out on Track Records, which would also be distributed through Polydor. Furthermore, the four members of the band were each given a 10 per cent stake in the label.

The band who would be Track's next signings put out their first single on the same day as *A Quick One*. An American-British trio, The Jimi Hendrix Experience's version of what was already a sixties staple, 'Hey Joe', barnstormed to Number Six on the UK chart. The Experience's manager, The Animals' original bassist, Chas Chandler, had actually sounded out Entwistle to join the band but without success, before opting for the twenty-two-year-old Noel Redding. All of the Experience's fireworks, however, came from Hendrix himself; twenty-four at the time and outrageously gifted on guitar, he was a former soldier with the 101st Airborne Division, based out of Kentucky, and a native of Seattle.

Chandler had brought Hendrix over to London from the States just the previous September, and now The Who were at last about to travel in the opposite direction. 'The Who will definitely go to America for ten days in April – after they have completed their six-day run at London's Saville Theatre with The Koobas and The Jimi Hendrix Experience which starts 10 April,' the *Melody Maker* reported in its 21 January 1967 edition. In fact, the paper was a month out with its dates and The Who flew out to New York on Tuesday, 21 March on a 4.00pm flight from London.

Chris Stamp had fixed the band up with an American booking agent, a twenty-eight-year-old Staten Islander named Frank Barsalona. He had founded his Premier Talent company in 1964 and booked the first American tours by both The Beatles and The Stones. Paunchy and balding, he was unimpressive-looking in person but just what The Who needed, since he was also shrewd, persuasive and dynamic. That February of 1967, Stamp flew back to New York to open up an office for Lambert and himself in the same building as Premier Talent's at 200 West 57th Street, and to rubber-stamp the first deal that Barsalona had done for the band.

In America, these were seismic, divisive times, the country fracturing along fault lines set off by President Lyndon B. Johnson's escalation of the Vietnam War, the anti-war movement that this had inflamed, the booming of a counter-culture and the deprivations of its black citizens. That summer, the powder-keg would go off with race riots exploding in Tampa, Buffalo and Detroit, where six nights of mayhem left forty-three people dead and 1,400 buildings razed by fire. Out on the West Coast, a soundtrack of folk-rock and acid-rock was gearing up. In just the first three months of that year, there would be début albums from The Doors and The Grateful Dead, a psychedelic-sounding second from Jefferson Airplane, *Surrealistic Pillow*, and The Byrds' first venturing towards country-rock on *Younger Than Yesterday*. From New York, there came another début album that mixed a darker and more decadent brew, *The Velvet Underground & Nico*.

The Who's entry point to America was nothing like so seditious. Barsalona had wrangled to get them on to an Easter package show staged annually by a self-aggrandising New York disc jockey, Murray the K. The K was yet another bewigged character and had been among the first DJs to spin The Beatles' records on US radio, enough for him to lay claim to being 'the fifth Beatle'. His 'Music in the Fifth Dimension' shows went ahead at a 1920s movie theatre in Manhattan, the RKO, at 58th Street and Third Avenue. The Who were to feature on a bill topped by blue-eyed soul man Mitch Ryder, and also including R&B powerhouse Wilson Pickett, Motown's Smokey Robinson and the Miracles, fellow Brits Cream, recently formed by ex-Yardbird Eric Clapton, and a comedy troupe, The Hardly Worthit Players. During the span of their ten-day engagement, they were contracted to play three ten-minute sets daily, four at the weekends.

Arriving in New York, they were ferried to a plush midtown Manhattan hotel, the Drake, that they could ill afford from their $5,000 fee. Writing up his recollections of the trip, Entwistle began:

How the fuck is a middle-aged American considered the fifth Beatle? Keith and I pondered this fact as we were checked into the Drake Hotel.

As usual, we were sharing a room and as the bellhop ushered us into our eleventh-floor home for the next two weeks, we both gasped in stereo. It was a palace. 'Party room!' we chorused, and instantly set out to make it so. Along one wall was a huge table, which we assigned to the buffet. We extended the wet bar by butting it up to another table that we purloined from opposite the lift on the tenth floor. We placed our bottles of duty-free whisky on the wet bar and stood back to survey our handiwork. 'Pathetic,' sneered Keith and he began to make up a list of food and drink. Then, Keith dialled room service. 'Right, we want vodka, brandy, wine, gin, bourbon,' his voice droned on, as if he was stock-taking at a liquor store. 'And a whole turkey,' I interrupted. 'Oh, yes,' Keith agreed, 'with caviar and champagne.'

When the order arrived, we realised the enormity of our crime. Six trolleys were lined up outside our door, each of them being pushed by a separate waiter. I was handed the bill in a long, thick leather folder. I opened it gingerly and immediately slammed it shut. Wide-eyed, I beckoned Keith into one of the bedrooms. 'It comes to $1,500,' I whispered. Keith made a sound like someone being struck in the throat with an axe. The head waiter obviously heard him. 'Is there something wrong?'

he enquired. 'No . . . no,' I stammered back. 'Um . . . I was just wondering how much to tip?' 'It's normally 15 per cent,' he informed me. A quick, panic-stricken calculation told me our bill would now be $1,725.

We signed. They left. We groaned. We jumped . . . Someone was knocking at the door. It was another of the waiters. 'You've got the food and drink – how about some grass to help the party move along?' he asked. We answered in stereo again: 'No,' on my side and, 'Yes,' on Keith's. $50 later, Keith was rolling a joint. There was another knock on the door. Keith ran into the bathroom to flush the joint; I ran in circles around the room trying to fan away the smoke. A key turned, the door opened. 'Nice smell, boys,' sleazed waiter number three. '$100 and I won't have to call the cops.' We had been stitched up like a pair of kippers.

The press reception was the usual boring round of introductions and cold, floppy, wet-fish handshakes. Pete, as usual, was surrounded by journalists. He'd worn a jacket woven with hundreds of little fairy lights in case they hadn't noticed him. 'Someone should stick an angel on his head,' Keith suggested. 'With a pair of boots made out of Christmas wrapping paper,' I added. We both meowed at the same time. We stared down at a plate of cheese and pineapple sticks and concurred that the spread in our room was vastly superior to this shit. We stalked back up to the eleventh floor, mouths watering, to find that all of our food had gone. Room service had decided that we were finished. Instantly, Keith was screaming into the telephone, 'Where's our fucking food? What do you mean it was all dried up? You only delivered it an hour ago. I want it replaced this minute! Put me on to the manager! Not here? I'M PHONING MY LAWYER – RIGHT NOW!! . . . Well, OK, that's more like it.' He turned to me with a self-satisfied grin on his face. 'That got the bastards. They're bringing it all back up.'

I woke up the next morning with a curling turkey sandwich on my pillow and an empty bottle of Scotch on the bedside table. I glanced, bleary-eyed at my door. Keith's silhouette was framed in it. 'I was just about to order breakfast – eggs benedict, champagne and orange juice?' he trumpeted. He ducked as my now-lethal turkey sandwich flew past his head. 'Can I take that as a no?' Today was the day we were to meet the great man himself – Murray the K, the king of WOR Radio, our benefactor and boss for the next ten, fun-filled days. He looked like a cross between Perry Como and a Jewish tailor. He shook hands with us with as much sincerity as a man running to catch a bus, posed for a couple of photographs and scurried back into his studio. As the door slammed shut behind him, I turned to the others and casually remarked, 'Nice crown-topper.' There would be no respect for this man coming from The Who's direction.

The next day, we turned up at the RKO for rehearsal. Chris Stamp had been wheeling and dealing to borrow equipment for us to play through and I found myself plugged into a Baldwin combo – two 12in speakers and 30 watts of unleashed fury! 'I'll blow this piece of shit up in five minutes,' I told Chris. In the event, I did it in five notes. Chris got on the phone to the Vox amplifier company and, within twenty-four hours, we had 600 watts of power at our disposal. By then, Chris had also examined with horror our hotel bill and he moved us out from the Drake to the Gorham, a huge step down-market and one of those bring-your-own-lightbulbs, don't-feed-the-'roaches hotels.

Saturday, 25 March – we waited for the curtain to rise on our first show. We'd been chosen to go on just before the main act, Mitch Ryder. We were resplendent in our tight white suits, ready to take New York by storm. The curtain went up. We broke out 'I Can't Explain'. Straight into 'My Generation'; then we smashed our equipment and walked off. The stage was swathed in the fog of our smoke bombs. The audience were stunned – some standing cheering, others still sat and trying to comprehend what had happened. With Mitch Ryder and his band waiting in the wings to go on, our sound man, Bobby Pridden, was scurrying around the stage picking up bits of equipment – a Stratocaster neck here, a drum part there. Bobby would have to have it all back together by the next show in three hours' time, but we had complete confidence in his ability to perform miracles with match wood and toothpicks.

Soon enough, Murray the K pushed our set up from two songs to five. By that point, he knew that the majority of the audience was coming to see The Who. Unwinding between the shows was impossible. If you went back to the hotel, you found yourself pacing around the tiny room, thinking about the next show. If you went down the street, you would end up going into a bar, spending money you didn't have and getting drunk. Finally, we decided that parties in our dressing room were the answer. Roger was usually 'otherwise occupied'. He had met Heather, a tall, red-headed model from Connecticut who, although he didn't then know it, was his wife-to-be. Pete would be there sometimes, but he had made some friends in Greenwich Village and spent a lot of time down there. Most of the parties it was just Keith and me, although we were often 'otherwise occupied', too.

Time flies when you're working too hard and we found ourselves about to play the last show. Equipment-wise, we were scraping the barrel. The last surviving Vox amps were lined up onstage, ready to meet their maker, and Keith was down to his final clean pair of Y-fronts. It ended up being one of our 'everything has to go' shows. I even put my bass through my speaker cabinet, only to find out later that no one saw it through the smoke. We all said goodbye to our 'otherwise occupieds' and jumped on the plane back to merry old England.

The ripples made by The Who on that first visit to New York soon dispersed out across the wider country. Their new single, 'Happy Jack', became their highest charting in the States, peaking at 24 on the *Billboard* Hot 100. Likewise, after its belated American release that May, the *A Quick One* album went on to eclipse the performance of *My Generation*, albeit topping-out at an unremarkable 67 on the US chart. The American version of the album was also retitled *Happy Jack*, as Decca sought to capitalise on their minor hit single and, equally, to protect American morals from suggestive double-entendres.

Back in Britain, The Who had touched down in London on the evening of 3 April, for just long enough to record what was to be their next single. Cut at IBC on 5 April, Townshend's 'Pictures of Lily', with Entwistle featured on French horn, was a whimsical, primary-coloured confection that would not have sounded out of place on the album it preceded by just a month, The Beatles' *Sgt Pepper's Lonely Hearts Club Band*. Both of them were heralds of the so-called 'Summer of Love' about to burst into bloom in London.

'Pictures of Lily' also provoked America's moral guardians when it was released there that June. The mere suggestion of teenage masturbation in Townshend's lyric was enough for it to be banned by several American radio stations. In Britain, it was to be the band's first release on Track, although for The Who, this turned out to be a somewhat inauspicious occasion all round, since it arrived several weeks after the label's launch offering, The Jimi Hendrix Experience's 'Purple Haze', and ended up charting one place lower than that incendiary single. There was a further indignity heaped on Entwistle, wrongly credited by Track for his B-side composition, 'Doctor, Doctor', as 'John Entwhistle'.

Two days after the 'Pictures of Lily' session, the band headed off to West Germany for a two-week tour beginning at the

Messehalle, Nuremberg, on 8 April. For Entwistle and Moon at least, this was an eventful fortnight. After the 13 April show in Munich, the attentions of one apparently unhinged, excessively amorous young female fan caused Entwistle to barricade himself in his hotel room while his pursuer ran amok outside, charging from floor to floor, banging on doors and screaming out his name. 'And shortly after I met my German loony,' he expanded in his memoir notes, 'Keith met his Lotte, a beautiful blonde from Sweden. She decided to shit in his suitcase. Then she stood out on the window ledge until two men in white coats burst in and took her off in a straitjacket.'

Home again, the two of them traded in their old Bentley for a later and more expensive S1 model. 'Wiggy' Wolff re-fitted the new car with his Tannoy, mic, amplifier and turntable system, although in any event, it couldn't have failed to turn heads, since the bodywork was painted in two eye-catching tones, the bottom half of the vehicle gleaming white, the top a vivid maroon. Entwistle was also occupied with the planning of his wedding to Alison, scheduled for June after the band had made their second trek to America. Before The Who flew off again, sessions started up for a new album. They also undertook a handful of out-of-town shows, managing to stir up the denizens of both the London satellite town of Stevenage and Oxford University's Pembroke College.

At the Locarno Ballroom, Stevenage, on 17 May, the band concluded their forty-minute set with their now-familiar bout of auto-destruction, Townshend almost braining a watching usher when he hurled the remnants of his broken guitar into the wings. The local paper, the *Stevenage News*, headlined its report on the show: THE WHO STORM OFF. The piece went on to quote the Ballroom's general manager, Maurice de Jonghe, who branded the band's act 'ridiculous. If this is what they have to do to put on a show – smashing thousands of pounds' worth of equipment – then that is their business . . . It was a terrible spectacle. We would certainly think twice about booking them again.' Neither did Entwistle enjoy the Stevenage show; back in the dressing room afterwards, he punched a wall and broke a finger.

Entwistle's injury didn't prevent him from playing with the band ten days later at Pembroke College's annual May Ball. That night, it was an audience of undergraduates done up in their evening suits and ballgowns that invoked The Who's collective ire. 'We were getting very effed-off with them,' Entwistle told Richard Barnes. 'They were real prannies, some of them trying to dance. I mean, dancing to The Who? They didn't clap or anything. So Keith got up and went and threw his drums into the audience. Next thing, he falls on to the stage, holding himself in pain. Keith had strained his stomach muscles.'[10]

Essentially, they were heading back out to America to appear at the Monterey International Pop Festival on the evening of Sunday, 18 June. Held over that weekend at the Monterey Fairgrounds, a hundred miles south of San Francisco, Monterey Pop was to be the first major rock festival of the sixties. It was the combined brainchild of a Los Angeles money man, Alan Pariser, and The Mamas and Papas' producer, Lou Adler, and their chief songwriter, John Phillips. Originally, these three had meant for the festival to be a showcase for the cream of the West Coast's new rock royalty – The Grateful Dead, Jefferson Airplane, Janis Joplin with Big Brother and the Holding Company, and The Mamas and the Papas all wound up appearing. However, the bill had expanded to take in the likes of New York duo Simon and Garfunkel, The Butterfield Blues Band from Chicago, Indian sitar maestro Ravi Shankar, and The Who's new sparring

---

[10] Taken from *The Who: Maximum R&B* by Richard Barnes, Plexus (2000)

partners, The Jimi Hendrix Experience. The Stones' manager, Andrew Loog Oldham, had brokered soul man Otis Redding on to the line-up; sensing an opportunity to accelerate the band's American profile, Stamp got Oldham also to lobby for The Who's inclusion.

Prior to Monterey, the band were booked to play four warm-up shows at the Fifth Dimension Club, Ann Arbor, Detroit, on 14 June, the Cellar club in Arlington Heights, Chicago, the next night, and then a brace at the Fillmore Auditorium, San Francisco, on 16 and 17 June. 'We got to Detroit knackered,' Entwistle wrote in his memoir notes:

> But on arrival at the hotel, we were informed that we were to be the guests of honour at a local club, the Roostertail – free food, free booze – we revived immediately.
>
> We were ushered with great ceremony into the club. A long white tablecloth and cut-glass crystal goblets were laid out sumptuously before us. Sitting at the table already was our old friend Mitch Ryder. Keith sat to the left of Mitch, and me to the right. 'We have roasted a whole suckling pig in your honour,' a bowing, scraping waiter informed us. We drank several bottles of wine very quickly in the next two hours. The suckling pig arrived, an apple stuck in its mouth, and remained untouched . . . a charred centrepiece for our bottle-cluttered table. Mitch mumbled something appropriately meaningless as his head fell into his salad plate.
>
> Our performance the next night at the Fifth Dimension club went amazingly well considering we were rather hungover and using our usual borrowed Vox amplification. It had been a bone of contention between the band – particularly me – and Kit that The Who could not sound like The Who without The Who's equipment. We had so often failed to make the same impact on foreign soil without the stage set-up we had bullied and cajoled

Marshall to invent for us. I warned Kit before the trip that Hendrix would not be so stupid as to leave his amps at home, and so would find it easy to blow us and our little Vox Beatles amps away at Monterey. 'We can't, John, it's too expensive,' Kit had replied in his usual offhand, brush-off manner. The only satisfaction I would get from this altercation would be in being able to say, 'I told you so,' after Monterey.

Chicago went much the same way and we moved triumphantly across America to San Francisco. We were excited about finally playing California and it lived up to our wildest expectations. The American kids had totally immersed themselves into the idea of peace and love. Haight Ashbury was a mass of hippie shops, flowers and friendly people, although I found myself choking on the sickly smells of incense and patchouli oil. Our own thoughts of peace, love and good vibrations turned to panic when the Fillmore's promoter, Bill Graham, told us to play two forty-five minute sets. We rehearsed continuously before the first show in our hotel rooms and the Fillmore dressing room, learning as much new stuff as we could to pad out our forty-minute show to one-and-a-half hours. We fell back on some of our old blues songs – 'Smokestack Lightning' and 'Dimples' – as well as learning how to perform live for the first time our mini-opera, 'A Quick One, While He's Away'. We were helped by the large Fillmore sound system and actually played one hour thirty-five minutes the first night. The following night was even better. The audience reactions ranged from being completely dumbfounded to raving and ecstatic. We were jubilant.

Arriving back at the hotel that night, I rushed up to my room to phone for room service. I was starving. But I was told that the kitchen staff had gone home an hour earlier. There was nothing for it: I would have to raid used room-service trays.

As I popped my head round my door, Keith's head appeared around his at the other end of the corridor. We proceeded to work our way towards each other, picking up anything edible from the leftovers on trays other guests had deposited outside their rooms. We met in the middle. Keith had draped a napkin over his tray and, with a devilish grin, enquired, 'Whatcha got?' 'Two rolls, two ketchups, a packet of crackers, two pats of butter and half a baked potato.' 'Splendid,' Keith said. 'Would you care to join me for supper – I've got a pork chop and a lump of chicken?' 'Delighted to – I'll pop back to my room and fetch my bottle of Old Grandad and see you in your room.' After supper, we decided to drink a few toasts to our success. 'Here's to Monterey – and fuck Hendrix!'

We were picked up the next day by a native Californian girl named Barbara Schare who was to drive us to Monterey. She had one of those typical American faces: blue eyes, perfect teeth, long, straight hair and a large mouth. When we arrived at the Fairgrounds, Keith and I had to wander through the audience to get to the backstage area. Peace, love and acid. 'Jesus loves you and you'll love these, too,' countless members of the crowd told us, thrusting pills of every shape and colour into our outstretched palms. By the time we reached backstage, we were dropping pills all over the ground. Mama Cass came to the rescue. This wonderful woman seemed able to recognise every variety of pills on – or off – the market. She had a quick rummage through our collection: 'Drop that . . . Take that . . . Forget this . . . Take these before you go to bed . . . That's an Aspirin . . . That'll kill you . . . I'll have those two.' Keith and I swallowed the remainder and finally got around to hugging Cass hello. 'Everybody in the world is back here,' she said, pointing out members of The Byrds and Jefferson Airplane. 'Now, let's find you something to wash those last pills down with.' I followed Cass to a garbage can full of ice and soft drinks. I chose a Coke to mix with the bottle of bourbon in my bag.

Neville, our replacement roadie, was signalling me from the other side of the tent. 'I've just told Pete,' he confided. 'I overheard Chas Chandler talking to Hendrix. He's on before you and he's going to smash his guitar – steal yer act.' I was angry – very fucking angry. We hadn't put ourselves through all these trials and tribulations – paying off huge debts, living on puny wages – only to have some arsehole come along and steal our act at our first big American gig. We confronted John Phillips with our predicament. He apparently misunderstood our motives for not wanting to follow Hendrix. We'd followed Hendrix enough times at the Saville Theatre to know that we were quite able to do so. And I'd never had any qualms about following Noel Redding – not ever!

What happened next is part of rock-'n'-roll history. It was finally agreed by the toss of a coin and we went on first. We opened up with 'Summertime Blues'. It blasted the audience into oblivion. Or as far into oblivion as those pieces of shit Vox amps could blast them. We followed that with possibly the worst version of 'A Quick One, While He's Away' that we ever performed in our career. 'Happy Jack' was next and we finished with 'My Generation'. I despaired all through our set. My speakers sounded as though they had no backs on them – and a later inspection revealed that, in actual fact, they didn't. Pete smashed his three hundredth guitar. His guitar lead became disconnected as it ricocheted off the amps and on to the stage. I stood in my Royal Standard flag jacket and continued making noises and notes until Keith had smashed his drum kit. Thankful it was nearly all over, I played my last note, grabbed my Fender Precision by the back of the body and threw it ten feet into the air. By the time it landed with a crash and feedback, I was off the stage and glad of it.

Hendrix went on next and also smashed his guitar, but then he set fire to it, too. As it happened, though, we were both a whole lot closer to superstardom. And I was able to tell Kit, 'See – we sounded like shit and Hendrix brought over his Marshall stacks. I TOLD YOU SO!'

8

Outside It's America

Three days after The Who arrived back in London from California, on the afternoon of Friday, 23 June 1967, Entwistle married Alison Wise at Acton Congregational Church. On the morning of the wedding, Entwistle, stepfather Gordon and his cousin Ian Gillingham, who was serving as an usher, stood together for a photograph in the tiny back garden at Lexden Road. The three of them are pictured done up in their grey morning suits and top hats, the scene as stiffly formal-looking as an old Victorian family portrait. Entwistle had insisted on the top hats, but this was to be the only time that he wore his all that day. He was always most particular about not having his hair messed and, the night before, he'd had Alison give it a fresh black dye just for the occasion.

They were met at the church by Entwistle's father, Bert, and his wife, Dora. Entwistle had chosen Bert as his best man. 'Bert loved Alison to bits and was incredibly proud that John asked him to be his best man,' says Entwistle's stepbrother, Bernard. 'Although I'm sure that it must have put Gordon's nose right out of joint, which John most probably intended.'

After the church service, the wedding party moved on to the reception, a sit-down meal followed by music and dancing, which went ahead at a restaurant above a pram shop, Daniel's Store, in West Ealing. Moon and wife Kim attended the reception together; Townshend, who would marry his art school girlfriend, Karen Astley, the following spring, came along alone; Daltrey was invited, but didn't show up. 'I remember chatting to Moony and thinking that he was really stoned,' recalls Ian Gillingham. 'But then, Moony never behaved himself. He was an absolute nutter always.'

The next day, the Entwistles moved together into their new, detached house, which they had bought for £8,100. It was located a mile to the west of Lexden Road at Pope's Lane, Ealing, and backed on to the verdant, 180-acre expanse of Gunnersbury Park. Their bedroom was the only room that Entwistle had found the time to decorate and, that same morning, he went out and bought the two of them a television set. However, he soon set about turning the Pope's Lane house into the kind of home that he had dreamed of living in these last few years, and one that was to fully reflect his newly-appointed status as master of the house.

First, he gave the house a name – The Bastille. Then he converted the box bedroom into his home studio, spending a hot summer's afternoon labouring with Alison on gluing soundproofing to the walls. He bought a pair of Scottish deerhounds, naming the great, bounding beasts Jason and Hamish, and acquired his first, small pieces of antique armour for the dining room. The ceiling of the dining room he had painted black. As the *pièce de résistance*, he had a one-way mirror installed in the downstairs bathroom that let the occupant of the loo look out unseen.

'One of the unwitting victims of that mirror was my twin sister,' says Alison. 'She was stood in front of it, adjusting her boobs and John was in the toilet, watching her. Christine was rather embarrassed about it when she found out, but he wasn't. John's sense of humour was wicked and I let him get away with it. But he was a very funny bloke in other ways. After Christopher was born, he would never let him go into the bathroom with him, or ever see him naked.'

The toys, gadgets and trinkets enabled Entwistle to live in the moment, and stopped him succumbing to the nagging certainty that this would all be snatched away from them, here today, gone tomorrow. Years later, he reflected, 'We always thought we'd have about a year and that would be it. That's what was happening in those days . . . you would suddenly plummet from the charts.'[11]

With The Who due to depart for America on 7 July, the Thursday following the wedding, the Entwistles boarded RMS *Queen Elizabeth* at Southampton Docks. They spent their honeymoon aboard the luxury liner, sailing to meet up with the others in New York. The newlyweds occupied themselves reading, playing table tennis and going dancing at night in the ship's grandly appointed Queen's Room ballroom. For mealtimes, they were sat at the ship's doctor's table, for which Alison was to be particularly grateful. The six-day Atlantic crossing was a rough one on choppy seas, and the doctor gave her an injection to ease a bout of acute seasickness.

Their only other interruption was a ship-to-shore phone call for Entwistle from Kit Lambert in London. In his absence, Townshend, Daltrey and Moon, with Lambert producing, had speedily recorded a cover of The Rolling Stones' 'Under My Thumb' as a gesture of support for Mick Jagger and Keith Richards, just then standing trial in Chichester on drugs charges.

---

[11] Taken from 'Madness with Quadrophenia', *Circus Raves* article by John Swenson, March 1974

Entwistle was summoned to the ship's radio room at 3.00am to be asked for his approval for the song to be released. He gave a terse reply: 'You can release acid into the Thames for all that I fucking care.'

The Who's first full American tour was to be a nine-week, cross-country stint as the opening act for fellow Brits Herman's Hermits. Hailing from Manchester, the five-piece Hermits had scored their first British Number One in 1964 with an overly saccharine pop ditty, 'I'm Into Something Good'. The following year, they repeated the feat in America with the even more irksome 'Mrs Brown, You've Got a Lovely Daughter'. From the outset, it appeared a mismatched pairing, which the first meeting between the two camps in New York did nothing to dispel. Entwistle arrived expecting to have Alison join him on the tour, but ran straight up against Herman's nineteen-year-old singer, Peter Noone. Writing up the encounter, Entwistle recalled:

Herman [Noone] was exactly as I expected him to be: young, obnoxious, condescending and toothy.

It was the day preceding the start of the tour. We were introduced in a hotel room by tour manager, Ed. I guess the idea was to get to know each other before going off on the road. Noone's words – 'No girlfriends and wives' – made my heart sink. I knew they were addressed directly to me and the smirk on his face as he spoke confirmed my worst fears. The kid was a spoilt brat. The Herman's had had a short string of American hits and this had obviously gone straight to his head. He was to do nothing on the ensuing tour to make me change my opinion. With his thin Mancunian voice, he reminded me of George Formby, but without the endearing qualities and humour. In fact, every time I watched the Herman's onstage, I saw a spectral ukulele hanging around his neck.

I skulked back to my hotel room and confronted Alison with the news. After a brief discussion, it was decided that she would have to return to London. But luckily, after mulling over a few possible alternative options, Barbara Schare suggested that Alison go and stay with her at her apartment in Los Angeles. The two of them could possibly meet up with us at a few points on the tour that were within driving distance. Alison and I were used to being separated, but we were disappointed at the short amount of time we'd been able to have together after the wedding.

The two girls left for Los Angeles. I cursed myself for being so fucking stupid. How could I have expected to be able to take a woman out on this musical nightmare? And why hadn't I triple-checked? It had been Kit Lambert's casual suggestion: 'Why don't you bring Alison along with you and combine a sea voyage to New York with your honeymoon?' He had never even considered that it was Herman's tour, Herman's audience and that we would have to play by Herman's rules. But then, neither had I. Well, OK . . . bollocks.

No one's outlook was improved when the tour opened with a matinée and then an evening show in Calgary, Canada, on Thursday, 13 July. The two British bands were joined on the road by an American one, the five-piece Blue Magoos, proto-psychedelic rockers from the Bronx, New York. Their coast-to-coast sweep took in convention centres, high school arenas and sports halls – venues too big and ill-equipped for the also inadequate sound system that the Herman's were hauling around. The Who were allotted just twenty-five minutes each night for their set. Worse, the bands were made to travel on board a decrepit Douglas DC-8 prop plane that groaned down the runway and, once in the air, was continually subject to violent shaking and buffeting.

As they wound on through Oklahoma City, Baton Rouge, Madison, Wisconsin and Omaha, Nebraska, Entwistle took a jaundiced view of the America that he found outside the great metropolitan centres of the East and West Coasts. 'They all looked like Beach Boys fans,' he said of the audiences on the tour. 'Everybody seemed to have a ginger moustache. I suppose we were flamboyant and outrageous. We were very arrogant about the way we looked and sounded. We thought that we dressed and played differently from everybody else.'[12]

Next to the good-natured Blue Magoos and toothsome Herman's, they couldn't help but stand out. Nightly, revving up with a breakneck sprint through 'I Can't Explain', ending with the smashing and strewing of their equipment over the stage, they left these self-same audiences shocked, awed. Whatever Middle America had heard up to then about peace, love and good vibes, it hadn't smoothed the way for something as violent and nihilistic-seeming as The Who in full, unfettered flight. Offstage, they found new ways to wreak mayhem. In Montgomery, Alabama, the Herman's took Moon and Entwistle out shopping for Cherry Bombs, an especially potent brand of firework. The pair of them hot-footed it back to their hotel room and let one off in the bathroom, blasting the toilet to smithereens and blowing a gaping hole in the floor.

'We'd never seen anything like Cherry Bombs in England and we loved them,' says Peter Noone. 'They were just like a little bomb, the size of a conker, and actually explosive. You lit one and it blew up. On our first American tour, Bobby Vee and his band, guys like Jim Gordon and Bobby Keys, had thrown these things into our car. For me, that whole tour was great fun. I watched every gig. The Blue Magoos had these suits with nine-volt

---

[12] Taken from an uncredited interview on YouTube dated 20 March 1986

batteries in them that were meant to light up, but didn't when they were supposed to most nights. Then The Who would go on. My band had done a deal with Fender for equipment. That was the gear that The Who smashed up each night, and then every third day, Fender would send us out a new consignment.

'We didn't see a lot of Pete, because I think he was off writing, and Roger was always taking care of himself. He didn't show up for any of the mayhem. John always showed up and sort of kept Moon from hurting himself. He was kind of his minder in a way. There was a lot of speed on the tour, so you could stay up all night and still be lucid. We had a roadie called Bob Levine who was real old school; he had worked for Ike Turner. Whenever we were going to have a party, he would go to the manager of the hotel and say, "Do you have a room that needs redecorating?" He would tell these guys that we would pay for the damage before there was any. They would negotiate a number and then put us in what they would call the "Party Room", with no chairs and just tables. Every night was like the last one on that tour. I've got pictures of us all waiting for the bus in one or other hotel and, apart from Pete or Roger, we all look like we've been fucked by nine men. We really were dragging ourselves around.'

Among these parties was one that went ahead at the Holiday Inn in Flint, Michigan, on 23 August to celebrate Moon's twenty-first birthday. That night, Entwistle wasn't able to protect Moon from himself. By that point well-refreshed and half-naked, Moon came back to earth with a literal bump. 'We had been drinking all day and had ordered up some fifty cakes to throw at each other,' Noone elaborates. 'Moon jumped up on one of the tables. We were all throwing cakes at him, trying to hit him in the balls; even the girls, who none of us knew, and he slipped. My minder saw him go down and grabbed at him by the back of his underpants. Moon would have been better off if he had let go of

(left) Queenie and Bert Entwistle with toddler John, shortly before the end of their marriage.

(above) At the Coronation Holiday Camp, Hayling Island, 1955. By coincidence, Ken Russell used the camp in scenes for the *Tommy* movie nineteen years later.

Entwistle went on his first family summer holiday in August 1955. 'I was left to my own devices and, when I wasn't emptying my favourite penny machine, I'd hang out by the ballroom, sucking on a banana milkshake, and listen to the resident dance band,' he later wrote.

The bird boy of Acton. 'He was such a thin, straggly thing … all fingers.'

(above left) Acton Congregational Church Boys' Brigade's lead bugler, circa 1957.

(above right) Second year pupil Entwistle (back row, centre with French horn) in the Acton County Grammar orchestra and with some of the first intake of girls to the school. 'I had already worked out,' he wrote, 'that by the time I was sixteen there would be two-hundred little cuties looking goo-goo eyed at us older boys.'

(left) Mother, son and the 'sour, ugly' Scruffy at 81a Southfield Road.

(above) Entwistle and Pete Townshend in The Detours circa 1962: according to early supporter 'Irish' Jack Lyons, 'The bass player was obviously the one with the most talent.'

Turning twenty-one with fiancée Alison, father Bert and stepfather Gordon. Keith Moon arrived at the family home later with a bottle of Pernod. 'We didn't see much of John after that,' says his cousin Ian Gillingham.

Caricature of then-girlfriend Alison Wise's twin sister, Christine, drawn for the school magazine. Says Alison: 'She never forgave him for it.' *(courtesy of Alison Entwistle)*

An early gig with new drummer Keith Moon. 'Two things you were always guaranteed: a fight and that The Who would be brilliant.'

(*above*) Dedicated followers of fashion, The Who circa 1964: 'John started to go to Carnaby Street and in one swoop would buy twelve pairs of mohair trousers and the same number of jackets and shirts. He'd wear these clothes once and then wouldn't want them anymore.'

(*left*) Young love: Entwistle and Alison at the Gower Coast, South Wales, mid-1960s. Says Alison: 'He was my boyfriend, my fiancé and then my husband. Then, he was horrible. But, you know, you forgive all of that.'

To Mum with love. Entwistle with Daltrey, Moon and Townshend, circa 1966: 'In those days, we were breaking up every week,' said Entwistle.

Queenie and Entwistle on the morning of his wedding to Alison, 23 June 1967.

The wedding party outside Acton Congregational Church. Father Bert (top right) was Entwistle's choice as best man. 'It must have put Gordon's (top left) nose right out of joint, which John probably intended.'

(above) The Who in all their 'Tommy'-era onstage glory.
(© Henry Diltz/Getty Images)

(left) The infamous skeleton suit, circa 1969. 'The most outrageous thing I ever wore,' Entwistle opined.
(© Jorgen Angel/Getty Images)

In 1971, Entwistle paid £14,500 for Corringway in Ealing. *(courtesy of Alison Entwistle)*

Corringway, Entwistle's very own Cadillac Ranch. However, he much preferred to drink than drive and so never held a driver's license.

The Ox, in typical at-home pose. Says erstwhile producer and friend, John Alcock: 'He would buy stuff to cheer himself up.' *(© Terry O'Neill/Iconic Images)*

In his home studio at Corringway. 'He spent a lot of time plonking, as I used to call it,' says Alison Entwistle. 'The bass would be booming out. He didn't do anything quietly.'

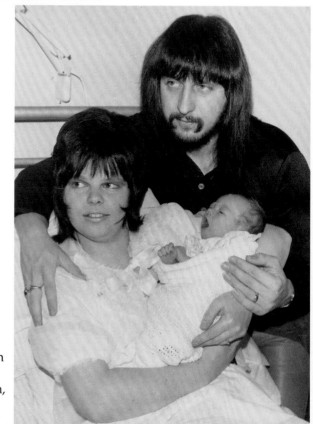

The new parents with baby Christopher, Queen Charlotte's Hospital, Chiswick, 23 January 1972. Recalls Alison Entwistle: 'John walked into the delivery room and the first thing he said was, "Humph, you've made me miss the end of *Upstairs Downstairs*."'

him, because he fell forward and knocked out half his front teeth on a table-top. The party instantly stopped, because you could see that Moon was really hurt. There were blood and bits of tooth everywhere.'

As it happened, Alison Entwistle wasn't driven out to any of the shows, but met up with her husband when the tour decamped to California for the penultimate date at the Anaheim Convention Centre on 8 September. The next day, she was able to fly on with Entwistle to Hawaii for the last show in Honolulu. After that, the couple stayed over in Honolulu for the best part of a week, resting up on the beach. They returned to Los Angeles to make the 15 September rehearsal for The Who's US television début, which was to be on a prime-time weekly variety show, *The Smothers Brothers Comedy Hour*. Fronted by a couple of erstwhile folk musicians, Dick and Tommy Smothers, the latter of whom had compèred Monterey Pop, the CBS show was just into its second season. The fact that the hosts had made the odd reference on-air to people having sex or else taking drugs had been enough for the show to be seen as mildly subversive. That perspective was only embellished by The Who's fateful appearance.

Invited by Tommy Smothers to repeat the *Sturm und Drang* of their Monterey set, Moon took matters into his own hands, bribing a stagehand to stuff his drum kit with an excessive amount of pyrotechnic flash-powder. He had this detonated at the end of a climactic 'My Generation'. The force of the blast blew his kit apart. Moon got sliced and diced with shrapnel, Townshend was deafened in one ear and, backstage, so legend now has it, Hollywood grand dame Bette Davis fainted into the arms of her fellow guest, Mickey Rooney. At all events, as this chaos went on about him, Entwistle didn't so much as flinch. Rather, he gazed on inexpressively, stoic and impervious, a soul apart.

The other song The Who performed that night was a new composition of Townshend's that they had cut in New York back in August and upon which they broke new ground. 'I Can See for Miles' seized the psychedelic-pop baton laid down by The Beatles on *Sgt Pepper's* . . . and ran off with it. All at once, it was artful and playful-sounding, but its surfaces were harder, the nimble interplay between Townshend's guitar and Entwistle's bass adding weight, depth, acceleration and dynamism. In short, it was an extraordinary song. It was released that October as The Who's next single, backed by the first Entwistle song that Daltrey had sung, 'Someone's Coming', a slice of tuneful, but more conventional sixties pop put down at the same New York session. In America, 'I Can See for Miles' reached Number Nine on the *Billboard* chart and signified a breakthrough for the band. Yet in the UK, Townshend's self-proclaimed 'ultimate Who record' stalled at Number Ten, well below the peaks of 'My Generation', 'Substitute' and 'Pictures of Lily'. This did nothing to alleviate Entwistle's foreboding that their time would be fleeting.

Completed that November, the band's new album celebrated an already disappearing age. Brought about by Harold Wilson's Labour Government that August, the Marine Broadcasting Act had effectively shut down the offshore pirate radio stations that had first championed the music of The Who and countless others. Stations such as Radio Caroline and Radio London were instrumental in shaping the sound of British pop in the sixties. In their stead, the Government licensed the BBC to launch a national station, Radio 1, which had begun broadcasting on 30 September with a music policy geared towards an older and more conservative audience. Lambert had schemed to have the band record a jaunty radio jingle advertising Coca-Cola, and this was the impetus for The Who to set about making a record that paid tribute to the bounding spirit of pirate radio. As the writer

Nik Cohn described it at the time, the album would also end up being 'a sonic parallel to Andy Warhol's soup cans – laced with irony in the best pop-art tradition'.

Conceived to sound like a pirate radio broadcast, *The Who Sell Out* was punctuated with both actual jingles taken from Radio London and also spoofs created by the band. In particular, Entwistle and Moon delighted in setting themselves to this latter task. In the afternoons, the pair of them would brainstorm ideas, huddled in the pub next door to the band's central London studio on Kingsway, the inspiration directly proportionate to the amount of alcohol that each had consumed. Liquidly inspired, they would hurry, cackling, back to the studio to put their jingles on tape, madcap odes to such 'household names' as Heinz Baked Beans . . . a fictitious acne cream, Medac . . . one of their preferred drinking dens, the Speakeasy . . . and to Premier Drums and Rotosound Strings. The last two of these self-made jingles they also successfully used to broker free gear for themselves from the manufacturers. The same tactic failed them when extolling an Ealing car dealer, John Mason, in the hope that he would gift them a Bentley. 'He gave them some dirty photos instead,' Townshend remembered. 'They dropped the jingle and stopped taking his phone calls.'[13]

Musically, *The Who Sell Out* was in its entirety a further vaulting step ahead. Following on from *Sgt Pepper's* . . . once again and also The Beach Boys' luminous *Pet Sounds* from the previous year, it was a spearhead towards the album being regarded not merely as a loose jumble of songs, but as a cohesive, joined-up body of work. As variously ingenious, rhapsodic and finely detailed as either of those two other records, The Who's album carried a harder punch and retained what they hadn't – the human, flesh-and-blood intimacy of a four-piece band.

---

[13] Taken from *Who I Am* by Pete Townshend, Harper (2012)

Like 'I Can See for Miles' – the album's signature track, blown in from the American West Coast – the other ten songs had the same shadings of psychedelia found on *Sgt Pepper's* . . . and on another record released by a British band that summer, Pink Floyd's début, *The Piper at the Gates of Dawn*. But they also had the taut, unyielding undercurrents of the American R&B records that first inspired The Who. Then again, they reached towards an even more expansive sound. The trace elements of what would come next, lurking just over the horizon and concerning a deaf, dumb and blind boy, can be found in the shifting movements of Townshend's closing track, 'Rael', and the sinister character sketch Entwistle painted on his other contribution, 'Silas Stingy'.

Comprised of four luridly-coloured portraits shot by a young buck American photographer, David Montgomery, the album's lavish packaging made its own statement about the band members and its hierarchy. The two front sleeve panels are occupied by Townshend and Daltrey. Townshend, bare-chested, brandishing an over-sized stick of deodorant, is on the left-hand, focal-point side. For his portrait, Daltrey was made to sit for forty-five minutes in a bathtub filled with cold baked beans. 'The beans had come out of the fridge and were freezing,' he described. 'I went home and – bosh – pneumonia.'[14]

Entwistle and Moon take up the back sleeve. Moon is pictured sad-clowning with a tube of the made-up Medac. Entwistle is done up as a cartoon caveman in leopard skins, one arm cradling a teddy bear, the other a barely-clad blonde, a triumphal smile on his face. Of the four, he is the only one to appear as if in his element.

---

[14] Taken from *Thanks a Lot, Mr Kibblewhite: My Life* by Roger Daltrey, Blink (2018)

As a whole, *The Who Sell Out* spoke of boldness and progression. It was also, though, too clever, too arch for its own good. Released on 15 December and with none of the warm-hearted spirit of Christmas, it peaked outside the Top Ten in the UK, while in America it didn't fare significantly better than its immediate predecessor, *A Quick One*. The Who's hymn to commercialism had proven to be their least-selling record to date.

■ ■ ■

As ever, perpetual motion kept them distracted from such harsh realities. From the end of October and up to 11 November, they undertook a theatre and ballroom tour of the UK, backed by two other young, questing British bands, Traffic and The Herd. Entwistle and Moon amused themselves one night by leaving the Herd's seventeen-year-old guitarist, Peter Frampton, chained to a radiator backstage. On 15 November, they flew off to America for a two-week tour in advance of their third album, leaving the usual trail of wreckage in their wake. For Entwistle, now that he was married and settled down, going off on tour was a means of escape into a parallel life. In this one he was made more assured and more attractive, the recipient of attention and adoration, and absolved of responsibility. No wonder it gave him his reason for being, as long as he also had the sanctuary of the other, more normal existence.

'John hadn't wanted me to go back to work and it was horrible for me when he had to go off,' reflects Alison. 'We used to write letters to each other. He was a very romantic man, but then, he was always away. Even if he was recording, I wouldn't see him all day. It would be four, five o'clock in the morning when he came home and then he would sleep through to the afternoon.

'When they were on tour, Kim, Keith's wife, would come and stay with me at Pope's Lane. She'd had their daughter, Mandy, by then and we were company for each other. Occasionally, we'd go down the Speakeasy with the boys. John could hold his drink, but Keith would be paralytic under the table and we would just be sat there, eating scampi and chips.'

Lambert and Stamp had promoted 'Wiggy' Wolff to tour manager, so hired a new driver for Entwistle and Moon. Peter Butler was another young local Mod from nearby Uxbridge and his mane of shaggy blonde hair soon led the two of them to christen him 'Dougal', after the hirsute dog character appearing in a children's TV show, *The Magic Roundabout*. 'My job was basically driving John and Keith to gigs and recording studios,' says Butler. 'Then, it would be the Speakeasy afterwards. John would probably go home and tell Alison that he'd been recording all night, but half the time he'd have been in the Speakeasy.

'John liked his brandy and his women. He found it hard to keep his trousers on, so to speak. It would be three, four in the morning and he'd have me drive a young lady home. They would be sat together in the back of the car. I'd have to wait in the car while they went inside and had another "chat", as they say. Then I'd take him home. That happened loads of times and you couldn't say anything. It was understood – mum's the word. I did get invited round to Pope's Lane. It was a nice little detached house . . . at home, John was a very two-feet-on-the-ground kind of man.

'John and Keith used to go to see a Dr Robertson in Harley Street – the famous one The Beatles wrote about as "Dr Robert". They used to get Drynamil and sleeping pills from him. Because they were on prescription, if you got pulled up by the police, you just got out your little brown pill bottles. John got off the uppers and downers after he got married. Humour bonded him with Keith. They were both very quick-witted – Pete, too – Pythonesque and all three of them would turn any situation into a laugh.

'Also, they didn't like Roger. On tour, you would never see Rog. After a show, he might moan about how the sound was shit and kick a speaker, but then he would just go off to his room in a tantrum. That wasn't all the time, don't get me wrong, but the other three, and most normally John and Keith, would sit in the bar, chill out and have a laugh. Or else go up to one of their rooms and drink till three in the morning. John and Keith would still be on that adrenalin rush, so that if they couldn't get hold of room service, or they wouldn't do sandwiches for them at that time, the phone would go out the window and the room would get trashed. They say the quiet ones are the worst and John was just as bad as Keith in that respect. He would smash up a room exactly the same; stick a Bowie knife in furniture and rip it to bits.'

The Who began the New Year on tour in Australia and New Zealand with fellow Londoners and kindred spirits, The Small Faces. The two bands' antics, which included an epic bout of hotel rearrangement to mark Small Faces singer Steve Marriott's twenty-first birthday, earned them a rebuke in the Australian Parliament.

The Who were also sent packing with a telegram from Australia's newly-elected Liberal Prime Minister, John Gorton. Recalling this missive, Entwistle wrote: '[Gorton] said that it was disgusting that rowdy foreign bands should be allowed into Australia to cause trouble and take home hard-earned Australian dollars. We flew home with what added up to £100 each, tourist class.'

On 21 February, The Who kicked off a six-week tour of North America. Entwistle's and Moon's former driver, Richard Cole, was working in New York at the time. Entwistle called Cole ahead of the band's arrival and instructed him to go down to a Greenwich Village club, the Salvation, and look up a girl who worked there called Devon Wilson. Cole remembers, 'He told me, "Send her my love and tell her we'll be back soon."' Such assignations aside, Entwistle passed time on the tour in ever-escalating cahoots with Moon. At one stop, the pair procured for themselves a school of piranha fish that they set to swimming in a hotel bath tub, but with underwhelming results. Belying their aggressive reputation, the piranha proceeded to swim listlessly about, mouths agape. Next, they got hold of a python. An altogether livelier purchase, the snake managed to slither off into the air-conditioning duct of another hotel, never to be seen again.

Yet for all the stimulation that Entwistle got from being in this altered state, he also made sure to keep himself fixed to the other aspect of his life and from which he was absented. En route to Detroit on 8 March, he wrote a letter addressed to his mother, stepfather and pet budgie at Lexden Road:

Dear Mum, Gordon and Ollie, hope you are all well.

Sorry this is a bit late, but you know how I hate writing letters and we've been pretty busy. I rang Alison yesterday and she told me about Grandad being ill. I was a bit worried, but when she told me he had started arguing with her again, I thought he must be getting better. Alison also told me about Scruffy being ill. If, by any chance, he has to be put down, I'd like to buy them another Yorkshire terrier as soon as possible. They'll miss him so much.

Keith and I went downstairs to the bar in our hotel in Edmonton yesterday. We sat down to order and the barman came up and told us 'dirty, long-haired hippies' to get out, or he'd throw us out. He pulled our chairs out from under us and we left, as he was three times as big as me. Apparently, the bar had been invaded one night by rough hippies and the whole place had been wrecked. We complained to the assistant manager that he'd better get bar staff who could tell the difference between 'gentlemen' (heh-heh) and hooligans. I had gone into the bar wearing my blue tonic suit and black shirt and tie.

Anyway, must sign off. I have just spilt my scotch and Coke and am now sitting in soaking wet trousers with the seat cushion upside down. Lots and lots of love, John.

PS: Give my love to Alison. And try to cheer the little nit up. The last time I saw her she was crying her eyes out on the doorstep.

9

The Mayor of Ealing

The Who wrapped up their latest American tour in New York City. There, they played a two-night stand at Bill Graham's Fillmore East over the weekend of 5 and 6 April 1968. At such a prestigious venue, this brace of shows made a statement about their growing status in America. As an extra burnish, their opening acts those nights were a pair of bluesmen they revered – Buddy Guy and BB King. Yet they flew back home beset by the same uncertainties that had dogged them over the past five years, principally concerning money and the delicacy of their position.

Although the tour had grossed around $100,00, once their expenses had been deducted, they were left with just $3,000 each to show for their six weeks' work. Their royalties from Track were also being consumed by the ballooning costs of replacing equipment and repairing hotel rooms. In just the two days that they were in New York, Moon ruinously let off Cherry Bombs in suites at the Gorham and Waldorf Astoria hotels. Fittingly, the first show that they played upon their return to London was at the Marquee Club, so they were not so far from being right back where they had started.

'Debts were piling up,' says 'Dougal' Butler. 'I'll tell you how bad things were – John used to bring back guitars with him from America, Fender Strats or Telecasters, so that he could sell them on to a guitar shop in South Ealing. He might bring back a couple each time and make himself a couple of hundred quid a pop. It was anything but strawberries and cream in those days.'

In general, Entwistle was in a sour mood. While in New York, he had met up with Richard Cole and voiced to him his frustrations at The Who and doubts about going on with the band. It wasn't the first time he had expressed as much, nor would it be the last. And he didn't act upon it then, or ever. However, his outlook was not improved by the business surrounding The Who's next single, a knockabout slice of psychedelic whimsy Townshend had titled 'Magic Bus'. Coming after 'I Can See for Miles', it sounded lightweight and regressive. They put the track down with Lambert at IBC at the end of May. It was not an occasion that Entwistle regarded with any affection.

'I played "Magic Bus" on a Vox Violin bass – an absolutely revolting thing, but it had the right sound,' he recalled. 'It looked more like a mint humbug, a stripy thing. Onstage, "Magic Bus" always was a complete bore for me. It was me playing "A" for six minutes. It wasn't boring when we recorded it, [but that was] because it was only three minutes long. Roger and Pete are having a great time and I'm playing "Humpty Dumpty" all through it. There are some points where it sounds like I'm going to sleep.'[15]

Neither was the indignity to end there. That October, when it was time to launch the single, Chris Stamp and Track's PR man, Vernon Brewer, together hatched an ill-conceived publicity stunt.

---

[15] Taken from an audio interview with Johnny Black, Rock's Backpages.com, August 1994

Stamp had Brewer hire a vintage, green London bus, which on the morning of Wednesday, 9 October set off from the BBC's Lime Grove Studios in Shepherd's Bush on a circuit of west and central London. On board were the four members of the band, a retinue of under-dressed girls freezing in mini-skirts and, courtesy of a company called Animal Actors, a baby elephant, a cockatoo and an elderly male lion. The wobbly old vehicle trundled along Oxford Street, Regent Street, Piccadilly and Fleet Street with its odd cargo and blaring out 'Magic Bus', but without attracting more than the occasional curious glance from passers-by.

The song itself passed in and out of the British charts just as inconsequentially, peaking at 26, although it was a modest hit in America. That June, the band had returned to America for another nine-week tour. Once again, the greater majority of the money that they made was sunk into new gear and placating hotel managers. For the most part, their routine on the road was now set in a fixed state of organised chaos. 'I always said that you couldn't manage The Who,' opines 'Wiggy' Wolff. 'John and Keith was a match made in humour heaven, but they would also be winding each other up all the time. Then there was their rivalry with Roger. Pete wrote the songs, so that left the pair of them to constantly snap at Rog's heels.

'At the start of that tour, I introduced a black-light effect onstage. Well, Rog had got his front teeth knocked out when he was younger and the black light nullified the reflection coming from off his false ones. It picked them up instead as a big, black spot. The first night, people in the audience were pointing up at him and laughing. Rog went berserk. He came storming offstage and ranted at me, "No more fucking black light!" Of course, John and Keith loved that, but to them Rog always was fair game. The English scene was grimy, hard work, lots of fighting going on, but the States was a revelation. Everything about it was exciting but, at the start, the biggest reason for going was to pull birds. And John loved that.'

In the months between the two US tours and 'Magic Bus', Townshend had begun to cook up something that was weightier and much more progressive. The roots of *Tommy* stretched back to 'A Quick One, While He's Away' and Lambert's pushing of him towards a longer-form narrative concept, their so-called 'rock opera'. For his subject, Townshend found his inspiration in the teachings of an Indian mystic, Meher Baba, to whom he had become devoted. In essence, Townshend's story of a deaf, dumb and blind boy who becomes a messianic figure was a metaphor for the higher states of consciousness that Baba preached to his followers to find and attain. No matter that the detail of this was as lost to the rest of the band as it would be vague to even the most attentive listener. As Entwistle told writer Dave Marsh, besides Townshend, 'nobody knew what it was all about. I had absolutely no idea what the story was, who the characters were or what they did.'[16]

Yet for all that Townshend's plot for *Tommy* lacked clarity, he more than compensated with the adventurousness of the music that he composed. Shifting back and forth from gentle acoustic passages to full-on, strident hard rock, he linked together a song cycle that was richly detailed with melodic flourishes, dramatic counterpoints and recurring themes. He was also spot-on with his timing. That year of 1968 was the first in which more albums than singles were sold in the UK; and among the former were such questing long-players as The Band's *Music From the Big Pink*, The Beatles' *White Album*, The Kinks' *Village Green Preservation Society*, Van Morrison's *Astral Weeks* and *Electric Ladyland* by The Jimi Hendrix Experience. Major works, they were linked by a

---

[16] Taken from *Before I Get Old: the Story of The Who* by Dave Marsh, Plexus (1983)

boldness of ambition and singularity of vision. Following on from these, *Tommy* was to seem like the next evolutionary step towards the rock album becoming the highest form of pop art.

■ ■ ■

On 19 September, The Who went into IBC's Studio A with Lambert to start work on their new album. The sessions went on for the better part of the next six months, with the band, Lambert and their crew camped out at the studio Mondays through to Fridays. Time was eaten up with intense, protracted discussions between Lambert and the band over the intricacies of *Tommy*. Even by his standards with The Who, Entwistle was absent from home so much that he had Alison practically move over to the studio.

'I was Aunty Alison to the roadies,' she says. 'They would come to me with all of their problems. When the recording was going on, I had a card school running with the crew guys outside the studio. Kit Lambert would be hanging around a lot. He was frightfully posh. I always remember how he drank brandy out of a paper cup.'

Bobby Pridden adds, 'Kit held the whole thing together in a lot of ways, because we all but lived at IBC during the week. It was Kit who would come up with the ideas. But in the studio, Pete and John were the mainstays of the band. Both of them were extremely musical and they shone on *Tommy*.'

Since the studio costs were yet another drain on The Who's parlous finances, at weekends they had to carry on doing gigs to replenish the coffers. On the weekend of 11 and 12 October, they travelled north for a brace of university shows in Sheffield and York. They did two more on 6 and 7 December, playing at Manchester University's Christmas Ball the first night and the second at Bristol University's Going Down Ball. On Tuesday, 10 and Wednesday, 11 December, they broke off from their own recording to film The Rolling Stones' *Rock & Roll Circus* TV special, lining up alongside The Stones, John Lennon, Eric Clapton, Marianne Faithfull and Jethro Tull at a TV studio in Wembley. Before an audience of a few hundred competition winners, The Who stormed through 'A Quick One, While He's Away', so comprehensively stealing the show from under the noses of the dishevelled headliners that The Stones had the footage shelved and kept from release for twenty-eight years.

In mid-November, they had taken a more routine respite from the studio to play a handful of theatre dates with such varied opening acts as The Small Faces, Joe Cocker, Free and nascent prog-rockers Yes. On 19 November, they travelled from Newcastle to Glasgow to play two shows at the Paisley Ice Rink. Entwistle recalled that journey in notes for his memoirs: 'Visited a Newcastle joke shop [with Moon]. We buy a pair of blow-up women's legs and fit with a pair of fishnet stockings. We drive through Newcastle with legs waving out the back window of the Bentley with Keith [on the Tannoy] making screaming girlie noises. I notice a policewoman on a walkie-talkie.

'After the show at Paisley Ice Rink, two policemen ask me if I am Mr John Entwistle, owner of the Bentley. A Newcastle policewoman has reported a woman in distress. We are escorted back to the hotel where Keith has arranged the legs sticking out of the bath tub with a blanket over a pillow. The police are much relieved when they nervously remove the blanket. We chat to the police who are now very friendly.'

The Saturday morning after that, Entwistle and Alison returned to Acton County Grammar and where he had been invited to open up the school's Christmas fête. 'I took him along to open a couple of church fêtes, too,' claims 'Dougal' Butler. 'That was John. He would go out of his way to please people. The other members of the band used to call him the Mayor of Ealing. When he found out they were taking the piss out of him, he stopped. I did think to myself, "John, what the fuck are you doing at a church fête on a Saturday morning? You're in The Who. It ain't rock-'n'-roll. Four nights ago, you were screwing some bird up against a wall in Manchester. Are you asking God's forgiveness?"'

At IBC, *Tommy* came together between feverish bouts of creativity and more drawn-out spells of prevarication and inertia. Townshend dashed off home one night and came back the next morning having written 'Pinball Wizard'. Stuck when it came to striking a vicious, pitch-black tone to depict two of his more depraved supporting characters, Tommy's brutish Uncle Ernie and bullying Cousin Kevin, Townshend turned to Entwistle for help. 'Could John compose a song about an Uncle Ernie abusing a boy?' Townshend wrote. 'He said he would try and came up with "Fiddle About". I liked it very much; it was disturbing, relentless and powerful. Again, John made "Cousin Kevin" brutally comedic, but this time the music was poignant, moving and frightening.'[17]

Entwistle's unsparing contributions certainly made *Tommy* a more potent drama. On 'Fiddle About', his lead vocal a malevolent cackle, he made vivid 'wicked Uncle Ernie' who menaced his young charge: 'Down with the bedclothes, up with the nightshirt!' If Entwistle's opening of a school fête suggested a gentler, more traditional facet of his own character, what was on display here was its macabre counterpoint.

Musically, *Tommy* actually benefited from The Who's lack of ready cash. For the first time, they had an eight-track facility at their disposal, but three of these wound up being left blank. They were held over for an orchestra that Lambert had intended to add on later, but which he ended up not being able to afford.

---

[17] Taken from *Who I Am* by Pete Townshend, Harper (2012)

The missing tracks, though, left *Tommy* with a more intimate and tightly-wound feel; space given over to the band's playing, and with a sense of spontaneity and coarseness preserved; it better served the songs. Entwistle, though, did later complain that Lambert had made Moon's drums sound like biscuit tins.

It wasn't until five months into the new year of 1969 that they unveiled the finished album, a double. Released in the UK on 23 May in a lavish, gatefold sleeve designed by a fellow Baba follower of Townshend's, Michael McInnerney, *Tommy* divided critics. The music weekly, *Disc and Music Echo*, instantly hailed it a masterpiece, while a review in the rival *New Musical Express* sneered: 'Pretentious is too strong a word . . . but sick certainly does apply.' Irrespective, *Tommy* soared to Number Two on the UK chart. It also hit the same peak in America, where it came out eight days later on 31 May, shifting 100,000 copies in its opening fortnight on sale.

■ ■ ■

Once The Who took *Tommy* out on the road, it became a different animal again. Now, it was louder, more ferocious and exultant. They began touring in North America and, in advance of the album's release, playing six weeks of shows that started with a brace of back-to-back, three-night runs, the first at Detroit's Grande Ballroom from 9 May and then again at Fillmore East from 16 May. Armed with a new, state-of-the-art sound system assembled by Bobby Pridden, they launched off each night at maximum volume and velocity.

They opened their sets with an Entwistle composition, the hard-driving 'Heaven and Hell'; 'I Can't Explain' was next up, followed by a full-blooded cover of Mose Allison's 'Young Man Blues'. Then they went into a thirteen-song selection from *Tommy*, revving up from 'It's a Boy' through to 'Pinball Wizard', and building from there to the explosive, orgiastic climax of

'We're Not Gonna Take It'. The encores were two more pulsating covers, Eddie Cochran's 'Summertime Blues' and 'Shakin' All Over' by Johnny Kidd and the Pirates, backward-looking nods that acted like twin pressure releases.

In July, they came back and played seven shows in the UK, including one at London's Royal Albert Hall on 5 July. Again, they flew back over to America on 10 August for two festival appearances on the East Coast. The first of these was promoted by Bill Graham and went ahead on Tuesday, 12 August at an open-air venue in Tanglewood, Massachusetts, more used to staging classical music events. The Who joined a bill that also featured headliners Jefferson Airplane and BB King. These facts aside, the Tanglewood Music Festival has passed off into history, vanished beneath the looming shadow cast by the festival that The Who were to play next. This one took place over the weekend of 16 and 17 August on fields belonging to a forty-nine-year-old dairy farmer, Max Yasgur, located just outside the village of Bethel, a resort in the Catskills Mountains of upstate New York. In full, it was named the Woodstock Music and Arts Fair. Initially, The Who had baulked at the offer of doing Woodstock. However, mired in debt, they were swayed when the festival's twenty-four-year-old co-promoter, Mike Lang, guaranteed to pay them $11,200 in cash.

By then, Lang had already secured the likes of The Band, The Grateful Dead, Janis Joplin, Santana and Hendrix for his festival. However, The Who could have been forgiven for having second thoughts soon after they rolled out of New York on the afternoon of 16 August. By the point they were embarked on their hundred-mile road trip up to Bethel, the Woodstock site and the surrounding areas had begun to resemble nothing so much as a disaster zone with the crowd there having swollen to a quarter-of-a-million people, far exceeding Lang's most optimistic advance estimate of 60,000.

Thousands of vehicles had been abandoned all along the two-lane highway that ran into Sullivan County and traffic was gridlocked for miles around. A series of downpours had turned the festival site into a quagmire, a situation exacerbated when the woefully inadequate toilet facilities overflowed. Supplies of water and the food concessions had also run out. The chaos extended to the actual staging of the festival. With the situation backstage gone from beyond anyone's control, the show was running hours behind schedule. Not that this made too much difference to the vast majority of those in attendance. The stage itself was too low and the PA system barely fit for purpose, so that most of the crowd weren't able to hear, much less see any of the acts. Worst of all, that very morning a seventeen-year-old, Raymond Mizak, had been killed on the site when a tractor ran over him in his sleeping bag. Such was the scene unfolding when The Who reached the outskirts of Bethel at 4.00pm under a sullen, darkening sky.

'It was the best of festivals . . . it was the worst of festivals,' Entwistle wrote of Woodstock:

> About to go bankrupt, we'd agreed to do two festivals to raise enough money to get temporarily out of trouble. We owed a quarter-of-a-million pounds in debts and taxes. The taxman was knocking at our door. In fact, the door hadn't stopped knocking for the last two years. The rock star helicopter shuttle service had turned into an emergency overdose service, flying out the victims of LSD-spiked fruit juice and STP-spiked coffee (God, you would have OD'd if you had fallen face down in the Woodstock mud). So we had to drive in. It took us three hours, but we were due on at 6.00pm and so arrived in good time.
>
> Four hours previous, I had been lying on my hotel bed watching TV with Alison. A loud tapping on our ground-floor

window made our heads whip round. Janis Joplin was jumping up and down outside with that wide-mouth grin of hers. She had bounced off, waving towards a waiting helicopter, probably the last one to ferry out performers. We had been waiting for a phone call from our tour manager, John Wolff, to tell us whether we were going to play or not. An ugly rumour was going around that the promoter hadn't enough money to pay the groups. We were insisting upon getting ours up front and before we made a move towards the festival. Anyway, the call had come and we had set off.

Arriving on site, we were shown to our log cabin dressing room. Apparently, it was everyone else's dressing room as well. We were backstage in the middle of Armageddon. 'I'm afraid the schedule's running a bit behind,' a promoter's assistant nonchalantly informed us. 'How far behind?' asked John Wolff, matter-of-factly. 'Oh,' was the reply, 'about nine hours.' I gazed around me and contemplated an exciting nine hours guiding my white Beatle boots through the mud. Keith and I headed out. We weren't at all prepared for what we saw. The toilets were a row of six, tall wooden cabins. All the doors were flung open and shit and newspaper were piled high to the ceiling in every one. We decided to shit in the woods.

Keith met up with an old girlfriend and wandered off in the direction of the woods. I watched a couple of bands – Creedence Clearwater Revival and Sly and the Family Stone. Bored during the prolonged equipment changeover and having snatched up a bottle of Old Grandad, I decided to walk out around the back of the audience. I ended up running into so many people I knew that it took me three hours. I hate neat bourbon, so gratefully accepted the kind offer of a can of Coke to mix it with and somebody else had a bucket of ice – sheer luxury. 'Where did you find this?' I asked the Coke donor. The answer was backstage at the fruit juice stand. I screamed silently. What else would be in it? Acid? STP? A mixture of both? I made it back to the dressing room, drank the rest of the Old Grandad bottle and passed out.

It was near dawn the next day by the time The Who took to the stage. With Entwistle, Townshend and Moon drunk, stoned and sleep-deprived, they sounded as ragged and untogether as they looked. All of those frayed, jangled nerves also made for an ugly mood up onstage. They were midway through the *Tommy* section of the set, about to go from 'Pinball Wizard' into 'Do You Think It's Alright?', when Yippie activist Abbie Hoffman stalked onstage and seized a microphone. Hoffman meant to make a speech protesting a ten-year prison sentence that had been handed down to White Panther leader John Sinclair for marijuana possession, but never made it that far. Enraged, Townshend got to him first, swiping at him with his guitar and then, with a boot up the backside, sending him tumbling down into the photographers' pit.

On The Who charged, Townshend's guitar strafing fire over Entwistle's and Moon's artillery bursts, lifting those in the wretched, battle-weary crowd who were able to hear them to their feet. Townshend in white boiler suit and Doc Marten boots; Daltrey, bare-chested, tassel-sleeved, corkscrews of hair spilling down; Moon, a blur of arms and teeth; and Entwistle, rigid, implacable, ink-black hair against a brilliant white jacket, their still, mooring point; the four of them frozen at the very moment they became the archetypal rock band. Not four weeks earlier, Neil Armstrong had become the first man to set foot on the moon. Now, here at Woodstock, amidst the ruin of the hippy idyll, The Who were rocketing off on their own extraordinary, perilous and ultimately doom-laden adventure.

10

A Dark, Violent Year

Two weeks on from Woodstock, The Who topped the bill at the Isle of Wight Festival on the evening of Saturday, 30 August. On this occasion, the band was ferried by helicopter out to the island in the English Channel, but they were paid a much more modest fee of £1,100. As at Woodstock, though, they produced a resounding performance, their thunder considerably amplified by a 2,500-watt PA system. Up on stage that night, and for all that Daltrey lassoed his microphone and Townshend and Moon thrashed at their instruments, it was Entwistle who stood out. He walked onstage kitted out in a jet-black jumpsuit that was painted over in white with a full body skeleton. 'The most outrageous thing I ever wore,' he remarked years later.[18]

With *Tommy* becoming a fixture on the *Billboard* chart, the real glory – and riches – was to be found in America. That autumn, The Who returned there for a triumphal five-week tour. This run started on 10 October in Boston and included an unprecedented six-night stand at Fillmore East that was attended by both Bob

---

[18] Taken from an uncredited interview on YouTube dated 20 March 1986

Dylan and Leonard Bernstein. Onstage, the band was tighter, mightier-sounding than ever, but off it their divisions had got more pronounced. Townshend increasingly operated in his own fiefdom and, with Daltrey isolated, Entwistle and Moon continued to present the band's only united, if bleary front.

'Dad told me once how it was with The Who on the road,' says Christopher Entwistle. 'Him and Keith would go off and cause trouble; Pete would go off and write songs; and Roger would be off shagging somebody. That was basically it.'

Cotswolds-born Mick Bratby joined up with the band's crew for the tour, and was detailed to look after Entwistle's and Townshend's guitars. He says, 'On tour, it was a totally different life. I liked John straight away. He and Keith used to joke about together. In Washington, we stayed at the Watergate Hotel and Keith let off all the fire alarms at 3.00am. Keith and John fed off each other. Pete and Roger wouldn't have much to do with their antics on the road, so they didn't mix much.

'I liked Pete, too. But Roger could be a nasty bugger sometimes. Later on that tour, we played another show in Boston, at the Tea Party, which was not a huge place. I was squatting down behind the PA when all of a sudden these huge cabinets came toppling down on top of me, straight on to my head. Roger wasn't pleased with the sound, so he'd done a flying leap at the cabinets and kicked them over. I had my head cut open. Another time, I also had a big punch-up with Roger. It was all over a girl. I thought she was my girlfriend, but Roger started sniffing around. He was like that.'

The band saw out the year doing a handful of shows around the UK. After the heightened experience of America, it was a comedown of sorts. The venues seemed small to them and grubby, the scenery all too familiar. Although across the Atlantic, a shroud was laid over the sixties by an event that took place the night after The Who had played at the Palace Theatre in Manchester. On 6 December, The Rolling Stones staged a free concert at a racetrack sixty miles east of San Francisco, the Altamont Speedway. The events that unfolded that Saturday at Altamont have become infamous – there was a general mood of menace that culminated in the murder of an eighteen-year-old black man, Meredith Hunter, by a gang of knife-wielding Hell's Angels. Hunter's killing was the ending of the peace and love generation's Age of Aquarius, and the signal of the dread, ill wind that was to blow in through the next decade.

1970 was a dark, violent year. The Vietnam War raged on; at Kent State University on 6 May, Ohio National Guardsmen shot and killed four students protesting President Nixon's expansion of the conflict into nearby Cambodia. In that country, the Khmer Rouge seized power and began a campaign of almost unimaginable brutality against the Cambodian people. After Altamont, rock music also seemed to have lost its free-loving, freewheeling soul. It was to be the year of The Beatles' rancorous split and when Jimi Hendrix and Janis Joplin ran out of road, both of them dead and gone at just twenty-seven. For The Who's part, 1970 also started with a senseless and terrible death.

On the evening of 4 January, Moon, his wife, Kim, his driver, Neil Boland, together with another couple, attended a disco in the London satellite town of Hatfield. When a group of local youths took exception to Moon's presence, the party hurried back to his Bentley which the baying mob surrounded. In the mêlée, Boland got out of the car to confront their tormentors and Moon, who couldn't drive and had been drinking, jumped behind the wheel and tore off out of the car park. The twenty-four-year-old Boland was either pushed, or fell, under the wheels of the departing car and died from the head injuries that he sustained. Moon was devastated. A subsequent inquest all but absolved him of Boland's death, but he knew the mortifying truth. Just as damning for Moon, so, too, did his closest ally. 'Everyone was devastated,' Entwistle told Moon's biographer, Tony Fletcher. 'But they all told the same story. They tried to stop Neil getting out of the car. Keith blamed himself, because he actually did the fucking thing. He admitted doing it.'

The tipping point of Moon's helter-skelter descent could be traced back to that awful night in Hatfield. He was always driven to excess but, after Boland's death, there was a more dangerous, fatalistic edge to his indulgences. It was as if he wanted to numb himself now, come what may. This also drove a wedge between him and Entwistle. Moon's protector, Entwistle would eventually weary of his manic episodes the more they occurred, to the point that a distance grew between the two of them. Ultimately, the consequences of this would for both of them be devastating and irreversible.

Not that any of this was apparent just yet. Moon was riddled with guilt but ever the clown, hiding behind his near-permanent, gap-toothed smile; Entwistle went on being his partner in crime. And The Who stormed into their imperious phase. At the end of that same month, they took *Tommy* off on a short tour of European opera houses. If this was validation of Townshend's pretensions towards making art, their next move was meant to reinforce their reputation as a loud, thrilling and uncompromising rock-'n'-roll band above all others.

Townshend had instructed Bobby Pridden to tape a number of shows on their last US tour, but then couldn't face listening back to them. Instead, he had Lambert and Stamp arrange five low-key UK university gigs for that February and hired the Pye mobile unit to record two of them – at Leeds on Valentine's Day, and the next night at Hull. There was a fault with the tapes at Hull but, by then, The Who already had captured magic in a bottle. Released on 16 May in a cardboard-coloured sleeve so as to look like a bootleg, the *Live at Leeds* album comprised just six tracks, half of them covers – 'Young Man Blues', 'Summertime Blues' and 'Shakin' All Over'. No more was necessary, since what was there, split over two sides of vinyl, amounted to a relentless sonic assault. *Tommy* had expanded The Who's horizons, but this was them pared back down to blunt, savage basics. Such was the pulverising nature of Townshend's, Entwistle's and Moon's playing that on a near-fifteen-minute battery of 'My Generation', they all but invented hard rock and heavy metal.

■ ■ ■

Like *Tommy*, *Live at Leeds* went on to be a smash hit and confirmed The Who's reputation as rock's most formidable live band. This they reinforced on their next – seventh – American tour, which began with an afternoon and evening show at New York's Metropolitan Opera House on Sunday, 7 June and climaxed in front of an 18,000 crowd back in Tanglewood, Massachusetts. As the audiences grew bigger and the air they were breathing got to be more rarefied, so, too, were the levels of pandemonium escalating offstage.

When their 22 June flight from Memphis to Atlanta was delayed on the runway, Townshend became agitated at the pilot's whistling over the intercom. Eventually, he snapped, jumping to his feet and shouting out, 'All right! All right! I'll tell you where the bomb is!' That got Townshend hauled off the plane and detained at the airport for questioning. The other three were left kicking their heels in their dressing room at Atlanta's Municipal Auditorium until he showed up three hours late. The show finally got going at midnight before an ill-tempered, diminished audience. Recalling the gig some years later, Entwistle said, 'Moon and I were sitting around the dressing room getting totally pissed, saying we didn't care and we'd take it out of [Townshend's] share. But Daltrey was stone sober, fuming off in a corner.'[19]

At the Philadelphia Spectrum on 24 June, their opening act was an American power-trio, The James Gang, fronted by a hot-shot young guitarist named Joe Walsh. The two bands hit it off straight away and The James Gang ended up becoming a regular opening act for The Who. 'Our two bands just bonded,' Walsh remembers. 'But then, we were fairly crazy, and so were they. Our bass player, Dale Peters, started hanging out with John and I was kind of buddying up with Pete. Eventually, though, I started to hang with John more and more, because Pete is Pete. Sometimes he's right there with you, and sometimes he's in Pete land. You never really knew which Pete you were going to get, which was OK.

'John and I had the same kind of dry humour and we talked a lot. We talked about music – John was a brilliant musician; he could read and write charts – and also relevant craziness. Moon decided that he liked me, too, and that was pretty terrifying. He came and got hold of you, and said, "Take these pills; we're going out!"

'John was a perfect gentleman, or at least he could be. He dressed impeccably. He didn't say much but, if you got to know him real good, over the course of an evening and a few brandies, he would kind of open up. He could sum up a complex situation in one line that was spot on and absolutely nailed it. He was brilliant in that way, too. He was The Ox. If John decided to give you a hug, he would have his arms wrapped around you until *he* decided to let go. Sometimes that was an amount of time and

---

[19] Taken from a *Crawdaddy* magazine piece by John Swendon, published January 1974

he was a big fucking guy. Also, I didn't know anybody who he couldn't out-drink, except for maybe Keith.

'Onstage, I would just stare at him, waiting to see him move or give some kind of facial expression. Maybe once I saw him smile. It might be when Keith kicked his drums over in the middle of a song, or else if Pete jumped in the air and fell down. A little corner of John's mouth would turn up. That motionlessness, that expressionlessness, it was a big part of his aura. Practical jokes, there were a bunch of them. Lots of room trashing. I want to say good, clean fun, but . . . You know, Keith was scary and all the stories are true. You just did not fucking know what he was going to do. John was more controlled, but he had a sick sense of humour and he loved practical jokes. He and I would get the guys in the crew. You fill a waste basket with water, lean it against somebody's hotel room door and then knock. The two of us took great delight in thinking up ways to get people. And back in those days, it was still just all kinds of boy-scout stuff.'

The more records that they sold, the longer The Who were kept inside their touring bubble. After America, they did a sprinkling of dates around the UK, which included a second consecutive headline appearance at the Isle of Wight on 30 August. This time, coming on after The Doors at 2.00am, they turned a bank of blinding white spotlights on the 600,000 crowd during 'Go to the Mirror!'

Another run round Europe followed, and then a full UK tour starting on 6 October in Cardiff and ending on 29 October at London's Hammersmith Palais, The James Gang their support act. Occasionally, reality did intrude. During the British tour, Entwistle's beloved grandmother, Daisy, died after a brief illness. 'John came home from a gig that night and drank a whole bottle of whisky,' says Alison Entwistle. 'And he was still stone, cold sober.'

Entwistle had liked to drink from when The Detours were first doing the pubs and clubs. Now, though, he drank all the time and in serious amounts. Alison says, 'The only thing he did end up doing was to change his drink from whisky to brandy. If he was drunk on whisky, he could get really nasty. So he stopped drinking whisky and he never got nasty again – not on drink, anyway.'

Bill Curbishley went to work at Track at the end of that year. The eldest of six, Curbishley hailed from Canning Town in London's notoriously tough East End, the Kray twins' stomping ground up until 1968. In 1963, Curbishley was wrongfully convicted of a security van robbery and had just then been paroled from Wormwood Scrubs prison. 'John was a strong guy and a lot of it with him went unspoken,' he says. 'I started to go out with him and Moon a lot. I always had a good time with John.

'The problem with all that was that John didn't drink that much more than me at the time. But he had the luxury of being able to wake up at whatever time he wanted, especially on the road. Drinking was part of the culture. I was brought up around the docks in the East End. If you went into a club, you would end up with ten drinks in front of you. The pubs opened at 5.30 in the afternoon. John might turn over in his grave, but I haven't had a drink in thirty years now. It's the reason why I'm still alive, I think. You either come to a crossroads, or you don't.'

Drink would also sometimes loosen Entwistle's tongue just enough that he would moan to others about his lot in The Who. Specifically, how Townshend wouldn't consent to using more of his songs in the band. Perhaps it was the booze that emboldened him, but whatever the cause, at the end of that year he decided to do a solo album. Squirrelled away in his box-room studio at Pope's Lane, he had assembled a stockpile of songs and secured a budget from Track to go off and make a record. With Entwistle also producing, the sessions began at Trident Studios in Soho on Monday, 30 November. He roped in his old running mate, Cy Langston, to play guitar and also enlisted the services of Humble Pie's drummer, Jerry Shirley.

Smash Your Head Against the Wall, as the album ended up being called, was completed in just two weeks. Even still, Entwistle ran a relaxed, well-refreshed operation and led regular sojourns to the local pubs. One afternoon, Moon dropped by the studio with a new drinking buddy, Viv Stanshall of the Bonzo Dog Doo-Dah Band, and Entwistle had the two of them beat out a Latin-tinged percussion for one of his songs, 'No. 29 (Eternal Youth)'. That tune encapsulated the general tone of the album. A playful, quintessentially early-seventies kind of rock romp, it was coloured by Entwistle's own brass parts and sung by him in the style of a knowing nod and wink.

All round, it turned out to be a good, solid record and one that testified first of all to Entwistle's musical craft, and then again to his black humour. Typical of this is 'Ted End', an engaging, lilting vignette about the lonely death of the titular Ted. The version of 'Heaven and Hell' that he cut for the album missed Moon's propulsion and the abrasiveness of Townshend's play-ing. Conversely, the opening track, 'My Size', packed the near-industrial, hammer-on-anvil wallop of the first two Black Sabbath albums, both of which had come out earlier that year. At least as much as to anyone else, the record was a revelation to his band-mates in The Who. As Townshend went on to note, 'We learned more from John making his album than we had in all the years that he'd played bass with us. Because he *did* it and it spoke to us.'[20]

---

[20] Taken from *Before I Get Old: the Story of The Who* by Dave Marsh, Plexus (1983)

When it was time to release the album the following year, Entwistle had Track put out the lead-off single, 'I Believe in Everything', on April Fools' Day. In another of Vernon Brewer's publicity stunts, that same morning Entwistle personally delivered copies of the single to a record shop on Fleet Street, pulling up to the premises in a horse-drawn carriage. The album's front-cover artwork was also designed to make an impression. It featured a portrait photograph of Entwistle, wearing a death mask, transposed on to an X-ray of a heart patient's chest cavity that he had wangled out of his doctor. None of this, though, was enough to make the single or the album a hit. On Decca in America, *Smash Your Head Against the Wall* would eventually go on to sell steadily, if unspectacularly, but in the moment it appeared to have come and gone.

'It was a really good album, much better than it was given credit for at the time,' maintains Keith Altham. 'But in some respects, maybe it was too good. It was an album for musicians, rather than a punters' album.'

Around the same time that Entwistle knuckled down to work on *Smash Your Head Against the Wall*, Townshend presented the band with his latest concept. He called it *Lifehouse*, and so far as the others could tell, it appeared to be a piece of dystopian science-fiction about an autocratic society in which rock music was banned.

Townshend planned to rehearse the work over a series of interactive, 'total music' concerts to be staged at London's Old Vic Theatre beginning in early 1971. At a press conference to announce the shows, Townshend revealed that the band would be working with a quadrophonic sound system and synthesisers. '[An invited audience of] 400 people will be involved with us and we aim to play music which represents them,' Townshend told the somewhat baffled gathering. 'I'll act as a computer, and everything will be fed into me and processed, then put back out again.'[21]

In the event, The Who did five shows at the Old Vic between 14 February and 26 April. None was advertised in advance, the audience largely being drawn from local youth clubs and with just a smattering of tickets going on general sale. Battling technical issues with the £30,000 quadrophonic sound system, and faced with mounting confusion from both the audiences and his own colleagues, Townshend didn't judge any of them a success.

The first recording session for *Lifehouse* also left him reeling. In mid-March, Lambert convinced him to fly the band out to New York to work at the Record Plant studio in midtown Manhattan. Lambert was already holed up there producing the début album from an American all-girl vocal group, Labelle. As a result, Lambert was missing for most of the week that The Who spent recording. Added to that frustration, Townshend still hadn't been able to get Entwistle, Moon or Daltrey to comprehend his vision for the project. Still fresh from taking charge of his own record, Entwistle brooded over the haphazardness of it all and also the presence in the studio of three American musicians – Dylan sideman Al Kooper, who had also played on *The Who Sell Out*, Mountain guitarist Leslie West and a jazz pianist, Ken Ascher, hired by Lambert to supplement The Who's sound.

'John didn't seem to care for me and was clearly being spiteful and mean,' Kooper recalls of the session. 'Once I understood that for sure, I avoided being in his presence.'

---

[21] Quoted from *Dear Boy: the Life of Keith Moon* by Tony Fletcher, Omnibus (2005)

As for Entwistle's perspective, he later on told Richard Barnes, 'That was the period when Pete was reading the dictionary. He said he was going to learn a new word every day to expand his vocabulary, but he didn't really bother to learn the meanings of them. Everything for him was a 'traumatic experience', and me and Keith went out and bought dictionaries and looked up "traumatic".'

Retreating to London, Townshend wrote to Glyn Johns, who had gone on to engineer for The Rolling Stones, The Beatles and Led Zeppelin, inviting him to work on the project. Townshend enclosed copies of his own demos for *Lifehouse* and an outline script. Johns also found himself bemused by what Townshend was striving for, but he was bowled over by the raw material and agreed to meet with the band and Bill Curbishley, who was representing Lambert and Stamp. The outcome of this meeting was that Townshend shelved *Lifehouse*, but agreed that The Who should use its strongest songs for a stand-alone album. That April, the band and Johns began recording at Mick Jagger's mansion in rural Berkshire, Stargroves, using The Stones' sixteen-track mobile studio and set-up in the high-ceilinged hallway.

This arrangement lasted just two days, but gave rise to one stunning take. Beginning with a nagging, thirty-second synthesiser drone, after which the band crash in, joined by a strutting, chest-out vocal from Daltrey, 'Won't Get Fooled Again' unravelled over more than eight, tumultuous minutes. It combined the dizzying musicianship of the *Tommy* material with the heads-down attack of *Live at Leeds*. A notoriously demanding taskmaster, Johns later on recalled listening to the band cut the track and his 'hair being parted by what was coming out of the speakers'.[22]

---

[22] Taken from *Sound Man: A Life Recording Hits with the Rolling Stones, the Who, Led Zeppelin, the Eagles . . .* by Glyn Johns, Plume (2014)

From Stargroves, they moved on to Johns' preferred studio, Olympic in Barnes, a leafy corner of south-west London. Over three more days that April and a further couple in June, the *Who's Next* album took shape at Olympic. From Townshend's batch of songs, they put down a second, synth-led barnstormer, 'Baba O'Riley', as well as a couple more reflective tunes that showed off a new-found lightness of touch – 'The Song is Over' and 'Behind Blue Eyes'. Wanting to retain the directness of Townshend's original demos, Johns asked Entwistle and Moon to rein in their playing on these tracks. Afterwards, Entwistle insisted that he had disagreed with Johns' approach. In the studio, though, it doesn't appear that he ever challenged the engineer.

'I didn't encounter any resistance,' Johns maintains. 'Both John and Keith went along with what I asked them to do, and Keith a little more begrudgingly. I only found out later that John wasn't happy about it. I mean, to the extent that he didn't want me to make the next record. I think he was overruled.

'It was very upsetting to me, because I would never, ever try to force a musician to do something that they weren't comfortable with; one can't, because it defeats the object if you're a producer. I felt that the particular material required a fuller, heavier bass sound to make it work well. That's what I asked John to give me, and he did. He never once said to me that he was unhappy about it.'

An almost pathological aversion to conflict would become a recurring theme of Entwistle's professional and personal lives. Indeed, towards the end of the sessions for *Who's Next*, he brought in a song of his own that described him fleeing the scene of a domestic dispute. A jaunty, gambolling rocker that Entwistle took the lead vocal on, and to which he also added piano and brass, 'My Wife' brought the kitchen-sink drama of his other life into The Who's realm. 'My life's in jeopardy,' he lamented in the opening verse, singing with a kind of sly, amused detachment. 'Murdered in cold blood is what I'm gonna be . . . I ain't been home since Friday night, and now my wife is coming after me.'

'I was still working for John at the time,' says 'Dougal' Butler. 'One night at Pope's Lane, he had a set-to with Alison. I happened to ring the house and Alison was in tears and angry, so I thought I had better go over. I drove to the house and Alison told me that John had gone off to the pub down the road. I went and found him there. He was sitting in the boozer all by himself; there were a few other people in the place, but nobody knew who he was. I got him a drink from the bar and we sat and had a chat.

'The band had just come off an American tour. He told me that Alison thought that he'd been with another woman and had confronted him about it. He had got the hump and stormed out. Then he said, "Ah, I denied it, but I was seeing this girl and blah, blah, blah . . ." I told him, "You know what, mate? You want to turn this around and make it into a song."'

'How accurate is that song? I'm not telling,' Alison counters. 'But, well, yes, I would get quite upset when he did something wrong. He used to go off and compose in his upstairs studio. He spent a lot of time "plonking", as I used to call it. The bass would be booming out. He didn't do anything quietly. He wrote "My Wife" in his upstairs studio at home. And whenever I listened to what he'd written, I would say to him, "Why are you saying such things?"'

11

Hey, Big Spender

On 14 July 1971, The Who threw a press party at Moon's new home to launch *Who's Next*. Inevitably, Moon's property, Tara, was a showy affair. Set in rolling grounds near the Surrey town of Chertsey, it was a minimalist, near-transparent bungalow comprised of white walls and glass, and a roof that peaked in five pyramids. Just as predictably, the party that ensued, which all of the band attended, ended up being a thoroughly riotous affair, and Moon's unfortunate neighbours ended up summoning the police to quieten it down. It was the first time that Entwistle had visited his friend at home, and was also to be the second to last.

When it was released that August, *Who's Next* was greeted with ecstatic reviews on both sides of the Atlantic. A rave by *Rolling Stone* critic John Medelsohn was indicative of the general tone of these notices: 'An old-fashioned long-player containing intelligently conceived, superbly performed, and sometimes even exciting rock-'n'-roll,' Medelsohn wrote. 'A monumental testament to their greatness ... Townshend playing with exemplary efficiency and taste, [and] Entwistle dreaming up all manner of scrumptious melodic and rhythmic flourishes (listen especially to what he plays beneath the chorus of "Won't Get Fooled Again").' Boosted by such acclaim, the album went on to become their first – and only – Number One in the UK. In America, it sold even better and had a more resounding impact. Along with The Rolling Stones' *Sticky Fingers*, released that April, and Led Zeppelin's untitled fourth album, which was to come out three months later, *Who's Next* was in the vanguard of the movement towards a new, mass-market, stadium-rock era that would endure into the next century.

The Who were already off on tour again by the time *Who's Next* was released. Indeed, the photograph that adorned its cover was shot off the cuff as they sped between dates in the UK that July. Tearing up the A1 with an American photographer, Ethan Russell, along for the ride, Townshend spotted four concrete structures looming over the landscape outside the north-eastern mining city of Durham. Pulling over to investigate, they came across Easington Colliery, the pillars rising up out of its slag heap. Russell had the band line up and pee against one, rainwater substituting for those who couldn't deliver to order. Apart from that one iconic image, grasped from such an unlikely situation, the British dates went ahead as a kind of curtain-raiser for the more grandstanding business in America.

The US tour opened with two sell-out shows in front of 14,000 people a night, at the Forest Hills Tennis Stadium, New York City, on 29 and 31 July. The Who, equipped now with the largest, most overwhelming PA on the circuit, a 3,000-watt monster, were roaring up to the height of their powers. There was about them a pulsating, electric air, magnetic and dangerous even. On the first night in New York, with rain pouring down from an angry sky, a security officer, George Byington, was knifed to death outside the stadium by a deranged young man. Byington's attacker had approached him screaming that he would kill somebody if he wasn't able to get a ticket for the show.

From New York, the tour carried on up the East Coast, thrilling audiences at each stop. Altogether, it was a three-week adrenalin rush and fuelled, too, by harsher stimulants. 'My capacity for booze onstage was enormous, especially if I stuck to cognac,' Townshend wrote of the period. 'But I still refrained from using the drugs my friends were; cocaine was everywhere backstage, and both John and Keith combined it with Mandrax, which couldn't have done their hearts much good.'[23]

In Entwistle's case, Townshend's claims may be premature. Entwistle was an intensely private man in many respects, which extended to his drug use. Certainly, he would go on to develop a taste for cocaine, but it was not something that he would ever do out in the open, in front of others. A number of the band's close aides insist that it was not until four years later that he first started doing cocaine, so far as it was possible for them to tell. One thing that was certain was that The Who had at last begun to make real money and, in that particular area, Entwistle never did hide his consumption.

In Detroit, he sought out a Cadillac dealer and forked out for a 20ft-long, low-riding Lincoln Continental, black with tinted windows and two sun-roofs; he paid more again to have it shipped back to England aboard the *QE1*. By the time he got home, he would have a new driver for the Lincoln, too. During the tour, he asked Mick Bratby to become his personal assistant as 'Dougal' Butler was moving on to nursemaid Moon.

At the end of that trek around America, Entwistle wound down in New York City. The first afternoon off, he trooped along to a Manhattan music store, Manny's, and bought himself

---

[23] Taken from *Who I Am* by Pete Townshend, Harper (2012)

armfuls of brass instruments, which was the start of yet another spending spree.

Richard Barnes happened to be in New York at the same time. He recalls, 'I met up with the band at the Navarro Hotel on Central Park South. That was about the only hotel left in New York that would have The Who and Moon. Pete was leaving for England and I was staying on. He gave me a crumpled $200 bill to tide me over. Everyone else from the band and crew left, too, apart from John and Mick Bratby.

'I went down to John's room, and John had clearly sent Mick out to fetch him some money. On the table were these piles of cash, all neat, brand-new and with green bands around every wad. He must have had $20,000, which was a fortune in those days. John said to me, "Right, we're going out spending!" They'd just done a long tour and that was his reward to himself.'

Back in London that September, The Who headlined a charity concert for the Bangladesh Relief Fund at the Oval Cricket Ground. Entwistle brought along the Lincoln Continental to show off backstage. As Barnes remembers, in the interim he'd had the car customised and fitted with a television, fridge, three tape machines and a fully-stocked bar. Entwistle invited Barnes to sit with him in the expansive rear seats and plied him with cognac. Soon after, the *Daily Mirror* newspaper agreed to do a photo shoot of Entwistle's 'rock star car'. For the occasion, Entwistle arranged to be driven over to Moon's Tara; this was to be the final occasion that he would go there and Moon had a surprise waiting for him.

'In advance of John arriving, Keith and I had called up the management and told them that we wanted some money to buy a milk float,' regales Butler. 'I got hold of some hardboard and a load of polystyrene, painted it black and covered three sides of the milk float. Next, I cut out a Rolls Royce grill and stuck it to the front and put up chintzy wallpaper and a picture of the Queen on the hardboard walls. We'd also bought an old-fashioned armchair, second-hand.

'When John turned up, Keith was sitting in the armchair on the back of the milk float. He'd slicked his hair back with Brylcreem, had a smoking jacket on and was puffing from a cigarette holder. What John didn't realise was that the whole thing was a piss-take of his car. I'm not saying he didn't see the funny side, but he didn't get what it was pertaining to.'

In any case, Entwistle had other things to occupy him. Alison had found out she was pregnant with their first child and the prospect of being a father thrilled Entwistle. That autumn, the couple also moved out of Pope's Lane and into a bigger, newer house in more upmarket Ealing. Entwistle paid £14,500 for the double-fronted, red-brick property at Corringway and got straight down to organising renovations. One of the upstairs bedrooms he again had converted into a home studio; another he used to store his growing collection of guitars, which now numbered near a hundred. Downstairs, he had a room wood-panelled and converted into a bar replete with optics, stools and a bar billiards table. He also acquired one of the earliest Philips video recorders, a big, unwieldy box-type thing that he loved to show off.

'We had a big extension done and a huge garden, too,' adds Alison. 'At home, he would do the washing up. Once in a blue moon, he used to cut the grass as well, but he hated doing the garden at all and he certainly wasn't a decorator.'

The Who rounded out 1971 in America once more, arriving in New York on 18 November and touring through to Seattle on 15 December. Moon continued with his japing. One night, he dressed himself up as Entwistle. He had his hair trimmed for the occasion and sported a drooping, stick-on moustache, just like

Entwistle's. Bill Curbishley recalls, 'John was shocked when he walked into the dressing room, couldn't take it in really. Moon was such a great mimic that he had all of John's idiosyncrasies off pat. Like the way John would hold his cigarette in between his thumb and forefinger.'

There were, though, other aspects of the tour that, should anyone have been taking note, were ominous portents of things to come. Flying from Los Angeles to San Francisco on 12 December, a near-comatose Moon required a wheelchair to get him on to the plane having sunk a dangerous cocktail of brandy and barbiturates.

Keith Altham was now working as The Who's publicity manager and recollects the general acrimonious mood of the tour: 'One of the lessons that you learned early on with The Who was to keep out of the way when they were working and wait for the dust to settle. When I started, I did make the hideous error on the first or second gig of going backstage to the dressing room. Chris Stamp was standing outside the door, nonchalantly smoking a cigarette. From inside, you could hear shouting, screaming and yelling going on. I said to Chris, "Is it alright to go in?" He replied, "Do you *want* to?" Well, I did go in and it was like World War Two in there. Daltrey had Moon by the throat and was shaking him vigorously. Townshend was shouting at Roger, "Leave him a-bloody-lone!" And Entwistle was sort of sat to one side, cleaning his nails.

'They needed time to come down and they cared about their performance to such a degree that they would have an autopsy about it right after the show. These affairs would get quite boisterous to say the least. They wanted it to be perfect. Being on the road with them was a kind of miasma of devastation – to guitars and hotels. Townshend on one occasion didn't change his clothes for a week. He would just go back to the hotel after a show, lie down on the bed and wait for the call to tell him they had been thrown out for whatever Moon had done.

'John wasn't such an extrovert in the accepted sense, but he was busy behind the scenes. I oversaw a couple of interviews with him at Corringway. When you walked into the house, there was a full suit of armour stood up in the hall, and which he named Henry. He was just bizarre.'

■ ■ ■

On Sunday, 23 January 1972, Alison Entwistle gave birth to a son, Christopher, at Queen Charlotte's Hospital in Chiswick, west London. Home from America, Entwistle went with Alison to the hospital. He had booked her a private room and, as she went through the initial stages of her labour, he sat watching an ITV costume drama, *Upstairs Downstairs* – the *Downtown Abbey* of the early seventies – on the television. 'I got taken off to the delivery room and, when I was imminent, John was called and gowned up,' says Alison. 'He walked into the delivery room and the first thing he said was, "Humph, you've made me miss the end of *Upstairs Downstairs*." He always did make jokes about everything. But he was a very gentle person, too. I remember coming back from the doctor's with John when I had just found out that I was pregnant. He got out of his seat and came around and opened the car door for me. I was special that day.'

The Who's new-found wealth was the other fundamental change to Entwistle's circumstances. One afternoon around this same time, he had Mick Bratby drive him into the West End to visit the band's accountants. Entwistle came out of the meeting and, smiling, promptly informed Bratby that he had just been declared a paper millionaire. 'But he didn't go on about it beyond that,' says Bratby. 'John was a pretty down-to-earth chap really.' Indeed, Entwistle on one level appeared entirely unaffected by this leap in his status. Throughout his life, he retained his tastes for simple, ordinary things: chocolate biscuits; fish and chips; model trains; a cup of tea and a fag in front of the telly. And yet, he also revelled in having money and, most of all, being able to spend it at will. It was as if he were making up for every penny of pocket money, every second of attention that his stepfather had pinched from him, as if the joy he got from blowing through his riches for each new acquisition was directly proportionate as an act of revenge towards Gordon.

He bought yet more cars; to the Lincoln Continental he added another Cadillac, a convertible Eldorado, white with red-leather interiors and an 8-litre engine. He bought sports cars – a Citroën Maserati and a Swiss Monteverdi fitted with a muscle car Chevrolet engine. Each and every one of them stood out a mile in conservative, suburban Ealing. But then, Entwistle loved to be recognised and, in his mind, what else was a rock star supposed to do but be chauffeured around town in a flash car?

'You know, I think at one point John had the longest car in England,' says Ian Gillingham, laughing. 'I was a salesman by then and used to work that area. We had kind of lost touch, but I drove past their house one day and pulled over to look at the Caddy. The front door of the house opened and Alison came out. She said, "*Ian?* You silly sod – get in here!" From then on, I would call in for a cup of tea every couple of weeks. John could be quiet and into himself, but then you'd get him talking and you couldn't shut him up. I wouldn't say he was an introvert, not at all. He had a very sharp mind and sometimes a spiteful sense of humour, but so long as you gave it him back . . .

'He had a thing about teapots. He would go into a shop and be like, "I'll have that teapot, and that one, and that one and that one." He loved his gadgets, too. I was at Corringway one day and he showed me this digital watch that he'd just bought. This was the early seventies and I'd never seen a watch like it. The time lit up in red numbers. He pressed a little button on the back and it turned into a calculator as well. John told me very proudly how he had bought it in New York and that it had cost him $2,000. Anyway, within eighteen months you could buy the exact same watches for thirty-nine quid in Dixons on the high street. I did remind him of that, but he wasn't amused.'

In fact, Entwistle demurred from pointing out to his cousin that these high street watches were different from his own in one fundamental aspect – they were not made of solid gold. Entwistle also found other extravagant ways of indulging himself. He had a fish pond dug out in the garden at Corringway and filled it with fifteen massive Koi carp. Like his dogs, the fish were to be one of his great joys. When he was at home, he made sure to feed them daily and would regularly spend two or three hours meticulously occupied with cleaning out the pond. As a matter of course, he started to shop at Harrods, too. From the richly appointed Knightsbridge store, he bought furniture, pictures, frames, ornaments, a tiger-skin rug to go in front of the fire at Corringway, and a polar bear skin, too.

More . . . there was always more. He had a well-known luxury jeweller, Michael Fishberg of Golders Green, make him a silver spider necklace encrusted with two ruby eyes and, to go with it, a fly necklace with emeralds for Alison. When eventually his guitar collection overflowed from the bedroom at Corringway, he simply shelled out for a three-bedroom semi round the corner. He moved the guitars into this new house and Mick Bratby in there as well to look after them.

'Could I control his spending? No, don't be silly,' says Alison. 'He bought things all the time. He wasn't big-headed about it, but he enjoyed his money and spending it on nice things. He was very generous, too. Oh gosh, I didn't have to ask. If I wanted it, I got it.'

'As with everything John did, there was an element of humour to his spending,' insists Bill Curbishley. 'And for me as an observer, it was great to see them all enjoying it – that's what it's all about, really.'

'Dougal' Butler takes a somewhat different view. 'They all started to change when the money rolled in,' he says. 'John would buy nothing but tailored outfits from this place called the Skin Room – ridiculous amounts. Then I put him on to a tailor's in Fulham, Major Hayward's, where Tony Curtis, Roger Moore and all of these other film and TV stars had their suits made. Fuck me, John had loads of suits and jackets made up for him there, denim jeans, too, and he spent thousands upon thousands of pounds. Which is fine, don't get me wrong, that's up to him. But when you're on the outside looking in, you're going, "Is that because he never had that growing up as a kid?" And it was the same with the women. "I can have who I want because of who I am."'

Even still, not all of this consumption, nor his new son, nor anything nor anyone else could ever completely fill the empty, black hole that he felt inside whenever he was off the road and not seen to be being John Entwistle, the rock star. His job, his calling, it was that which fortified him and pumped the blood through his veins. The trouble was, now that Townshend was also raking in additional money from song-writing royalties, he didn't want to tour so much. Townshend much preferred to be at home and to be creating apart from the band. Entwistle, like Moon, could only endure a domestic state for so long and then he would get restless, bored. He would have to, *need* to, step back into his other life. Bratby would be summoned and off they would drive up town to the Speakeasy, or one of Entwistle's other favourite after-hours clubs.

'I could never have a drink because I would be driving, so those always seemed long nights and John would get sloshed,' says Bratby. 'He would get out a big wad of money and tell me, "Pay the bill." I could have easily ripped him off, but I didn't ever. One night we came out of the Speakeasy and he said to me, "You've got to take this bird home for me." It was 1.30 in the morning and I had to drive her to bloody Brighton. That was the sort of thing he would do.

'John saw his life as being in two separate compartments. There was his life at home, and then his road life. I don't actually think he found it that difficult to separate the two. When he was on the road, it would be as if home didn't exist. At home, it was the same thing in reverse. That being said, I know that when he used to come back from America, he wouldn't touch Alison for two weeks just in case he'd picked something up.'

'Really, John wanted to be onstage the whole time,' Alison furthers. 'He loved the adrenalin rush and, well, he liked to perform. It was good for him. He couldn't bear just sitting around the house. Not that he did just sit around. He was always composing, or drawing. He loved to do his caricatures. He just led two different lives and in our one together we had wonderful, happy times.

'I got on with it because I had to. When John was away, I had Christopher and the dogs. The hard thing for me was, when John was off touring, I would get to have a little bit of life with friends and stuff, and then when he came back, he wouldn't want me to go out. I had to go back to just being with him. It was tough for him to slot back in as well. He wouldn't want to go anywhere, because he had already been off travelling and partying. And then *I* was bored.

'If we went on holiday, we had a pact. One night we would go to a restaurant for me. The next, he would get us room service and watch the television. There was one time that I said to him that maybe I would just turn up on tour. Straight off, he told me,

"Well, if you do, I shall slam the door in your face." He didn't want me to go out with him. He couldn't pull if I was there, could he? I suppose that I did have a vague idea of what he was getting up to, but I didn't really want to know.'

■ ■ ■

Apart from The Who, Entwistle was also determined to go on forging a solo career. In the two months following Christopher's birth, he sketched out a clutch of songs at Corringway, working out loose arrangements on piano. The material followed on in the same unfussy, insouciant vein as *Smash Your Head Against the Wall*, but with even more biting lyrics. 'Ten Little Friends', 'Thinkin' It Over' and 'Feeling Better' were punchy melodic rockers respectively written about a set of troll figures Entwistle had been gifted by Moon, a man contemplating suicide, and an unfaithful lover.

On the plangent ballad 'Apron Strings', meanwhile, his perspective was that of a bereaved son, or widowed husband. 'What am I gonna do?' he sang, mournful at first. Then a bitter, sardonic twist: 'If I said I'm sorry that you've gone, I'd be lying. I feel more sorry for myself [sic]; I'm crying.' There was even a sly nod and a wink in the title that he ended up giving to the album; *Whistle Rymes* was meant as a dig at Track and others who had habitually misspelled his surname.

Entwistle recorded the album at Island Records' west London studios at Basing Street that April and May. He had Peter Frampton come in and play guitar and also Jimmy McCulloch from Thunderclap Newman, for whom Townshend had written a 1969 Number One, 'Something in the Air'. Rod Coombes from Jeff Beck's band and session man Graham Deakin played drums, with Moon once again dropping by to make mischief and add percussion. To co-produce the album with him, Entwistle enlisted someone else he had met through Townshend – John

Alcock. 'Pete and I had set up a company together, Track Plan, specifically to build recording studios in rock stars' houses,' says Alcock. 'Pete said to me, "Ah, you should go and talk to John about this."

Coincidentally, I lived very close to John in Ealing. I went over to his house and we started hanging out. The idea of getting him a proper home studio built never got off the ground, but we became very good friends for many years. Fun was a very big part of why he wanted to do solo albums. The drink would flow in the studio. He loved people to drop by, whereas I hated it. I mean, I liked the social aspect, but it got in the way of the actual work. It's very hard to get an album done when you've got a perpetual party going on in the control room. Frampton was there . . . Townshend came down once or twice, so did Moon. Roger never came. Then, after the sessions, we would go along to the Speakeasy and then, of course, we would meet up with a whole bunch of other people.

The songs were worked up in the studio. John brought in backing tracks with very rough vocals on top, but they were no more than twenty per cent done. His songs, though, were pretty well structured in terms of the verses, choruses and lyrics. The lyrics were pretty much set and written down. 'I Feel Better' would have been a great Who track, I think, and there were others with that little bit of a twist to them that he'd had kicking around. Yet, for whatever reason, the band hadn't wanted to do them. There was no ready outlet for those songs and John felt strongly about them.

He was kind of a meek and mild guy. You rarely saw him get annoyed – he would turn and walk away. He also hated to talk about money. So it was great for John to have somebody like me around who would first of all do all of the organising for him. I would talk to the musicians about how much they were going to get paid. Then, if the right parts weren't being played in the studio, John would sort of whisper in my ear and I would deal with that as well. I was like his minder and did what had to be done to make the session run smoothly. Also, I enabled John to take more of a back seat and relax.

John was a very unlikely rock star. He loved the fame, but he was also a very retiring person. He had a split personality. The John Entwistle who would sink a bottle of Rémy and be up all night was the rock star. Then, the next day, he would be back walking his dogs and being the good neighbour in Ealing. At home, you could almost picture him back at the tax office. He kept things inside.

Not long after Alison had Christopher, I had a baby bass guitar built. It was a tiny little Gibson Thunderbird. I had 'Christopher' written on the headstock and it was fully functioning with mandolin pick-ups and strings. I went over to their house with this bass one night and gave it to John. He looked at it and had tears in his eyes. In all the years that I knew him, that was the only time I ever saw him be like that.

'John cried when Christopher was born, too,' adds Alison. 'He was quite open with his emotions, but when it was called for. He didn't do it in public either but, yes, when he was on his own with me.'

Whistle Rymes came out that November and did no better than its predecessor. Like *Smash Your Head* . . ., it ticked over in America, too, where it eventually shifted around 100,000 copies. In Britain, though, it sank without trace and nowhere could it be said to have made Entwistle a star in his own right. Alcock sensed that the commercial failure of *Whistle Rymes* wounded Entwistle deeply, but not that he was about to show it. 'John was a very sensitive guy, but hid it well,' he says. 'When he saw a bad review or comment, he didn't say much, but you recognised the signs once you got to know him and that it hurt his feelings.

'I think he expected that album to do better than it did but, the fact was, it was not promoted. There were a lot of politics going on behind the scenes. This is purely my personal suspicion, but I don't think the record company wanted to push it too much. It didn't fit in with their plans. I mean, their golden goose was The Who and they didn't want anything to disrupt that.'

12

Cell Number Seven

While Entwistle was overseeing the final mix sessions on *Whistle Rymes*, Townshend slipped The Who back into gear. Townshend had been stirred by three rousing songs that all topped the UK singles chart that spring of 1972: T-Rex's 'Metal Guru'; Slade's 'Take Me Bak 'Ome'; and Alice Cooper's 'School's Out'. Respectively, the plaything of former flower-power pop-pixie Marc Bolan, a bunch of erstwhile skinheads from the English Black Country town of Walsall, and an American band fronted by a preacher's son who had opened for The Who back in 1969, these acts were outriders of the glam-rock movement that had been gathering momentum since the previous year.

Townshend took the catchy irresistibility of their anthem-like, verse-chorus songs as a personal challenge, and applied himself to the task of writing in the same way. That May, he assembled the band at Olympic with Glyn Johns, with the intention of making a new Who album that would be just as instant and to the point. In the event, they managed half a record, but then the sessions ground to a halt.

'[It was] all very good, but put together sounded like shades of *Who's Next*,' Townshend told *Rolling Stone* later that same year. 'So I said, "Fuck this . . ." Well, everybody did, unanimously.'[24]

Townshend went off again to rethink his plan of attack. As a stopgap, The Who put out as singles two of the songs they had cut at Olympic, 'Join Together' and 'Relay'. Both sounded forced and not quite fully realised. It was as if Townshend were just too cerebral and he, Entwistle and Moon too deft as musicians to pull off something so route one. Neither song also measured up to the glam-rockers on the charts. 'Join Together' scraped the UK Top Ten when it was released in June, and 'Relay' didn't even do that five months later.

The picture was much the same in America, too. From Entwistle's perspective, the best to be said about the whole exercise was that it did at least also prompt Townshend back out on to the road. That August, The Who set off on a sixteen-date tour of Europe, their first trek around the continent in two years.

They were rusty and the tour wasn't long enough for them to get back up to full speed but, as usual, it wasn't without incident. The fourteenth date was in Paris on 9 September at a giant outdoor festival, Fête de L'Humanité, organised for the French Communist Party. 'Pete had invited Eric Clapton and his then-girlfriend, Alice Ormsby-Gore, to come along,' takes up Bill Curbishley.

> The entire festival site took in around half a million people. You had everything there – people selling washing machines, coconut shies and a rock gig. After the show, I had to settle all the monies so I sent them all off in cars back to the hotel. We were staying at the George V Hotel, which was the height of five-star luxury. When I arrived back later that night, there was a crowd gathered around the hotel bar. Moon had made a bet that

---

[24] Taken from *Rolling Stone* article published on 26 October 1972

he could drink nineteen margaritas and then he was going to get on the piano and sing 'Danny Boy'. So, I asked our security guy, Jim Callaghan, to keep an eye on him. Then I went upstairs and did my usual thing, which was to go and visit everybody in their rooms and make sure they were OK.

Eventually, I got to John's suite. I found him sitting down to a late dinner. He'd got a napkin tucked into the collar of his shirt and a waiter on hand. The waiter had obviously just decanted a bottle of wine into a carafe. As I was catching up with John, into the room came Moon with nineteen margaritas inside him. He was all over the place. He lurched up to the table and slurred, 'Hullo, John.' He put his finger into the pot of mustard and stuffed that in his mouth. Then he took the carafe, shook some pepper into it and threw it down in one shot. John was sat looking at him, but with no expression on his face. Moon took the silver-service cover off the plate in front of John. John had ordered a fillet steak. Moon snatched it up, took a bite out of it and put it back on the plate. It was like something out of a cartoon – there was the steak with a bite-shaped piece missing from it. Next thing, Moon turned around, walked over to the wall, pissed up against it and collapsed. The waiter couldn't believe his eyes. Moon was lying there on the floor out cold.

At that point, John very deliberately took his napkin off and went over to the prostrate Moon. Moon had hanging around one wrist a big room key on a dongle. John removed the room key from Moon's wrist and marched off to Moon's room, which was just across the corridor from his own suite. He opened the door, went into the room, and shut the door again behind him. All that you could hear for the next twenty minutes was smash-crash-bang-smash. Then John came back out, grabbed Moon under his arms and dragged him off to his suite. He threw the key on him and shut the door.

John had smashed every single thing in that room . . . everything – the television, tables and chairs – the lot. About 4.00am, I got a call from Jim Callaghan. He told me that Moon had woken up and thought that he had wrecked his own room in a drunken frenzy. He was worried I was going to kill him. I told Jim to take him to the airport, get hold of the Red Cross, tell them Moon was not well and have them give him something to help him sleep. After first settling the damages on Moon's room, the rest of us got to the airport around 11.00am for our flight to Rome. We got on the plane and Moon was cowering in the back, waiting for me to give him some verbal abuse, which I never did. Till the day that he died, Moon believed that he had smashed that room up. And it all went on his bill. John and I just couldn't stop laughing about it.

Back in London, Townshend bunkered down to prepare more new material that he now envisaged coming together in the form of another conceptual piece. The band would have a different environment to make it in, too. That same September, 'Wiggy' Wolff had been assigned £15,000 of The Who's cash to purchase for them a near-derelict Victorian church hall in Battersea, south-west London. Within weeks, Wolff was overseeing the renovation of the building to prepare it for a studio to be fitted. Initially, the band re-christened the place The Kitchen and then, decisively, Ramport.

As the building work went on and with Townshend tied up, Entwistle used the time to go off and record his third solo album. Put down over just three weeks at Nova Sound Studios, Marble Arch, with John Alcock again co-producing, it featured a slew of session musicians, including drummer Graham Deakin once more and a keyboard player, Tony Ashton, whose extravagant moustache put Entwistle's to shame. Entwistle meant to have

Rigor Mortis Sets In revive the gleeful, twist-and-shout sound of fifties rock-'n'-roll. However, the half-baked album that ensued fell well short of recapturing the spirit of his youth.

A mixed bag comprised of listless covers ('Hound Dog', 'Lucille'), slight originals ('Do the Dangle', 'Peg Leg Peggy'), and a perfunctory reworking of 'My Wife', it came out sounding tossed-off and untended. It was as though, having been seen to have tried and not succeeded with his first two records, Entwistle this time around wanted to appear anything but serious or determined to make it under his own name. By doing so, he could put up a protective shield around himself. Or then again, the fact that almost half the budget assigned to the album went on booze was perhaps the greater factor contributing to its lifelessness.

'Oh, that one was John's party record,' affirms Alcock. 'He just wanted to get out of the house, hang with people in the studio and have a laugh. It was enormous fun to do, too. I just don't think it was a particularly valid reason to make a record. In the event, he got a bit too close to making a parody album, which wasn't such a great idea.'

Released the following May, *Rigor Mortis Sets In* came out adorned with a front cover made up as a coffin. Intended to mourn the passing of a golden age, it was also a portent of the album's fate, since it was dead on arrival. More galling for Entwistle, preceding his record by a month was Daltrey's first, self-titled album. Daltrey's record was polished, easy listening and sailed to Number Six in the UK. Lambert and Stamp had resisted releasing Daltrey's album so soon in advance of the next Who set, so instead he enlisted Curbishley to manage the project for him. In the short term, the success of his album was a boost for Daltrey. However, the fall-out from it was to have much longer-lasting consequences for the whole band.

■ ■ ■

Two months before all that and in March 1973, The Who had got down to recording in earnest again. Johns had gone off to produce a second album for The Eagles, *Desperado*, so it fell to Townshend to run the sessions which carried on through to July. That same spring saw the release of such high-blown albums as Pink Floyd's *Dark Side of the Moon*, *Aladdin Sane* by David Bowie and *Tubular Bells* by Mike Oldfield. What Townshend had brought back to The Who in the demoed-up form of *Quadrophenia* was every bit as epically-minded as any of those records.

Townshend had delved back to his Mod days to imagine the story of a young 'face', Jimmy, who he meant as a composite of the four members of The Who. Like *Tommy*, Townshend foresaw the album being a double and one that would mark another artistic benchmark for the band, particularly in the way that it sounded. Speaking to *Rolling Stone* before The Who went into the studio, he cited Bowie and also fellow Brits Roxy Music as examples of artists 'who are really pushing recording experimentation to its limit. And we stopped doing that. We said, "We are The Who. Everything has got our stamp and so we don't need to experiment." So, I'd like to do some really crazy things.

'The album will be quadrophonic and each different part of the guy's character will be a reflection of one member of the group,' Townshend went on. 'One part of his character will be the good part – which is me. One part will be bad, which is Roger. Another will be insane and abandoned, which is Moon, and the other – surprise, surprise – romantic, which is John Entwistle.'[25]

Immediately, Townshend encountered problems with getting the multi-layered sound that he wanted for the album. Quadrophonic sound was being touted as the next leap on

---

[25] Taken from *Rolling Stone* article published on 26 October 1972

from stereo, but the technology was still then in its infancy and untested. Then again, in no way was Townshend equipped to render the sheer density of sound that he wanted. The stop-start work on installing a studio at Ramport was still incomplete, so he had no option but to hire a mobile unit from Ronnie Lane of The Faces and have it temporarily installed at Battersea. In addition to the band's parts, Townshend wanted to fill tracks up with 'found' sounds. He went off and taped such ephemera as a train whistling and waves breaking on the shore. Lane's studio was just an eight-track, so he had engineer, Ron Nevison, labouring day and night to advance it to sixteen. Even then, the nuts and bolts of the recording process were painstaking and hit-and-miss.

As for the others in the band, Daltrey played up to the 'bad' persona ascribed to him by Townshend. He turned up to sing his parts, but otherwise grouched about the whole business, or else stayed away from the studio. This left Townshend, Entwistle and Moon to plough on through the basic tracks. They set up in the same semi-circle arrangement they had onstage, Entwistle to the right and Townshend to the left of Moon's huge drum kit. For refreshment, they had a flight case stocked with bottles of brandy positioned over by the piano booth.

This time around, Townshend had arrived at the sessions with all of the songs written. That suited Moon just fine, since he didn't require much more from the band than to be enabled to thrash at his drums. Entwistle, though, had to have a purpose. He needed to be made useful and fundamental, and to be recognised for being so. In that sense, he viewed being in The Who in much the same way as he had the Middlesex Youth Orchestra or the Boys' Brigade band, which is to say that he didn't aspire to ultimate leadership, but to having a significant, well-defined role. On *Quadrophenia*, this came about when Townshend sought to add horn parts to the songs. Tasked by Townshend to organise the horn arrangements, Entwistle worked long hours writing out multiple detailed parts and all of which he then played himself. The work suited him to a tee. It required precision and a craftsman's skill, and he was able to apply himself to it alone.

Writing later, Townshend recalled that 'John gathered for the purpose at least twenty or so magnificent trumpets, horns and valve trombones. He could play all of them, writing out his parts on manuscript paper like an orthodox composer, and working through the recording meticulously until his lips started to go numb. He was wonderful to work with, disciplined, funny and inspired.'[26]

Ultimately, across its four sides of vinyl, *Quadrophenia* didn't have as many outstanding songs as either *Tommy* or *Who's Next*; neither was Jimmy the Mod's story any better defined than Tommy's. However, throughout it was brilliantly played and most especially by Entwistle who was operating at the very top of his game. On 'The Real Me', for example, his bass dances in and out of the main melody, like a shadow boxer, thrusting the song along with intricate, jabbing flurries as Townshend and Moon brawl away. Then again, on such forceful other highlights as '5:15' and 'Love Reign O'er Me', the standout instrument was Entwistle's bass, while his massed horns brought a depth and richness of sound to the piece as a whole.

Outside the studio, there was nothing like the same unity of purpose. Daltrey's dispute with Lambert and Stamp rumbled on in the background with the singer increasingly occupied by the state of the band's finances. Daltrey was alerted by the extravagances of the two managers and Lambert in particular;

---

[26] Taken from *Who I Am* by Pete Townshend, Harper (2012)

both Lambert and Stamp had flats in well-to-do Kensington. Lambert had also now bought a fifteenth-century Venetian palace, Palazzo Dario, sited on the banks of the Grand Canal. Daltrey began to press the others to have the band's books audited. To begin with, Townshend stayed loyal to Lambert, and Stamp also, and dismissed Daltrey's claims while he got on with completing *Quadrophenia*. With his marriage on the point of imploding, Moon was also otherwise occupied.

Yet Daltrey won over Entwistle. On the surface, theirs was an unlikely alliance. Notwithstanding their mutual antipathy, Entwistle appeared to take a thoroughly cavalier attitude to money. However, this only applied to how he spent it. In regard to what he was owed, Entwistle was as sharp with the details as Daltrey, if somewhat more tolerant. He was inclined to let things go, but only up to the point when he determined that he was being taken for a fool. Where that point actually was could be entirely arbitrary but, certainly, Lambert's Venetian extravagance crossed a line with him. With Entwistle's support, Daltrey forced the books to be opened up. What they discovered seemed to confirm their worst suspicions; both Lambert and Stamp had been siphoning off large sums of money, while at the same time failing to keep up with the band's royalty payments. Furthermore, none of the band's principals had received so much as a penny out of Track and certainly not the 10 per cent share of profits that each of them had been promised.

'Roger and John had got to be very distrustful of Kit and Chris. Not unduly, but Kit and Chris were victims of their own abuses,' opines Bill Curbishley. 'They would plunder different accounts. We also had Mammoth Records, into which went Jimi Hendrix's royalties – and those of other artists – and they took money out of that, too. I don't think that Kit and Chris in the end thought that they were stealing; they believed they were just borrowing.

The fact of the matter is that they were both drug addicts. And the biggest fear that you have as a drug addict is running out of money.

'I'll never forget that I took a phone call from John Wolff who was running things at Ramport. He said that the band were in desperate need of money. I took a look at the royalty statements and, sure enough, we did owe them quite a sum. I had a cheque drawn up for £100,000 and went to see Kit, who was actually about to leave for Venice. In fact, we owed them more than that, but I told Kit that he needed to countersign this cheque just to tide them over, which he did. Kit went off to the airport and I sent the cheque down to Ramport. Unbeknown to me, though, Kit stopped the cheque. That was the start of things really coming to a head. Even so, it wasn't until later when Pete discovered that he'd had money stolen from his publishing, specifically in America, that everything really fell apart.'

By the end of that year, the full extent of Lambert's and Stamp's profligacy would be made apparent to Townshend and Moon. Daltrey and Entwistle seized the day. In 1974, The Who as a group instituted legal proceedings to recover the missing royalties from their now former managers. Lambert and Stamp had by then moved their base of operations to New York and Curbishley had taken over the day-to-day management of the band. It would, though, be another three years before the case was settled in The Who's favour and their partnership with Lambert and Stamp formally dissolved in court.

■ ■ ■

As their relationship with Lambert and Stamp began to unravel more decisively in October 1973, The Who released *Quadrophenia*. Their last record to come out under the Track imprint in the UK, after which they switched directly over to Polydor, it sold strongly on both sides of the Atlantic. The album's success, though, was only a temporary balm and tensions erupted again just as soon as they prepared to go on tour. Townshend meant to perform *Quadrophenia* in its entirety onstage and spent weeks assembling backing tapes, so that their performances would sound as layered as the record. However, only two days were set aside for rehearsals before a nine-date UK tour got under way at Trentham Gardens, Stoke-on-Trent on 28 October.

There was simply not enough time to iron out the more technical aspects of the show. A fraught situation was also compounded by the fact that Townshend got drunk and then became aggressive at the first rehearsal. Whatever demons Townshend was working through, he decided to take them out on Daltrey. At one point, he charged at Daltrey, fists flailing. Just as he had once done with Moon, Daltrey responded by knocking Townshend out cold with a single punch. On this occasion, there was to be no retribution for Daltrey since the general consensus was that Townshend had it coming.

The UK tour that followed was no more harmonious. In Stoke, Townshend's tapes could not be made to come in on cue. By as soon as the second night in Wolverhampton, a third of the *Quadrophenia* songs had been scrubbed from the set-list and, at the fifth, at Newcastle Odeon, the tapes once again malfunctioned. This last incident caused Townshend once more to snap. In a blind rage, he stormed over to poor Bobby Pridden's sound desk and smashed up the unreliable tape machines, then stomped offstage, kicking over his amplifiers as a parting shot.

The air around the band was just as volatile when they moved on to North America the following month. Townshend had insisted that this run be kept to a manageable sixteen dates, which proved a blessing under the circumstances. On opening night at the Cow Palace, San Francisco, on 20 November, Moon lurched on to the stage as if in a daze and then once the show started couldn't keep up with the rest of the band, his drums an erratic, ailing heartbeat.

'Someone had spiked Moony's drink with an animal tranquiliser,' explains Mick Bratby. 'Pete was turning round to Moony and shouting, "Faster, you cunt, faster!" Moony would speed up for a bit and then, all of a sudden, start to slow down again. Then, he just passed out.'

Moon was rushed off to hospital to have his stomach pumped. In his absence, the band completed a truncated set with the help of nineteen-year-old Scott Halpin from Iowa, who volunteered himself from the sell-out crowd when Townshend asked if there was a good drummer in the house. Moon was back behind the drums for the next two nights at the Forum in Los Angeles and, from there, the tour reeled on cross-country and up into Canada.

The Who's reputation preceded their arrival in Chicago on 29 November. Among his archives, Entwistle retained an internal memo sent out from MCA Records' Chicago office to the band informing them that an after-show party planned for that night had been cancelled by their hotel management. Their 'unchangeable feeling', the memo read, 'was that there would be party-crashers, groupies and mass destruction'.

The essential accuracy of this assumption was borne out by events in Montreal three nights later. On this occasion, an MCA executive made the grievous error of throwing a post-show bash for the band in his own hotel suite. Townshend and Moon proceeded to smash up their host's room and, in the early hours of the next morning, a troop of Royal Canadian Mounted Police arrived to arrest the sixteen-strong Who retinue. Among them were Daltrey, who had retired to bed long before the mayhem kicked off, and also the wheelchair-bound Mike Shaw. Moon and Entwistle were bundled into a cell together and the whole lot of them held until Curbishley stumped up for the damages.

'It came to twenty-odd grand, a huge amount back then,' Curbishley says. 'But then, Moon and Townshend had thrown everything that was in this guy's room out of the windows. I was also asleep at the time. Next thing I knew, the door was being kicked in and police grabbed me out of bed. It was a Sunday morning and so there wasn't a bank open. I had to persuade the local promoter to go round to all of his friends and get cash. At times like that, John would always be pretty calm. He wasn't given to hysterics.'

Soon after, Entwistle wrote a song about the incident, 'Cell Number Seven': 'Six-thirty in the morning, I'd just gone to sleep,' ran his lyrics. 'I felt so tired didn't even count sheep. I woke up with six policemen standing by the bed . . . the voice of doom was rising in my head . . . Me and Moony were in cell number seven. He dribbled on my jacket – snored like a goat – ruined my coat.'

Like all of their other tours now, this one proceeded in a state of suspended reality, a ritual of random extremes and regular excesses that happened without any apparent lasting consequence and shut off from the outside world. At each stop, the four band members would be whisked from hotel to arena in a fleet of long, black limousines and flanked by an escort of police outriders. Driven into the bowels of the venue, they would move right on to their dressing room without having to come up for air. Backstage, a lavish spread would await them: all kinds of food, bottles of vintage champagne and brandies, bourbons and beer. Do the show . . . into the limos again . . . back to the hotel to inveigle themselves of whatever or whoever was on offer . . . and then do it all over again the next night and the one after that.

There was no one among them who seemed better suited to the endless repetitiveness of touring than Entwistle, since he, too, never appeared to be any different. Day after day, come what may, his demeanour would be just the same – dispassionate, unflappable, inscrutable and ultimately unknowable. And then, ever so occasionally, he would get a wide-eyed look on his face and it would be as if he had been jolted out of the tumult. Momentarily, he would be able to take in the bigger picture of their journey and the fantastical craziness of it all.

'I can remember us doing the Cobo Hall in Detroit on that tour,' remembers Dougal Butler. 'Driving to the gig, John turned to me and said, "You know, Dougal, we're getting half-a-million dollars for this show." And it *was* awe-inspiring. I mean, in America at that time they were bigger than The Stones. They had everything. The feeling I got from him was that John was actually saying, "Wow, we've come a long way since Acton, you know."'

13

Mad Dog and Zorg Women

Almost the last deal that Kit Lambert struck as co-manager of The Who was to have *Tommy* made into a film. Together with Townshend, he had been kicking the idea around for several years. He had fixed up for Townshend to have meetings with various American producers and directors, all of which proved fruitless. At one point, the two men had fallen out when Townshend discovered that Lambert had been peddling a version of *Tommy* without his consent. Eventually, Lambert's old friend Robert Stigwood came on board to produce the film. Stigwood got Columbia Pictures to agree to finance and distribute a movie and also hired an English director with whom Townshend was at last able to see eye to eye – Ken Russell.

At forty-six, Russell's reputation as the *enfant terrible* of British cinema had been established by his two previous films, each as provocative as the other. In *Women in Love*, his 1969 D. H. Lawrence adaptation, Russell had his two male leads, Oliver Reed and Alan Bates, wrestle naked. And in 1971, *The Devils* was a hysterical horror with Reed again as a mutinous priest and so explicit that Warner Brothers point-blank refused to release Russell's original cut. The white-haired Russell was in equal measure outrageous, flamboyant and iconoclastic, which was also just the vision he had for *Tommy*. Collaborating with Townshend, Russell cooked up a script over the course of that year. From the outset, Russell conceived the film as a full musical with no dialogue. To that end, he was never much more troubled than Townshend with making sense of the story, but rather with how to exaggerate and heighten the core elements of it, so as to be able to fashion something that was as brashly lurid as his other films.

By January 1974, Russell had a working script and a shooting budget of $2 million. He had also cast the film with a mix of professional actors and musicians. Playing Tommy's mother would be the Swedish-American actress-singer Ann-Margret, who had famously appeared alongside Elvis Presley in 1964's *Viva Las Vegas*. Reed was signed up to be monstrous Uncle Ernie and another American, Jack Nicholson – hot off an Oscar-nominated turn in Roman Polanski's film noir *Chinatown* – was signed up to play Tommy's doctor. In the title role, Daltrey would get to reprise his performance as Tommy on the record and there were also to be singing and performing cameos from Eric Clapton, Tina Turner, Elton John and Moon.

Before Russell started filming, Townshend was given the job of managing the soundtrack recording. This proved to be a chore, since the cast were singing their own parts and neither Nicholson nor Reed was able to carry a tune. Townshend had written four new songs to link the narrative together better and sessions commenced at Ramport on 12 January. For the purpose, Townshend assembled an all-star band with Clapton, Ronnie Wood of The Faces and Mick Ralphs from Bad Company also on guitars and Nicky Hopkins on piano. With Moon claiming to be ill, The Faces' Kenney Jones, Mike Kellie of Spooky Tooth and Graham Deakin covered the drums. Townshend also tried out a handful of session bassists, but Entwistle ended up playing on most tracks.

Talking about the sessions to *Rolling Stone* later that summer, Townshend said, 'In a way, [Moon's absence] was a blessing in disguise . . . Keith has his style, great as it is, but he can't do much outside of it. John, though, is good all round. We found some good bass players, but John is pretty unbeatable.'[27]

In a repeat of his role on *Quadrophenia*, Entwistle also wrote out and played the horn arrangements for Townshend. Once again, this was enough to make him feel pivotal to the project, without having to be under the same harsh spotlight glare as Townshend or Daltrey. It also meant that when the actual filming started in April of that year, Entwistle was happy enough to take a back seat and go along for the ride. Russell started off shooting in and around north London, before moving the production down to the English south coast. There, on Hayling Island, he shot the 'Tommy's Holiday Camp' scenes in sight of the very same Coronation Holiday Camp that Entwistle had been taken to as a child by his mother and stepfather.

Entwistle was only fitfully engaged with the filming. Fleetingly, he can be seen in the house band in a couple of the performance set-pieces, backing Clapton on 'Eyesight to the Blind' and Elton John on 'Pinball Wizard'. He also loaned Russell the use of his Cadillac Eldorado, along with driver Mick Bratby, for a scene with Daltrey and Margret. Off set, he formed an unholy alliance with Moon, by now relocated to Los Angeles but back to shoot his cameo, and Reed, who was every bit as much of a hellraiser as they were.

'Dougal' Butler recalls, 'Ollie Reed and his brother, Simon, who was driving him, Moon, John, Mick and I would go out

---

[27] Taken from *Rolling Stone* article published on 10 April 1975

together to pubs and restaurants, and we would have a fucking good night of it. I mean, you couldn't wish for a better crowd in a pub. When we were down in Portsmouth, we got separated from everyone else. The six of us got put up in a hotel in Southsea three miles away, because Ken Russell didn't want Ann-Margret or any of the film crew to be near to John, Keith or Ollie Reed.

'Well, there were still cabs and cars. After work, everyone would come out to our hotel and we would meet up with them in the bar. It was a fourteen-hour day, filming started at 7.00am. We would be drinking till gone midnight and then have to be on set for 6.00. Ollie Reed would only go to bed for three hours. Literally, he would have a cold shower and then go off to work. He drank like a fish, but he would always know his lines.'

'During the time that they were filming *Tommy*, the six of us got thrown out of every pub that we went into,' adds Bratby. 'It was simply not possible to exercise any control whatsoever over John, Moon or Ollie Reed. You could suggest that they didn't do something, but they wouldn't take any notice.'

As they had when making the *Tommy* album, The Who's principals also broke off from the shoot to go and do intermittent gigs. On 18 May, they played an outdoor show to a crowd of more than 70,000 at Charlton Athletic's football stadium in south London, headlining a bill that also featured Bad Company, Humble Pie and Lou Reed. The next month, they flew to New York to play four nights at Madison Square Garden on 10, 11, 13 and 14 June. First night at the Garden, there was a poisonous atmosphere backstage. Kit Lambert turned up unannounced, unwelcomed and drunk. Townshend and Daltrey, meanwhile, were at loggerheads all week over one detail or other of the show, their hostilities finally breaking out into a furious row. The background ructions seemed to sap the spirit and energy from the band and they gave a series of lacklustre and disconnected performances.

As so often, outwardly Entwistle didn't appear to be bothered in the slightest by the turmoil. Whatever the nature of the ruptures and ego battles kicking off around him, he kept out of the fray, impervious to all things, or else just plain bored with the carryings on. In any case, be it New York, south London or wherever, he was in his element being lifted out of the ordinary and freed into his own realm.

'I visited John in his room at the Navarro Hotel on Central Park South,' remembers Chris Charlesworth, then working as *Melody Maker*'s correspondent in New York. 'We sat and had a brandy together and chatted about playing in New York. John really loved the city and being on the road in general. But then, he did also have a beautiful, statuesque blonde with him who was obviously his companion for that entire week.'

■ ■ ■

Entwistle also made sure to keep himself occupied away from the film. With Townshend and Daltrey tied up, he was assigned by the others to supervise a compilation album of The Who's studio outtakes that was to be released in time for that Christmas. Assiduously, he waded through hours of tape to pick out eleven songs. He made sure to assemble them in a kind of narrative order, and was on hand to supervise the final mixes with the trusted John Alcock. The album that resulted, *Odds and Sods*, was released to positive reviews and went gold in America. Hailing Entwistle's work, *Rolling Stone* wrote that *Odds and Sods* as a whole was 'thoughtfully paced and annotated. [It] presents pop music raw, the rough edges intact.'

Altogether less successfully, Entwistle also wrapped up a fourth solo album with Alcock and many of the same musicians who had played on *Rigor Mortis Sets In*. He made *Mad Dog* just as breezily and, with it, ploughed the same revivalist furrow, but with even more slapdash-sounding results. Plumbing a nadir on the near-instrumental 'Jungle Bunny', *Mad Dog* also went on to vanish just as quickly when it was released the following year. The only thing that could be said for it was that it did slightly better than the other solo album to emerge from The Who camp during that same period. However, since this was Moon's wretched *Two Sides of the Moon*, which was eked out between – and in the midst of – the drummer's bouts of idle self-destruction in California, that wasn't saying much.

After the *Mad Dog* misadventure, Alcock persuaded Entwistle to play bass on another lightweight album that he was then producing. Conceived as a pretend stage musical score about a fictitious comic book hero, *Flash Fearless Vs the Zorg Women* was laid down over a couple of months at London's Wessex Studios and also featured contributions from Alice Cooper, Justin Hayward of The Moody Blues, Elkie Brooks, Nicky Hopkins, Moon and two other drummers, Bill Bruford of King Crimson and an American, Carmine Appice, then playing with Jeff Beck. Alcock recalls, 'John and Carmine just clicked. When those two started playing together in the studio, everybody got chills. After the sessions, John would rant and rave to me about how he would love to do his next record with Carmine and I hoped we might then be able to get into something really serious musically. But it didn't happen.'

In fact, it would be another six years before Entwistle released another solo record and, by then, Alcock would be out of the picture. Entwistle might also have thought rather less about this brief interlude than his producer surmised. He told the *New Musical Express* at the time, 'Basically, I saw it as a perfect opportunity to play some funky bass with a lot of other musicians while getting sloshed. I alone went through eight dozen bottles of wine.'

The first day that he was involved in the *Flash Fearless . . .* project, 9 October, also happened to be his thirtieth birthday.

Alison arranged a party for him at Corringway. She was determined that this would be an occasion kept to his other life and ensured it would be a quiet, family affair with Queenie and Gordon in attendance. No one from The Who camp or Entwistle's circle of musician friends was invited, but Alison did track down Mick Brown and persuade him along. It was the first time that the two old school pals had seen each other in nearly ten years and delighted Entwistle.

'I don't think John had changed particularly at that point,' Brown recalls. 'When Alison called me, she had said, "I want to be with people – and John *needs* to be with people – who knew him before he became 'John from The Who'." She seemed to me very keen to have that conversation and it was a pleasant evening.'

Not, though, that it was possible for Alison, or indeed anyone else, to keep Entwistle bound to a version of normality for very long. In advance of the release of *Mad Dog*, Entwistle decided to do a solo tour and set about putting together a band to take out on the road. He would be funding the enterprise out of his own pocket, not that this was ever likely to rein him in. The Ox, as he ended up calling the group, swelled through weeks of rehearsals to a twelve-piece and included drummer Deakin, a guitarist from Memphis, Tennessee, Robert A. Johnson, a four-piece horn section and two backing singers, sisters Doreen and Irene Chanter. Entwistle had them booked to do three UK shows that December at Newcastle City Hall, Southport Odeon and Sheffield City Hall. For these, he arranged to have use of The Who's full PA and crew, which added yet more to his outlay.

Some degree of financial prudence had at least taken hold of him by the time the shows rolled around, but only in the sense that he trimmed the horn section to a single sax player.

At all events, the venues they were playing were far too big for Entwistle and his band to be doing. Opening night in Newcastle, they performed to around 300 people in a hall that held 2,000. Attendances at the other two dates were just as sparse. The shows were barely an hour long and leaned heavily on The Who, opening with 'I Can't Explain' and featuring versions of 'Boris the Spider', 'Whiskey Man' and 'Cousin Kevin'. Keith Altham bussed a group of music writers up to the Newcastle gig, among them Chris Charlesworth. At their Gateshead hotel afterwards, Entwistle stumped up for a round of drinks for the assembled hacks, telling them, 'This has cost a bomb, so a few quid more won't make any difference.'

'It was immediately obvious that this was a foolhardy enterprise,' says Charlesworth. 'I believe John fell out with his guitarist, too. Onstage, this guy was trying to do a bit of a Pete Townshend and jumping around. John made it clear to him that he was the star of this band.'

'If John was disappointed about the attendances, he never conveyed that to my sister or me,' adds Doreen Chanter. 'The money side of things was simply not discussed. For me, the tour was really exciting. It was just unfortunate that I had to leave the band after those very first shows. I started to get a pain in my left ear. I had to go see my doctor about it and he told me that if I continued to sing with such a loud band, my eardrum could be perforated.'

Undeterred and at the start of the New Year, Entwistle had The Ox do a handful of smaller-scale university shows around the UK and then took them off to America for two months of dates as opening act for the J. Geils Band. In part, this allowed him to rekindle some of the questing spirit that had fuelled The Who on their initial sorties to that continent. The experience of travelling by bus with the band and crew for the first time since those heady days seemed to animate him. Then again, the whole Ox experiment ended up costing him something in the region of £60,000, a small fortune in 1975.

'John did it to be out there and playing,' says Bobby Pridden, who went along to run the sound on the tour. 'It was as if in some ways it would keep him ticking over. After a show, John would always hold court. He loved people and an audience. He used to love to tell stories and jokes. It would be late at night and there would always be a bottle of brandy around, and he'd go off on a tale. He would always sprinkle a little bit of fairy dust on to his stories, too, never tell them quite how things had happened, but be able to make them into something quite extraordinary.'

Left at home, it fell to Alison to deal with the actual realities of her husband's gallivanting. 'We had a day nanny for Christopher and sometimes I didn't know where her wages would be coming from,' she says. 'It got to be quite worrying, but John was just absolutely reckless and would go on spending money like water. To me, he would always use the excuse that he could write it off against tax. But then, you can only do that so much. And he would never buy, say, one pair of boots, but half-a-dozen at a time. We hadn't had money to begin with, and now we had a lot and it all went to his head a little bit.'

Also, there was the safety net of The Who for him to fall back on. Ken Russell had spent more than double his budget shooting *Tommy*, but the film was a smash when it went on general release that spring. In London, *Tommy* broke the house record at the Leicester Square Theatre and would go on to garner two Oscar nominations, one for Ann-Margret, the other for Townshend's score. Entwistle rejoined his band-mates at that year's Cannes Film Festival on 23 May where *Tommy* was screened as the closing film.

In Alison's family album, there is a photograph of the two of them at the première party in Cannes sitting alongside a beaming

Ann-Margret and Moon, dashing in a tuxedo. By contrast, Entwistle and Alison are wearing matching white, bejewelled outfits. He had these made up specially for the evening so that they would look like a Pearly King and his Queen. Frozen there in the moment, one could believe that these very best of times were how it always was, and would for ever be, for the smiling, blessed people in the picture.

■ ■ ■

As Entwistle sank himself in the mire with The Ox, Townshend was laying the ground for the next Who album, demoing up songs at his Twickenham home. At first glance, this time around he didn't appear to have had a big, connecting theme in mind. The two most immediate songs of Townshend's latest crop, 'Slip Kid' and 'Squeeze Box', were one-two punch rockers, the double entendre lyrics of the latter as subtle as a saucy seaside postcard. However, there were shadowy, discomfiting facets to other, more reflective songs such as 'However Much I Booze', 'Imagine a Man' and 'How Many Friends' and upon which Townshend had bared himself in streaks of self-disgust and self-loathing.

It was these songs that would make *The Who by Numbers* such a rewarding and revealing album, and one of the band's very best. When the sessions began at Ramport in mid-April of 1975, though, they were just as troubled and unsettled as Townshend's own mind appeared to be. Daltrey was off shooting his lead role in Ken Russell's next picture, *Lisztomania*, and late arriving. Moon also took time to get up to speed. Drying out from booze, he seemed in his new-found sobriety to have temporarily forgotten how to play the drums. Glyn Johns was back producing, but couldn't get to grips with the set-up at Ramport.

On 30 April, the band moved their base of operations to the Shepperton Film Studios complex on the western fringes of London. They had sunk a chunk of their booty from *Tommy* into buying one of Shepperton's cavernous soundstages and proceeded to work there with Johns for the next month, using the Island mobile studio. Entwistle took up his now established position at Townshend's right hand for the recording. His bass was the album's bedrock, bursting out for one extraordinary run on the closing track, 'In a Hand or a Face'. His horn arrangements, meanwhile, lifted off the more upbeat material and gave shading and a foundation to a fragile, almost hesitant track that Townshend otherwise performed solo, 'Blue Red and Grey'.

As he did with 'Cousin Kevin' and 'Fiddle About', Entwistle tailored his sole song-writing contribution to the album to fit Townshend's general tone. 'Success Story' came on as a knockabout rocker, but Entwistle's lyrics were a bitter, black pill and one seemingly delivered to The Who themselves. 'I may go far if I smash my guitar,' Entwistle sang, before concluding, 'You know, this used to be fun.'

'John was hugely respected by the other three,' considers Johns. 'He was also probably the only one of them who was able to have a positive relationship with all of the other guys in the band. On that album, there was tension between the other three for one reason and another, but particularly with Pete and Roger. Roger would have his tuppence worth as it were, and Pete would respond. Moon was always volatile, but there were also occasions when he wasn't together enough to remember an arrangement. John was a bit of a rock. He just didn't get involved in any of the normal problems that go on within a band, the ego battles and whatever else.'

Ironically, Entwistle's last act on *The Who by Numbers* also saved the band a considerable amount of money. He submitted a pen-and-ink, join-the-dots caricature of the four of them to be used as the album's front cover art. Later, he claimed that he had been paid the princely sum of £30 for this work, whereas the montage of black-and-white photographs that Townshend had commissioned from Ethan Russell for the *Quadrophenia* gatefold had set The Who back £16,000. *The Who by Numbers* was released that October to admiring notices and went Top Ten in the UK and US. To support it, Townshend assented to the longest tour The Who had mounted in four years, forty-one dates covering the UK, Europe and North America.

They began in Britain at the newly-built Bingley Hall in Stafford in the East Midlands on 3 and 4 October, moving on to Manchester, Glasgow, Leicester and then London, where they headlined three nights at the Empire Pool in Wembley. On these London dates, they unveiled a ground-breaking laser light show. However, the tour had got off under a cloud, with Townshend and Daltrey carping at each other through the pages of the music press. Back in May, Townshend had told the *New Musical Express* that The Who had sounded 'old' and 'dreadful' when they had played at Madison Square Garden the previous year. In the same publication that August, Daltrey hit back that 'the group was running on three cylinders . . . Townshend was in a bad frame of mind . . . and he didn't play well. He's talked himself up his own ass.'

Typically, Entwistle kept himself off to the sidelines of this latest conflict. But something else did rile him as the British shows wound on. Before The Who opened the European leg of the tour in Rotterdam on 27 October, he brought it to the attention of Curbishley. 'John came to see me and said, "My wife told me that she couldn't see me onstage,"' explains Curbishley. 'So I said to him, "John, you get exactly the same amount of lighting as anyone else onstage. But let's try something, shall we? Don't stand so far back. And by the way, I don't think we'd have headlines in the newspapers tomorrow if you weren't wearing black onstage." We started the European leg and one of the crew guys told me that I had to come and look at something. On the road, the band had the use of these big, free-standing wardrobes. The crew guy took me over to John's. Inside, there were hung up fifteen identical, but different sized white suits. In the waistband of the first five trousers in the row there was written an "F". That was for "fat", because John had put on a bit of weight before the tour. The next five trousers had written in them an "M" for "medium", for when he had slimmed down a bit. There was a "T" in the last five for "thin". John steadily worked his way through every one of those fifteen suits. That took him half the tour and then he reverted to black.'

They went to America that November. Entwistle carried with him on these dates a Zippo lighter that he had customised with a cartoon drawing of a spider. In bold red letters underneath, he had painted the words: 'If we mate, I'll have to kill you.' The US shows got off to the now-established uproarious start in Houston, Texas, on 20 November. After The Who's show that night at the Summit arena, their promoter threw a party for the band in the ballroom of the Houston Oaks Hotel. Townshend and Daltrey retired from the scene early to go to their beds, leaving Entwistle and Moon to make merry. Right there in front of the other guests, Moon got a blow-job from an accommodating young lady. He still had his trousers around his ankles when the cops arrived. Entwistle rushed to his comrade-in-arms' aid and was arrested for being drunk and disorderly.

At another show, a food fight erupted backstage. 'Everybody was getting pelted with food and joining in, except for John,' describes Keith Altham. 'John was just sitting off quietly in a corner, immaculate in his white stage suit. I thought he looked a little bit lost, left out. So I just gently lobbed a tomato off the buffet tray at his head, which he appeared to disregard.

'Five minutes later, John came up behind me with the entire buffet tray from the table and the lot went over my head. As I was brushing fried eggs off my shoulders and greasy bacon from my lap, Townshend wandered over to me and very quietly said, "Keith, I shouldn't play with John if I were you." John was laid-back but, if provoked, he would spring into decisive action.'

'Then again, there was a very generous side to John's nature,' Curbishley adds. 'In Toronto, there was an art gallery in the lobby of our hotel. I went in and was looking around, and I happened to spot a print of the ballet dancer, Baryshnikov, that I very much liked. I asked the assistant how much it was and it was a bit too expensive for me. Off we went and carried on the tour, but what I didn't know was that John had been in the gallery at the same time as me, lurking in a corner again. When I got home to England, there was the Baryshnikov print. John had bought it and had it shipped back for me.'

Onstage during that North American run, the band gave some of the most blazing performances of their career. It was a huge financial success for them, too. At the Pontiac Silver Dome, Michigan, on 6 December, they played to a near 80,000 crowd, setting an attendance record for an indoor gig and grossing over $600,000 for just that one performance. They returned to America in March of the following year and for another fourteen dates. By then, though, The Who's fire had dimmed because of the waning of Moon's powers.

Moon had not been able to stay off the bottle for long. Holed up at his rented home in Malibu in between tours, he had been on a bender of epic proportions. On 7 March 1976, he turned up at the Boston Garden for opening night looking bloated and vacant. Moon had spent the night before carousing at the Playboy Club in New York and was hardly able to make it up on to the stage. The abiding image of that tour was of him trying to pick up the beat of The Who's first number that night, 'I Can't Explain', and failing miserably, lost in a fog of his own making.

Moon lasted just one more song, before slumping over his kit and having to be carried off. Just as he had done so many times in the past, he bounced right back and was able to soldier on through the rest of the tour. Now, though, there were the clear warning signs that he wouldn't be able to keep on doing it for much longer. No one in and around the band was more acutely aware of this sobering fact than Entwistle.

'John was troubled by the decline in Keith, I know that,' says Mick Bratby. 'Dougal would have words with John and me . . . about trying to hide Keith's stuff from him, or flushing it down the loo. But there wasn't a lot that John or any of us could do about it. I expect John knew by then what was coming.'

Altham adds, 'Everybody made some sort of effort to get Moon back on track. But Moon was like a runaway racing car and on a downhill gradient. John especially, Townshend and even Roger would run around trying to stop the car going downhill; kick a couple of chocks under the front wheels. Then they would go away and Moon would gleefully kick them out again. He was determined to live his life at ten times the speed of everyone else.

'I remember going to visit Moon in hospital once. He'd had a suspected heart-attack of some sort and I said to him, "Moon, this is a fucking warning, man. You've got to slow down." His reply was, "Oh, dear boy, you know me. Mortality I simply never consider. Immortality I take quite seriously." That was the nature of the man. He was great fun to be with, but he burned himself out for your delight.'

14

Quarwood

Moon's incapacity forced them to postpone the Boston Garden show. The rescheduled date was tacked on at the very end of the tour and passed without incident on 1 April 1976. Right after that gig, the four band members went their separate ways for the next six weeks. At such down times and now that he could rely on getting ready cash from a tour, Entwistle would often whisk Alison and Christopher off for an extended holiday. These family breaks could be a challenge for all concerned since Entwistle would still be stuck in touring mode. That is to say that he would hanker for an unwavering routine and to have someone else take care of all of his essential needs.

His basic requirements would be twenty-four-hour room service and a swimming pool to idle around. There was one year that Entwistle took along Daltrey's masseuse as a child-minder for Christopher for the entire six weeks that they spent on the Bahaman island of Bimini and in Miami. In that regard, he may have been mindful of an incident on an earlier family holiday to Hawaii. On that occasion, Entwistle was meant to be supervising his young son; Christopher couldn't swim, but snuck off into the sea without his water-wings.

'Mother says it was Dad's turn to be watching over me, but he wasn't,' explains Christopher. 'I almost drowned. I have a memory of going down under the water. My mother, who also couldn't swim very well, came out like an Olympic swimmer and got me back to the shore. She saved me.'

Whenever he felt stuck at home, left to his own devices and growing increasingly bored and agitated, Entwistle would lift his mood by going out shopping. Such was the case that spring of 1976 and when he returned to Corringway directly from Boston. However, where in the past his post-tour splurges had extended as far as multiples of cars, guitars, clothes and gadgets, now he stretched all the way to a house. Nor was it to be just any old house. Entwistle desired a holiday home. Alison had in mind a quaint English country cottage with a thatched roof and garden gate. Since Mick Bratby hailed from the Cotswolds, knew the area well and had a ready base at his mother's should he ever be required to drive them to the area, it was there one weekend that they went house-hunting.

Entwistle found his perfect place just outside the sleepy, picture-postcard Cotswold town of Stow-on-the-Wold. 'Quarwood', though, was no cottage, but a grandly-appointed, sprawling old pile set on forty acres of land and upon which were also paddocks, barns, garages, fish ponds and seven workers' cottages. The main house had been designed by a Victorian architect, John Loughborough-Pearson, better known for his cathedrals and churches, and was built between 1856 and 1859 for the local parish priest, Reverend Robert William Hippisley. The current owner was a retail entrepreneur, Isaac Wolfson, who that same April accepted an offer from Entwistle of £150,000 for the house and grounds. It was almost ten times what Entwistle had paid for Corringway, but it bought him somewhere fit for a gentleman rock star, which was how he now defined himself.

'The thing with John was, he was like a kid whose dream had come true,' considers Richard Barnes. 'He was very successful, rich and he just over-indulged himself in every possible way. Also, he loved to show off and to have people look at him. With Quarwood, he got the lot. The view from the back must have been the best in all of the Cotswolds. You looked out over twenty or so miles of fields and hills, not another building in sight. And he had got himself a much more impressive house than any of the others in the band.'

'I wouldn't have discouraged him from buying Quarwood,' notes Bill Curbishley. 'That was a sensible investment, because the house would always have a value and it might even be doubled. That was how I looked at it. No problem there and rather that than him spend it all at Harrods.'

In fact, Entwistle immediately set about filling the fifty-five-room house with furniture and fittings that he bought almost exclusively from the Knightsbridge store. In time, he transformed Quarwood into something that was even more representative of his own character than Corringway. On the outside it would remain quietly dignified, while over the span of years that he was to live there, the interior of the house ended up becoming a fun-filled but seemingly random riot of extravagances, hoardings, self-indulgences and other features bought or done on an apparent whim.

Standing guard in the entrance hall was Henry, the medieval suit of armour that had also been stationed at Corringway. Henry's helmet wobbled in the Quarwood draughts, so to secure it, Entwistle had it stuffed with one of Alison's fur hats. Two more full suits of armour were stationed around a great long table in the ground-floor dining room. Swinging over the hall was

'Quasi', an effigy of the hunchback of Notre Dame that Entwistle had hung from a forty-foot bell rope. In one room, a full human skeleton reclined in a Regency chair with one of its bony hands reached out and attached to a telephone.

Another room on the second floor was taken up with Entwistle's comprehensive and intricately-detailed double-zero-gauge model train set, which was laid out over several raised tables. He had bought the set meaning to give it to Christopher as a birthday present, but then kept it for himself. More rooms he filled with his collections of teapots, porcelain, ornamental rugs and antique weaponry – shotguns, pistols and crossbows. His gold discs went up on the walls of the downstairs loo. On the first floor were four bedroom suites named after the colours in which they were decorated; Entwistle's and Alison's was the main Blue Suite, with a smaller bedroom next door for Christopher. The three other suites – Pink, Green and Gold – were guests' rooms.

Another bar was also added to the ground floor. This one was as authentically appointed and well stocked as that at Corringway, but around fifteen times bigger. Entwistle christened it 'The Barracuda Inne' and had it equipped with a 1950s Wurlitzer jukebox, a pinball machine and a Pianola piano that played itself. Entwistle loved to throw parties at Quarwood and, over the years, The Barracuda Inne would be the hub of all of these get-togethers; the host leaning over from behind the bar, cigarette in one hand, full glass in the other, doling out drinks in liberal measures and at the very centre of things. Playing up to his role as country squire, Entwistle bought shotguns and took up shooting – for clay pigeons at Quarwood, or else for pheasant and as a guest of the Wolfsons at their other country estate at nearby Burford.

In due course, he would have a full-time staff to manage the house and grounds for him. He also had his mother and stepfather to mind the place. Grandad John died just as the Quarwood sale was going through, so Entwistle moved Queenie and Gordon into the house as soon as he took up ownership. They were to reside at Quarwood in their own self-contained apartment that ranged over two floors in what were the old servants' quarters. With Entwistle, Alison and Christopher being weekend visitors, Gordon seized the chance to lord it up whenever they were absent.

'Gordon definitely thought the place was his,' says Christopher. 'And most people around the area thought that Quarwood belonged to him, too, because that's what he led them to believe. He always was the big "I am". Gordon was never happy when Dad was there for a weekend, because that would put a stop to his routine. Even so, we'd be in the house and Gordon would still follow Dad around the place, turning lights off after him. And Dad didn't really ever confront him about that.'

■ ■ ■

That summer of 1976 would go on to be a long, record-breaking hot one in Britain. The country underwent a drought for much of July and August, with some areas in the south of England going forty-five days without rain. Almost the last deluge to fall on London for three months poured down throughout Saturday, 31 May when The Who again performed at Charlton Athletic's football ground. This was the first of three stadium shows that they were scheduled to play around the UK on what was billed as the 'Who Put the Boot In' tour.

All told, it was an ugly, miserable day. As the rain bucketed down, warm-up acts such as Little Feat and The Sensational Alex Harvey Band battled both the elements and a tense, ill-tempered crowd. The mood in the stadium had hardly improved by the time The Who took to the stage, but they confronted it head on and by sheer force of volume. Onstage that night, The Who were measured at 120 decibels, almost exactly the equivalent of a thunderclap and enough to gain them entry into the *Guinness Book of Records* as the loudest rock-'n'-roll band in the world. Completing the otherworldly atmosphere, they were watched from the side of the stage by the actress Elizabeth Taylor, who had turned up backstage with her two daughters, Liza and Maria.

From Charlton, The Who travelled up to Glasgow to play Celtic FC's Celtic Park Stadium on 5 June and then down to the south of Wales for the climactic British date at Swansea City's football ground on 12 June. In August, they undertook a whirlwind tour of the US, playing four dates in six days in Maryland and Florida. While on a day off in Miami and instigated by Entwistle, the band hired a boat to go deep sea fishing. They had to cut the trip short when Moon pleaded seasickness, but Entwistle had by then already been inspired to pursue another of his life-long passions. Whenever he was in Florida, he would fix himself up with a boat and a skipper and set sail out into the Gulf Stream to fish for marlin, bonito, sailfish and other such big game, never happier or more at peace than he was on those fishing trips. He found a place in Miami that would make plaster casts of his catches and had them shipped over to England. Soon enough, all kinds of replica fish were swinging from the ceiling of The Barracuda Inne.

'Whenever you walked into the bar at Quarwood, you would feel like Jacques Cousteau, like you were underwater,' says Bill Curbishley. 'John had sharks and all kinds of shit hanging from that ceiling. These fish would all have been spray-painted. I used to say to him, "John, how do you know you actually caught *that*?" And he was paying thousands and thousands of dollars for these things. I know, because I would pay the bills for him.'

'John had one shark made into a kind of lampshade,' adds Keith Altham. 'Another fish that he had caught had been pregnant, so he had the babies stuffed and cast as well. Only Entwistle would have done something as grotesque as that. These were ridiculously expensive things, but he loved to buy stuff that was impractical really and simply because he could.'

That October, The Who went back to North America to complete the final leg of their tour, another nine dates in fifteen days, beginning on 6 October at the Veterans Memorial Coliseum in Phoenix, Arizona. Moving on to California on the weekend of 9 and 10 October they co-headlined with The Grateful Dead at Bill Graham's annual Day on the Green festival at the Oakland Stadium. Next to the Dead's free-form meanderings, The Who's sets both nights were like hard, sharp blows to the solar plexus. Onstage in Oakland, Entwistle unveiled a new prop that he would continue to use: two large, plastic drinks bottles with straws that he had attached together to his mike stand. He supped from them throughout each of these shows and at all the ones that followed. Like most observers, Bill Curbishley had assumed that these were water bottles and Entwistle never said anything to correct him.

'I found out later on that he was filling them up with Southern Comfort and brandy,' says Curbishley. 'The trouble was, John didn't have anyone else in the band that could pull him up about it, apart from maybe Roger, because they were all doing all kinds of stuff and acting like madmen. I mean, Pete was drinking like a fish, too. A lot of it I think was that they had convinced themselves that it was all part of the creative process, when it's not. But John wasn't Moon. He never fell over or collapsed. He would drink copious amounts, but you would never see him be totally legless.'

On the last night of the tour, on 21 October at the Maple Leaf Gardens, Toronto and before an audience of 20,000, The Who played a singularly triumphant show. Collectively, so commanding, so powerful were they that night that they seemed like an elemental force of nature. Later, Entwistle would describe this show and the eight that preceded it as being the very peak of the band's career. 'Right then, there was nothing that even came close to them,' affirms Bobby Pridden. 'Their feet weren't even touching the ground.' In one respect at least, Toronto was also a valedictory performance since it was to be the last that they gave in North America with Moon among them.

Back in Britain, something new and potent was brewing up that winter. On 1 December, a young, surly-looking rock band caused a national outrage appearing on an early-evening current affairs programme on ITV, *Today*. Riled by the taunting tone adopted by their interviewer, The Sex Pistols, or at least one of them, guitarist Steve Jones, responded by branding the forty-three-year-old Bill Grundy a 'dirty fucker' live on air. Grundy, who seemed drunk, compounded the matter by inviting Jones to repeat the insult, to which he duly obliged. The next morning, the country's best-selling tabloid newspaper, the *Daily Mirror*, splashed the four Pistols across its front page under the banner headline THE FILTH AND THE FURY, and punk rock was set loose in the UK.

Like The Who, three-quarters of the Pistols hailed from west London and they regularly covered 'Substitute' in their live sets. However, on the *Today* show, the Pistols' singer, Johnny Rotten, had sported a T-shirt emblazoned with the words 'I Hate Pink Floyd'. His band, and the others like them spitting and sneering out from pubs and clubs in London and the provinces, set themselves against rock's old guard. When the Pistols sang of 'Anarchy in the UK', it was interpreted as a challenge to no one so much as the young bucks from the sixties who had gone on to make concept albums, fill stadiums and be seen to become as distant and aloof as aristocrats. In other words, bands just like The Who.

In their early thirties now, Entwistle, Townshend, Daltrey and Moon were at a stroke being cast as 'dinosaurs'. Townshend fretted and worried about his own and The Who's validity and currency, but not so Entwistle. He seemed to carry on just as he always had, content to be above the fray, unapologetic about however he might be perceived, rich and not shy about flaunting it and, if a bunch of truculent upstarts took issue with all or any part of that, well then, so be it. He went on being blithely unconcerned with whatever the punks said or did, and was never more detached than when he was at Quarwood.

That Christmas and New Year, the first of many that he was to host at the rambling old house, he feasted and made merry and as if in utter defiance of these enemies at the gates. He spent another small fortune on food, booze and trimmings. He had a huge Christmas tree erected at the foot of the hallway stairs which rose up to the first floor. He paid for students from a local catering college to come in and cook a gargantuan traditional Christmas dinner for family and friends. He threw a splendid New Year's Eve costume party at which his guests ate, drank and danced the night away.

'Christmas always was a huge event for Dad,' says Christopher, who that year had been enrolled by his parents at a west London pre-prep school, Durston House. 'At Quarwood, you used to always have to climb up and decorate the tree from the stairs. I remember one party where every single room in the house was occupied and so all the kids had to sleep on shelves in the giant airing cupboard.

'Dad didn't really give me presents outside of Christmas or birthdays, but at those times he would really go to town. The Christmas following, he had just come back from America. He knew that I had got into *Star Wars* and he had bought me every possible item of *Star Wars* merchandise: every figurine, every mask, every spacecraft, every toy, he had put them in a massive box. That was the collector in him. Later on, when I was a teenager, *2000 AD* was one of the comics I used to get. Dad took a copy off me, read it and liked it, and then went out and bought every single issue from 1 to 600, because he had to have the complete collection.'

At the start of 1977, Townshend enforced a period of inactivity for The Who. He wanted to spend time with his family, so no live or recording dates were booked for the band. Entwistle busied himself with other projects. He had imagined a sci-fi-themed concept album, once again flagrantly disregarding the punks, and began to write songs for it at home at Corringway. He did a couple of studio sessions – one for a Lonnie Donegan album, *Puttin' on the Style*, and for which his parts went inexplicably unused; and the other for a track, 'Avenging Annie', that was to be included on Daltrey's third solo record, *One of the Boys*. The Daltrey album was cut at Ramport that February and March. On the day that Entwistle put down his bass part, Paul McCartney was a visitor to the studio.

'Paul walked into the control room while I was recording a particularly fast, flashy solo on "Avenging Annie", an Andy Pratt song,' Entwistle recorded in his memoir notes. 'After I had finished it, he came out on to the studio floor and said to me, "That was very nice. But I bet you can't play country and western." I replied by playing a lightning fast, slapping bluegrass passage. Paul muttered as he left, "Flash cunt."'

■ ■ ■

During the Townshend-imposed lull, one new Who project did start up. Typically, *The Kids Are Alright* emerged from a battle of wills waged between Daltrey and Townshend while Entwistle and Moon looked on from the sidelines. Daltrey had hired a young English film-maker, Tony Klinger, to direct a promo video for the title track of 'One of the Boys'. Klinger was just twenty-six, but had pedigree. His father, Michael, had made the hard-nosed British gangster classic *Get Carter* with Michael Caine in the lead role, while Klinger himself had just produced two films for Roger Moore, *Gold* and *Shout at the Devil*. Klinger impressed enough for Daltrey and Curbishley to hire him to produce a career-spanning documentary film of The Who.

Barely had Klinger shaken hands on the deal than Townshend announced that he had hired a twenty-two-year-old New Yorker, Jeff Stein, to direct the very same film. Stein was an enthusiastic Who fan, but had never made a film. Nevertheless, he also won over Curbishley, Entwistle and Moon with a seventeen-minute reel of the band's American television performances that he had edited together. Daltrey's man, Klinger, was instantly relegated to being co-producer with Curbishley and filming with Stein got under way at Shepperton that July. The £300,000 budget was put up out of the band's own pockets. Costs ended up spiralling as the production dragged on.

'There was a constant – I won't say war – but more like sniper fire going off between Roger and Pete,' says Klinger. 'You felt that if one said something was black, the other would say it was white, even if it was obviously black. With our film, they just happened to have signed two contracts for the same job. It was an impossible situation for everyone. Although I also had an intense battle with Curbishley, I think he had to be as tough as he was to make the whole thing function.

'When I met John, he actually was just like a big ox. He didn't really communicate a lot. It was only when he got to know me a little bit that he started to come across as very droll and I did grow to like him. Whenever those meetings took place with Roger's camp and Townshend's lot, though, John, like Moon, would kind of go over to one side or the other. It was ridiculous.'

Moon showed up at Shepperton in a wretched state – overweight, puffy-eyed and wholly unfit to play the drums for any length of time. Between them, Stein and Klinger agreed to get the rest of the footage required of him in the can first just in case the worst should happen. Early the next month, they flew out to Los Angeles with a small crew and spent five crazed, perilous, depressing days trailing Moon around his adopted hometown.

'We saw shed-loads of money go up Moon's nose,' Klinger says. 'He was very bright but, like a huge child doing mad things constantly, those five days were a twenty-four-seven fucking nightmare. One day, he drove me the wrong way up the Pacific Coast Highway, but it was like that with him all the time.'

Even 'Dougal' Butler, Moon's faithful and long-suffering assistant, had reached the end of his tether. 'I was going, "Hold on, I'm out here in Malibu, we're living in a beach house next door to Steve McQueen and Ali MacGraw, and yet we're skint." It had got to the point where I was having to hide $50 from Moon just so I could go out for a beer with a couple of guys that I knew. Over just a few months, he had borrowed ten grand off me and he was doing drugs like there was no tomorrow and from off people I didn't know.

'McQueen eventually shot out the lights in our house – literally. Moon kept leaving the bathroom light on all night and it overlooked their bedroom. One night, McQueen got out a shotgun and just went bang. That was enough for me. I rang Bill Curbishley and said, "Bill, that's me finished. Get him home, too, or else he's going to be dead within months."'

Back in England, Entwistle had by then also begun to cultivate a taste for cocaine. It was at an Eagles gig that April at Wembley Empire Pool that Mick Bratby first saw him overtly doing a couple of lines. Bratby says these were given to Entwistle by his old running mate Joe Walsh, now The Eagles' lead guitarist.

However, to all other outward appearances, Entwistle's life seemed to be as well ordered, if fanciful, as ever.

At the end of that August, he paid for and cut a record at Ramport with the seventy-four strong Newport Male Voice Choir, among whose number was his father, Bert. Entwistle picked out songs for the choir to sing at the session, including Elvis's 'Love Me Tender' and The Beatles' 'Yesterday'. He also put down bass on three tracks and had Rod Argent, who had played with him on Daltrey's most recent album, add keyboards. The following week, Entwistle took Argent with him to Wales, where he did overdubs with the choir and dropped in on Bert. The pair of them also made a beeline for the Cardiff pub that Entwistle's stepbrother Bernard was then running.

'The chauffeur rang me up and told me that John and a mate would be coming round,' says Bernard. 'It was a huge pub on the outskirts of the city called The Retreat. In John came, Rod Argent behind him. In one corner, I happened to have a Yamaha B3 piano. Argent turned to me and said, "Have you got the key to that?" This was before they had even had a drink. Then Argent said to John, "We've got to have a go, haven't we?" John had a bass in the car and they also happened to have brought a couple of amps along with them. So they sent out for them. As they were plugging in, I asked John what he wanted to drink. He said champagne, which we didn't sell in a pub in Cardiff. I had to get one of the barmen to go round the corner to the off-licence to fetch me a bottle. The cheapest one they had was thirty-two quid.

'There and then, the pair of them just started playing. It was like a jam session and they went on for about an hour. The place soon filled up, but hardly anybody knew who they were. At one point, I noticed that John's bottle was empty. Off the barman went to get another. John never did say to me, "How much do you want for that?"'

Early the next year, Stein, Klinger and their film crew travelled to the Cotswolds to shoot Entwistle's two scenes for *The Kids Are Alright* at Quarwood. They filmed one of him walking down the house's sweeping main staircase, the walls and banisters bedecked with his many guitars which he had brought out just for the occasion. In the other scene, he was shown outside on the croquet lawn, armed with a machine-gun and shooting up gold discs like clay pigeons. In these snatched moments, Entwistle appeared to be as wry and self-contained as usual. However, someone who knew him well might have detected something else now going on behind his mask: doubt, a kind of sadness, a sense of emptiness, or all of these things at once. These were the things that grew within him the longer The Who remained inactive, the more that Moon ruined himself, and perhaps the nearer that he felt to the edge of an abyss.

Klinger remembers, 'When we were doing the work, and especially true of John and Moon, there was a certain amount of play-acting. It became very hard to tell if things were for real. I think that with us John was living up to his black image. And also, he was playing at being lord of the manor.

'We had the same thing with Roger. He arrived for filming one day by helicopter. I said to him that this would make a fantastic shot and he went bananas at me. He told me, "I'm not going to look like those fuckers in Led Zeppelin – driving their Cadillacs across a bridge." And he'd got a fucking helicopter. The only one of them that was totally genuine was Pete. He was true to himself, whether you liked it or not.

'Intentionally or not, I don't think John was being truthful. In fact, I don't think I ever saw the real John. I think there might have been three or more versions of John and I got to see just one and a bit. It was a huge surprise to me to find out that he did drugs of any kind. I can't remember who told me, it might have been Roger, but I just hadn't realised. I guess I was quite naïve, but John was also more subtle, or clever about it than Moon. Up to then, I had thought that John was a steadying influence. I think it's just really hard for those guys to be normal. There's always somebody saying to them, "Here, have this, or put that up your nose." That's what fucks them up.'

Another visitor to Quarwood around this same time was Mick Brown. He recalls, 'John showed me round the place. It was room after room after room and all of them full of . . . stuff. What I didn't see from John was: "This is fantastic!" There was no enthusiasm coming from him. He just went around saying [in a dulled monotone], "There's this, and there's that." He looked a bit careworn, subdued maybe.

'He had a dining room table that stretched from one end of the room to the other, but we sat and ate burgers and chips in what would have been the servants' kitchen. That was the last time that I was ever properly together with him. Really, John was one of the greatest friends I never had. He just drifted up and away from me.'

15

Eclipse

Moon was persuaded to move back to London that September in time for The Who to begin rehearsals for a new album. He was still in no real condition to drum, but then he wasn't the only one of them in poor shape. Townshend, also drinking heavily at the time, hadn't been nearly so productive. When the band met up at Ramport on 19 September, he came along with fewer and much less substantive songs than usual. Entwistle, on the other hand, brought in seven tracks that he had demoed up, some of which were meant for his now aborted sci-fi album. On the finished record, he would end up having an unprecedented three songs to Townshend's six.

As a piece, the making of the *Who Are You* album proved to be a tortuous experience. The sessions at Ramport, with Glyn Johns producing and Townshend's brother-in-law, Jon Astley, engineering, dragged on for the next six months. Hollowed-out, Moon played like a ghost of himself, a zombie drummer. Not that most of the songs amounted to much. Townshend's contributions for the most part were pale echoes of former glories. Four at least were empty vessels underneath the slick sheen of Johns' polishing and a smothering of synthesisers, backing vocals and the guesting Rod Argent's keyboards. The same was true of Entwistle's 'Had Enough', which was sung by Daltrey. Putting down another of his songs at Corringway, '905', a leftover from his concept album, Entwistle had used one of the very first Polymoog synthesisers, but this was the only thing about it that stood out.

'Trick of the Light', Entwistle's third contribution to the album and in which he described an awkward assignation with a prostitute, did at least have some zip to it, thrust along by his distorted Alembic bass. Yet still it paled beside Townshend's six-minute title track, the album's one heroic – but not quite made – reach for greatness. The remainder of the songs sounded as if they had been forced out through tight spaces that they didn't fit, and Daltrey sang them as if through gritted teeth.

At Jeff Stein's begging, they broke off on 15 December to play a one-off gig. Stein had pleaded a dearth of good contemporary footage of the band for his film, so The Who arranged to play a mid-afternoon set at the Gaumont State Theatre in Kilburn, north London, before an audience of 800 and Stein's cameras. By no means was it a successful exercise. Moon's playing was catatonic and the band stumbled and flagged badly. Stein got nothing that he would be able to use. 'I was pissed out of me fucking head,' Entwistle told Moon's biographer, Tony Fletcher, of the show. 'I had a premonition that The Who weren't going to exist any more.'[28]

Entwistle had also doubled his workload since he had been put in charge of remixing old Who recordings for the *The Kids Are Alright* soundtrack. After hours on *Who Are You*, he would

---

[28] Taken from *Dear Boy: the Life of Keith Moon* by Tony Fletcher, Omnibus (2005)

In the spring of 1976, Entwistle went shopping for a country cottage in the Cotswolds – and came back with Quarwood.

(above) 'John's sense of humour was wicked,' says Alison Entwistle. 'But he was a very funny bloke in other ways.'

(right) Shortly after acquiring Quarwood and in lord of the manor guise.

Entwistle and friend take a turn around the Barracuda Inne dancefloor.

(above) Entwistle introduced a new stage prop, plastic cup holders, in 1976. 'He was filling them up with Southern Comfort and brandy,' says Bill Curbishley. (© Ross Halfin)

(left) Letter home from America. Christopher Entwistle: 'Dad told me once how it was with The Who on the road. Him and Keith would go off and cause trouble. Pete would go off and write songs. And Roger would be off shagging somebody.' That was basically it.'

YOUR VACATION ESCAPE

LEAVENWORTH ARMS

SERVICE WITH A FILE

LEAVENWORTH ARMS

ADDITIONAL ROOMS AT THE TOMBS

Dear Mum and Gordon,

Hope you are both well + I hope you got my last letter. We did a concert at Central Park last week + there must have been about 12,000 people there. We also did one at the Illinois state fair with a group called The Association and there we 25,000 people there.

Still you can only ever see the first 10 rows anyway. This will probably be the last letters I write over here as there is not too long to go now. (15 days). Thank you for your letter by the way I received it in New York.

JOIN THE GROUP AT THE PIANO IN THE "IRON BAR" AND DO THE SING SING ♪ THING

Entwistle, Alison and Christopher kitted out for a summer fete in Stow-on-the-Wold. *(courtesy of Alison Entwistle)*

Entwistle attending sports day at Christopher's west London prep school, Colet Court. Faithful driver Kenny Wyatt is reclining in the foreground.

(left) Father and son, together at Quarwood. 'He was away, or out for most of the time that he was living at home,' says Christopher.

(right) 'He was very successful, rich and he just over-indulged himself in every possible way.' Entwistle with Alison in his pomp at Quarwood.

(above) Outtake from Terry O'Neill's photo shoot for the cover of the *Who Are You* album, May 1978. Less than four months later, Keith Moon was dead.
(© Terry O'Neill/Iconic Images)

(left) Happy times at Quarwood: second wife Maxene (on blanket) and Entwistle with family friends Jennifer McClain (left) and Sue McClain. Recalls Maxene: 'I figured I had kissed a frog. I was just twenty-two, naïve and gullible, but I was ready for an adventure.'

Entwistle with Maxene. She says: 'John allowed me to take care of everything and most especially him … because he was like a big kid.'

(above) Lisa Pritchett-Johnson: 'It was Lisa that truly fucked Dad up,' says Christopher. 'I hate her for what she did to him.'

(right) Deep-sea fishing was one of the enduring passions of Entwistle's life. As here in Miami, he would never miss an opportunity to charter a boat.

An outtake from the photo shoot for the cover of Entwistle's 1981 solo album *Too Late the Hero*. Says photographer Gered Mankowitz: 'Yes, definitely, he was quite odd'. (© *Gered Mankowitz*)

Queenie, actor John Hurt and Entwistle at a New Year's Eve party at the Priory Lane house.

Hanging out in Hollywood with (*from Entwistle's left*) 'Cy' Langston, unidentified, Joe Walsh and friend Ray Ray. Says Walsh: 'We partied more and more and played and composed less and less, and because we could.'

Quarwood's regular barman, pictured with Marlene the Rottweiler.

Wolfhound Flynn and his adoring master.

The John Entwistle Band, mid-1990s vintage: *(from left)* Alan St Jon, Entwistle, Steve Luongo and Godfrey Townsend.

At rehearsals for The Who's 2002 US tour. Whereas Pete Townshend took Entwistle's sitting down as a sign of his ailing health, Bill Curbishley insists: 'I put [it] down to his being bored.' *(© Ross Halfin)*

Onstage with The Who at London's Royal Albert Hall, 8 February 2002. Entwistle's last-ever show. *(© Ross Halfin)*

be holed up with Cy Langston at CTS Studios in Wembley preparing the original mono tracks to be transferred over to a new format – Dolby Stereo. It was only the second time that Dolby had been used on a British film production and the work was again painstaking and time-consuming. The first mix alone took Entwistle ten days to complete, with Stein, Klinger and others from the film's production retinue standing over him; his band-mates also weighed in at various points.

'Everybody involved in the process was a perfectionist and it was horrendous – like picking at a scab, over and over again,' Klinger recalls. 'Pete wanted his guitar more upfront. Then Keith wanted the drums bringing up. Next, the bass wouldn't be upfront enough for John. We would all come in and then have to go away for another x amount of months, before coming back and going through the whole thing yet again.

'It wasn't about the music; it was about the egos and the whole balance of the band. I still can't believe it, but I was there – at one point each of them actually had stopwatches going to see how many minutes of screen time they had. They had people sitting there and timing it for them.'

Back at Ramport and with the exception of the studio's drinks cabinet, there were precious few moments of light relief to be had as the weeks dragged on. One afternoon, Paul McCartney dropped by again with wife Linda in tow. Once more, Entwistle inadvertently rubbed the former Beatle up the wrong way. 'I guess we always seemed to say the wrong thing to each other,' he wrote up in his memoir notes. 'Paul politely asked me what I was doing for the weekend. I replied without thinking, "Oh, I'm going home to Gloucestershire to shoot a few squirrels."' The McCartneys, of course, were strict vegetarians.

More typical of the sessions was the point at which Daltrey blew up. Berating Johns over one of his mixes, Daltrey threw a punch at the distraught producer before storming out. Johns left the album soon after that to go and make a record with Joan Armatrading. It then fell to Astley to drag them over the line.

'There was a lot of sitting around,' Astley says. 'In frustration, Pete put his hand through a window at his parents' house, slashed it open and had to take time off. Then, there were Keith's problems. I got to know John pretty well during that period, because he was the only one who was there all the time, day in and day out. He started to take me out to clubs. We would go to one in particular on the King's Road where John's tipple was Blue Nun wine. Just as soon as we arrived, a bottle of Blue Nun would appear at our table.

'John was a very, very patient man. If nothing was happening, he'd say to me, "Oh, let's do that bass part again." Then he would go down to the studio floor, set up and play the exact same part and just as perfectly as the first time. I mean, he tried to keep things moving. You could also see that he was concerned about Keith. Eventually, they all confronted Keith. We all went out to a Pizza Express and they turned on him. They told him that he had to get his shit together, otherwise he was out. Keith did sort himself out. He started to lose a bit of weight, get into shape and, in ten days, we were able to do all of his drum parts again from scratch. I think each of them, though, was just glad to have had John there all through the making of that album. He was the one that held the whole thing together.'

■ ■ ■

After they had at last wrapped up *Who Are You*, they tried again to give Stein his missing footage. On 4 May 1978, the director and his crew filmed them at Ramport overdubbing the title track. On the surface, they seem demob happy in the scenes shot that day, with Moon their ever-present court jester. Closer inspection suggests a kind of weariness, desperation even behind Entwistle's, Townshend's and Daltrey's fixed grins and, in Moon, the sadness of a clown.

Three weeks later, on the afternoon of Thursday, 25 May, they set up another impromptu gig for Stein to film. They took as few chances as possible this time around; the venue was home turf, Shepperton Studios, the audience smaller and by invite only. Stein got what he wanted from their opening number, a splenetic 'Baba O'Riley', and by brow-beating Townshend to do an extra, pounding run through 'Won't Get Fooled Again'. In between these twin peaks, the band's short set for the 500-strong audience was notable in the main for how overweight and vacant Moon looked behind his kit. Whatever improvements Astley had seen in him, they could only have been minor.

Dark omens also attended the release of *Who Are You*. That April, Track Records had gone into liquidation. And on 30 July, Peter Meaden was found dead at his parents' home where he had been living. He had died from an accidental overdose of barbiturates – he was just thirty-six.

Following on from Townshend with *Quadrophenia* and Entwistle for *The Who by Numbers*, Moon was given a turn to come up with an album sleeve for the new record. Unsurprisingly, he left it to the last minute, necessitating a hastily convened shoot with celebrity photographer Terry O'Neill that went ahead in the car-park at Ramport the day after the Shepperton show. In the image subsequently used, Moon is shown sitting astride an office chair, the better to hide his gut, and kitted out in riding gear. Entwistle and Townshend stand on either side of him, Daltrey stationed off to his right. Stencilled on to the back of Moon's chair, facing out to O'Neill's camera, were the words: 'NOT TO BE TAKEN AWAY'.

Who Are You was met with lukewarm reviews when it came out on 18 August. In *Rolling Stone*, Griel Marcus praised Entwistle's work as 'his best in years', but went on to note that 'Moon truly seems to have lost what he once had'. Marcus concluded, 'This is by no means a great record . . . The tunes lack a natural, kinetic groove.' However, the album was a hit, peaking at Number Six on the UK chart and Number Two in the US where it went on to sell more than three million copies. There was, though, no tour in the offing to back it up. Moon simply wasn't up to it, and now no one in the camp wanted to go out any more, not when they would be so handicapped.

Instead, wheels went into motion on yet another film project. Curbishley hired a little-known English TV director, Franc Roddam, to helm and co-write with Townshend a *Quadrophenia* movie. That August, Roddam and Curbishley set up a casting call at a cinema in Soho and, from this, plucked out a skinny, hyperactive nineteen-year-old, Phil Daniels, to be their Jimmy the Mod. A couple of days later, they threw a reception party for the media at Lee International Studios in Wembley to drum up interest in the film. That particular afternoon, it was Entwistle, The Who's so-called quiet one, who made the most noise. 'Irish' Jack Lyons attended the party and remembers, 'Everyone was there – media people, actors, punks, film executives and rock stars. Glasses were being clinked and finger food left all over the floor, and then there was an embarrassed hush as a shemozzle broke out on one side of the room. It was Entwistle, roaring at the top of his voice as he threw heavy ashtrays and glasses at the wall. Loudly, he accused his wife, Alison, of chatting up some guy.

'The guy in question, an angelic-looking young man with trendy blonde locks, was stood in the middle of the floor seeming petrified. The film executives were in shock, not being used to seeing a rock star throw one of his strops. Somebody ushered young blondie-locks out of the room as John's faithful driver moved about the place, hunched over, scooping up the debris with a newspaper. Sometime later, when the ever-patient Alison had calmed her husband down, he returned to the reception as if nothing had happened. He did, though, come over to me and say, "Jack, I want you to find out for me who that little bastard is. Because I'm going to make sure that he never works in the industry again."'

■ ■ ■

On 1 September, Entwistle was in Wembley again and at CTS Studios overseeing overdubs on to footage for *The Kids Are Alright*. One particular mute clip showed Moon setting about his drum-kit. Entwistle had asked Moon to drop by and play along to it so that they would have a usable soundtrack. A kit was set up, but when Moon arrived he wasn't remotely able to keep up with his old self. He had recently been prescribed a sedative, Heminevrin, to help counter the effects of coming off booze, and he seemed almost narcoleptic.

Five nights later, Moon and his Swedish girlfriend, Annette Walter-Lax, attended a party Paul McCartney was throwing at a West End club, the Peppermint Park, to mark the movie première of *The Buddy Holly Story*. That night, Moon was again subdued and the couple took a taxi back to the Mayfair flat they were renting from Harry Nilsson at around 1.00am. Walter-Lax cooked Moon a supper of lamb cutlets and he went off to sleep watching the television in bed. He woke at 7.30am and got Walter-Lax to cook him another meal, steak this time, before drifting off again.

Unbeknown to Walter-Lax, Moon had taken thirty-two Heminevrin tablets to get him off to sleep. The recommended daily dose was three. At 3.40pm that afternoon of 7 September when Moon still hadn't woken, Walter-Lax went to check on him in bed. Moon had died in his sleep at some point during the preceding eight hours. He was thirty-two. Freakishly, four years earlier, 'Mama' Cass Elliott had died in the exact same bedroom at 9 Curzon Place and also at thirty-two years old. When Nilsson had shared his concerns with Moon that the place was cursed, Moon had assured him that lightning would not strike twice.

'I would always say of Moon that I didn't see him making old bells, or growing old gracefully,' says Bill Curbishley. 'I discussed it several times with John. There was no self-discipline whatsoever with Moon. The problem was that he would just have to look at you with that artful smile of his and you would forgive him so many things.'

Curbishley called Daltrey first with the news. Daltrey then rang Townshend at his home studio and told him, 'He's done it.' Entwistle was at Quarwood giving an interview to a group of French journalists when Curbishley phoned; Alison took the call. She had to interrupt the interview to take her husband aside and tell him the awful news. 'He took it very hard, very badly,' she says. Entwistle tried to resume the interview, but when he was asked about the band's plans for the future, he broke down in tears, unable this once to keep himself buttoned up.

Moon was cremated at Golders Green Crematorium, north London, six days later. After the service, Entwistle brought Bill Wyman back with him to Corringway. Alison made them cheese and tomato sandwiches and they ate in front of a football match on the television that Wyman had wanted to watch. Entwistle had looked pale and drawn that day, but otherwise had re-established his stone-faced expression for the rest of the world. Only those who knew him best would ever be able to guess at the depths of his despair.

The mere fact that he had sat down to watch a football match was a strong indication. Normally, he could not abide the sport. It wasn't just that he had lost his co-conspirator and musical foil in the band. Entwistle regarded Moon as kin; someone who he could share with, protect, admonish, love in his own way and who just by being there had made him feel more secure, not so much an only child. Wayward and unstable Moon most certainly was, but Entwistle had connected with him. Fundamentally, he was weakened by – and never fully recovered from – the severing of that tie.

'Keith's loss *really* hit John,' considers Bobby Pridden. 'It was everyone's loss. In the band, Keith played a great big part in being the one who could defuse a situation. If there was an argument going on, he could put water on it with his antics and by doing something incredibly funny or stupid. John and Keith just clicked. They had a kind of telepathy between them, something you couldn't manufacture. You've either got it or you haven't, and they had it.'

'I saw vulnerability in John when Moon died,' Curbishley opines. 'There was something taken away from him that couldn't ever be put back.'

16

Hotel California

As an entity, The Who was hardly stopped by Moon's death. Directly after the funeral, Townshend met with Daltrey to discuss the idea of taking the band out on the road again and with a replacement drummer. Phil Collins of Genesis had quickly volunteered his services. But Townshend was friendly with Kenney Jones, without a band since The Faces had split three years earlier, and was set on trying him out for the gig. Townshend wrote in his autobiography that Entwistle was still too much in shock to attend this initial meeting, but neither would he have spoken out against the idea of The Who touring without Moon. 'He wanted to play,' notes Alison Entwistle. 'So, he had to get on with it, didn't he? And he always got on very well with Kenney.'

Towards the end of that year, sessions were convened at Ramport to try out Jones and with Entwistle now back in the fray. There must have been a ghost in the room over those few days in Battersea. The four of them – Townshend, Entwistle, Daltrey and Jones – were set up in the same space, and in the exact same arrangement, that just a few months earlier they had used to eke out *Who Are You*. Jon Astley was also once again engineering for them. Jones, though, was a very different drummer to Moon. Where Moon couldn't have cared less for the strictures of timing, Jones was tight, disciplined and kept right on the beat. Put another way, Townshend was seeking to substitute an explosive device with a ticking clock.

'I think we all felt it was a very odd situation,' insists Astley. 'But it was Pete's wish to have Kenney come in. You would very rarely get an idea from John of what he was thinking. He was just too enigmatic, but he did definitely miss Keith's playing, I think. He would say to me how Keith would have done this or that about one particular part or another.'

The official announcement that Jones had joined the band was made in late December 1978. They had also added a keyboard player to the line-up – a Texan, John 'Rabbit' Bundrick – who had previously worked with Bob Marley and Free. Whereas Bundrick was taken on as a hired hand, Townshend had lobbied for Jones to be made a full partner in the band. That move had instantly shown up the cracks in their new façade. Daltrey was a very vocal opponent of this handing over of preferred status to Jones, but Entwistle's casting vote swung the decision to Townshend. Almost at once, another fissure was opened up. Both Jones and Bundrick were prodigious drinkers, which made them natural allies to Entwistle and Townshend, while at the same time furthering the distance between them and the near-teetotal Daltrey.

For now, Entwistle could distract himself with other band business. He spent the lead up to that Christmas in Los Angeles and overseeing the Dolby mix of *The Kids Are Alright* soundtrack. Sharp, hard and loud-sounding, it made exciting what was an otherwise disjointed and oddly emotionless film; Moon's stereo-enhanced detonations serving as a much better, fonder tribute to him than Stein's footage of him fat and burned out at Shepperton. Following on from the film's première at Cannes the next May, the soundtrack album would go on to be a Top Ten, million-seller in the US.

'John told me that he liked the film a lot,' says Tony Klinger. 'So did Roger. Pete was a different beast. Sometime later, I got invited to a Who show in America. Pete saw me and gave me a bear-hug. An hour or two afterwards, at the after-show party, he walked straight past me like I didn't exist, as if I were a piece of shit. I have no idea what occurred between those two moments.'

As it happened, Entwistle had been no more straightforward with Klinger than Townshend. In his memoir notes, he devoted just five words to the film and these were: 'Directed by a guide dog'. In any event, during those last six weeks that he spent in Los Angeles tied up with *The Kids Are Alright*, he embarked upon an affair that was to have a much more dramatic and far-reaching impact on his life. After hours in the studio, he would invariably retire to the Rainbow Bar and Grill on Sunset Boulevard, a magnet for the city's rock-'n'-roll denizens and their attendant coteries of hangers-on. A pretty brunette working as a waitress at the Rainbow soon caught his eye.

Maxene Harlow was twenty-two and a native of Sacramento, California. Like countless others, she had moved to Los Angeles in the hope of getting an 'in' into the entertainment business. A talented seamstress, she had aspirations to become a clothes designer and stylist. For a spell, she had landed a job tailoring on a syndicated television variety show, *Sha Na Na*, which was hosted by a fifties-style rock-'n'-roll group of the same name. A fan of Sha Na Na's, Moon had several times guested onstage with them and, according to Harlow, once visited the set of the TV show when he was holed up in Malibu. At that time, Moon was also a regular at the Rainbow.

'When I started waitressing at the Rainbow, Keith and I became fast friends,' says Maxene. 'He would come in and just sit there; he was obviously homesick. Keith used to talk about John as if he was his big brother. So, when I later on met John at the Rainbow, I was a little intimidated by him, but at the same time fascinated. Everyone would be so attracted and drawn to John. Keith attracted the loons, whereas John was a magnet for all kinds of people.

'I liked listening to John talk, and watching how he presented himself. He asked me out, but I didn't want to be labelled as a home-wrecker. I knew that he was married. He persisted, though, and also he seemed to me very unhappy, so eventually I agreed to go on a date with him. After that, we were inseparable.'

Up until then, Entwistle had been able to keep his womanising almost wholly apart from the life that he had made for himself at home with Alison and Christopher. His serial flings were just that – passing fancies that came and went and to which he attached no great or lasting meaning. Unmoored by the loss of Moon, though, it was as if he needed someone else to fasten on to in his other world. Since that wasn't ever going to be Townshend, much less Daltrey, it would have to be someone from outside of the band's circle. And the newer and more exotic-seeming that person, the better.

Neither had he needed nor felt compelled to chase anyone before, but he did with Maxene. His pursuit of her was relentless, urgent even; it was as if the mere act of it might serve to restore a fundamental part of him, or else at the very least enable him to just go on being. To that end, when at last he had worn Maxene down, he didn't do then what he had done all of those other times before, which was to let go and move on. Now, he felt secured once more. He found himself entranced, captivated by Maxene, but also feeling like he was being torn in two. This much he did confide to Townshend when he got back to London, and who counselled him not to confess a thing to Alison. Entwistle didn't heed Townshend's advice.

'He came back home and I knew something was wrong,' says Alison. 'We were in bed and I asked him, "What's the matter, darling?" He told me that he had met someone else and that he was in love with both of us. That's how I found out. He asked me not to talk about it with anybody else. He said that he was going to make up his mind and asked if I could wait for him until he did.

'Stupid fool, I said yes. I just didn't know which way to play it. If I had been miserable and horrible all the time, he would have gone sooner or later. Whereas if I had got him to see the error of his ways . . . It was the hardest thing I've ever done. I mean, I had always been able to pretend that kind of thing wasn't happening, because I would know that he was coming back.'

■ ■ ■

After that, Entwistle was able to find reasons to keep going back to Los Angeles. No sooner was *The Kids Are Alright* soundtrack finished than he took on the role of Musical Director of the one for *Quadrophenia*, and set up a base in the city from which to do the remixing work. During the protracted spells that he was in town, Maxene would sublet her apartment to friends and move in with him to his hotel suite. At such times, Entwistle to all intents and purposes lived an entirely separate life and he would go on doing so for the next eighteen months.

'John's cousin, Ian, came to see me one afternoon when he was away and I did confide in him,' says Alison. 'He asked me when I was going to get a divorce and I told him that John didn't want one. Ian got so angry. He said, "Oh, he wants his bloody cake and to eat it, too, does he?"'

'I liked Alison and John hurt her,' affirms Gillingham. 'As far as I was concerned, she was family. He *did* want to have his cake and eat it. And, yes, I was mad about it. I was aware that he used to go to this Rainbow Bar to pick up girls. My old man used to say, "That's where he meets his hookers." It was just part of the life that he led, wasn't it?'

As he was winding down his stint on *Quadrophenia*, Entwistle next decided to embark upon a new solo album out in LA. He had a stockpile of song ideas and invited Joe Walsh to help him knock them into shape. Walsh accepted and also suggested a drummer, Joe Vitale, who had been playing in The Eagles' road band and with whom he had co-written the song 'Pretty Maids All in a Row' for their *Hotel California* album. Entwistle booked the three of them a studio in Hollywood – Crystal Sound – and they began to work out of there early in 1979. According to Walsh, the sessions were relaxed and unstructured, the musicians bouncing ideas off each other and largely improvising their parts.

'It was almost jazz-like thinking and John loved to play in that kind of free-form way,' Walsh says. 'That was when he lit up. If you really paid a lot of attention to what he was doing, you would have trouble playing yourself because it would be so easy to get lost. In other words, if John, Joe and I were all playing free-form for four bars, I had to concentrate on being right there on beat one at the start of the next four bars and stay with the drummer. John was *always* there but, if you listened to what he was playing, you couldn't be sure where beat one was. He was just brilliant. But you had to let him go off and play in his own little John world – and make sure your own shit was in order.'

'Those were crazy sessions, completely nuts,' adds Vitale. 'And we were as serious about the music as we were crazy about the fun times. We spent quite a while recording in LA. Each night, at the end of a session, John would always want to go over to the Rainbow. He had the use of a special room there and that was his favourite hang.'

One night, Walsh brought his girlfriend along with him to the Rainbow. She was also a striking brunette, but a southern girl from Memphis, Tennessee. Lisa Pritchett-Johnson was her name and when she had got a few drinks, and whatever else, inside her there was no mistaking that she was a firecracker. Entwistle liked her right away and, soon enough, whenever he was out on the town with Maxene, Lisa would also be a regular face on their scene, even after Walsh had to go back off to The Eagles.

With Walsh's departure, the sessions on Entwistle's album ground to a halt. There was yet more upheaval when he returned to London. One morning, Mick Bratby stormed into the kitchen at Corringway and quit on the spot. Of all things, Bratby was furious that he had been sent a late birthday card. In Entwistle's absence, Alison had fallen ill and had forgotten to mail him one on time. 'It was bloody stupid,' reasons Bratby. 'If I could change just one thing, I wouldn't have fallen out with John over that card.' Unspoken, but perhaps as likely, they were all of them poisoned by the heavy, toxic atmosphere that prevailed at Corringway those days.

In Bratby's place, Entwistle hired a character named Kenny Wyatt to be his driver and gopher. Wyatt and his wife Connie were the erstwhile proprietors of the Skin Room, the Ealing tailors that Entwistle had once patronised. If anything, Wyatt was even more taciturn than his new boss. Hardly a word would pass between the two of them as Wyatt chauffeured Entwistle about. For a time, the Wyatts' teenage daughter, Karen, was also tasked with child-minding Christopher. That arrangement came to an abrupt end when Alison discovered that the babysitter had been tutoring her six-year-old son to smoke cigarettes.

Once more, The Who was to be Entwistle's salvation and his best means of escape. Indeed, at that same time and even in spite of Moon's passing, the outlook for the band had never before seemed so robust. In Britain, something of a Mod revival was under way, spearheaded by a young three-piece band from Woking – The Jam – whose third album, *All Mod Cons*, had gone Top Ten at the end of the previous year. Their fourth, *Setting Sons*, would do even better and its November 1979 release coincided with that of the *Quadrophenia* film, which also went on to do strong business at the British box office.

That spring, The Who's reputation for pioneering and danger was reinforced by the release of their other film, *The Kids Are Alright*. To back it up, the band announced a thirty-five date tour of the UK, Europe and North America, their first with Jones. Tickets for the entire tour sold briskly and, in advance of it, Curbishley took the opportunity to renegotiate the band's deal with Warner Brothers in America on more favourable terms; these included a multi-million dollar advance. The one bump in the road was that Daltrey once again objected to Jones getting an equal share of this bounty. Jones, Daltrey insisted, hadn't contributed to the building up of The Who's name. Again, too, he was outvoted by Townshend and Entwistle, and Jones got his cut.

'That spoke volumes to me, especially when it came to John,' Jones later wrote. 'He was always getting himself into money problems, and yet was still happy for a four-way split.'[29]

Not eight months after Moon's death, The Who made their live comeback at the Rainbow Theatre in north London on 2 May. Backstage, various Sex Pistols mingled with Mick Jagger and Phil Collins. Onstage, with Entwistle done up like a matador, Daltrey's hair shorn for his next film role as redeemed convict John McVicar, and Townshend all kinetic energy and angled limbs, The Who were the same, but then again different. They

---

[29] Taken from *Let the Good Times Roll: My Life in the Small Faces, the Faces and the Who* by Kenney Jones, Blink (2018)

blasted off their twenty-one song set with 'Substitute', 'I Can't Explain' and 'Baba O'Riley', and carried on at full throttle right through to a solitary encore, 'The Real Me'. The band were as unrelenting as ever, with Jones's metronomic playing making them tighter, more focused, but also not so unpredictable and threatening. Entwistle also now had more space to play around in but, then again, nothing to spark off.

This new-model Who was reliable, dependable and proved to be a huge draw. Everywhere, they played to packed houses: at London's Wembley Stadium that Bank Holiday August; over five nights at Madison Square Garden the following month, slick and powerful shows that banished the memory of their last, dispirited performances with Moon at the hallowed venue; and on up America's eastern seaboard. For Entwistle, these were better times; he had his freedom out there on the road. In America, he also had Maxene with him, whom he took along as his assistant on the tour.

'I wasn't working for The Who, but for John – I dressed him,' she says. 'In that period of time, John hung out an awful lot with Kenney. John didn't like all the politicking that went on but, then again, he and Pete and Roger were very competitive. They all wanted to be the star. They all wanted to be front and centre. They wanted to be able to walk into a room and be the focus of everybody's attention.

'I used to say, "If you want to break up a party, invite The Who," because socially they didn't get along. With the dynamics and personality clashes, you would never know what was going to happen between the three of them. Roger was always sweet and wonderful to me. Pete scared the bejesus out of me. The first thing he said to me I thought was insulting; he called me a "lovely old toe-rag". I went running off to the bathroom and burst into tears.'

Whatever good vibes there were on the tour, they were blown away on the night of 3 December 1979, at the Riverfront Coliseum, Cincinnati. It was another sold-out gig and fans had begun gathering outside the venue from early afternoon that day, the better to secure a good seat from their general admission tickets. By the time The Who finished their sound-check at 7.00pm, the scene outside had degenerated into a mêlée. At 7.05pm, the crowd was let into the venue. However, just four of the Coliseum's sixteen outer entrance doors were opened up. As thousands of people tried to shove their way inside, they were forced into a bottleneck that squeezed up against the ticket turnstiles located just inside the entrance hall. At eighteen inches, these turnstiles were simply not wide enough for such a throng to pass through quickly and, within minutes, a deadly crush had built up.

Police found the first body at 7.54pm, twenty-six minutes before The Who took to the stage. Alerted by a fire marshal, Bill Curbishley went and saw for himself the carnage that was unfolding. By the time The Who came offstage, eleven people had lost their lives in the crush. Curbishley took the band off into a tuning room to tell them the awful news.

Richard Barnes was with them that night and accompanied them back to their hotel. 'John phoned round and got everybody into his room,' he later wrote. 'Some of the people there were still in shock and just sat silently; others had talked it all out earlier and were feeling empty. The TV was on and it was from that that we learned what really had happened. John had realised that nobody could just go to their room and sleep, and the gathering in his room worked in calming everybody down.'[30]

---

[30] Taken from *The Who: Maximum R&B* by Richard Barnes, Plexus (2000)

The band had flowers and messages of condolence sent to the funerals of each of the victims of the Cincinnati tragedy. Then, they rolled on – beginning on 26 March in Essen, Germany, and rounding up at the CNE Stadium, Toronto, on 16 July, they undertook another forty-two-date tour in 1980. On this run, Daltrey took against Jones's playing, believing that its very stability sapped The Who of energy. At the end of the tour, he orchestrated a group meeting at Curbishley's house in Essex at which he gave the others an ultimatum: it was either him or Jones. In response, Daltrey described, 'Kenney said nothing . . . Bill said nothing . . . John was quiet, too. But Pete didn't hesitate. Not for a second. He said it was no choice at all. Kenney would stay . . . Kenney stayed, and though I came to regret it, so did I.'[31]

For his part, Entwistle had finally to decide the outcome of his own ultimatum to himself – whether or not to save his marriage. That summer, he took Alison and Christopher off to Miami for a family holiday. By then, he had as good as made his mind up and it was a difficult, unhappy time for both husband and wife. 'I didn't know it, but they had already talked about splitting up,' says Christopher, then nine years old. 'I would go into their room and find that the beds were apart. They told me it was the maid's doing, but obviously that wasn't the case. My mother had wanted us all to have a holiday together before we went our separate ways.'

Upon their return to England, Entwistle moved out of Corringway. Since he couldn't bring himself to break the news to his father, he persuaded Alison to ring Bert on his behalf and it was she who told him that they had split up. Entwistle took on an apartment on the King's Road that Townshend had been

---

[31] Taken from *Thanks a Lot, Mr Kibblewhite: My Life* by Roger Daltrey, Blink (2018)

renting. Made up of two connected flats, it was an airy, spacious place above a Kickers store. On 31 October, Hallowe'en, Maxene arrived from Los Angeles and moved into the flat. 'When I first got over to England, he was my knight in shining armour,' she says. 'I figured I had kissed a frog. I was just twenty-two, naïve and gullible, but I was ready for an adventure. John honoured me and prided himself in me. He showed me off. I was his arm candy and he opened up to me a whole world that otherwise I could never have imagined or been able to gain access to. I'll never forget the first time he took me to Quarwood. That was hysterical. I got in the limo and he told me we were going to see his other house in the country. I thought it would be a quaint little cottage. Then we pulled up in front of this mansion. My mouth dropped open.

'In London, we played tourist. We went to the Tower of London. We used to go to Harrods all the time. John was such an avid shopper that he had been given a Harrods gold card. He got me a gold card of my own, too, which I still have. John was fun to be around. Those early days of our relationship were when I saw him at his best.'

Alison and Christopher remained at Corringway. For the first year that they were separated, Alison forbade John to introduce their son to Maxene. Every Thursday, Kenny Wyatt would pick up Christopher from school and drive him over to the King's Road to see his father. On those evenings, Maxene would be sure to be out shopping or sightseeing.

'Dad had to do something to entertain me, so together we went and saw just about every single movie that was on at the cinema during that year – everything from *Raiders of the Lost Ark* and *Chariots of Fire* to *The Fox and the Hound*,' recounts Christopher. 'We got to know each other quite well that way. In fact, that was when I properly did get to know my dad. He had been away or out for most of the time that he was living at home.

'After that first year, Mother let me go and stay with him every other weekend in London or at Quarwood. The first time that I met Max was in Dad's bar at Quarwood. He had got table-top video games in there and I was playing Asteroids. Max walked in, sat down opposite me and asked me if I wanted a game. She proceeded to be the only person that ever beat me on Asteroids. In fact, she beat the shit out of me. We're talking about a nine-year-old boy here and that basically enamoured me to her. And she was great with me. She used to take me shopping for clothes. She was brash, would take the piss out of me, and we got on really well throughout my childhood and teens.'

The October after they had separated, Alison started divorce proceedings and these would go on for the next three years. Their marriage was formally ended on 7 December 1984. By then, Alison had gone back to work as a secretary and administrator at Hammersmith Hospital. She had also entered into a new relationship. One afternoon in 1982, three years after she had last seen him, Mick Bratby turned up on the doorstep at Corringway and never left.

'Splitting up with Alison took a lot from John,' insists Bill Curbishley. 'And he was wounded by Alison ending up with Mick, because he had thought that there was something going on between them before that. Other than Moon's death, that was the only time I ever saw him be really exposed.'

'No, he didn't like it,' admits Alison. 'Once again, he wanted to have his cake and eat it, too. He wouldn't talk about it for years and would get really upset. There was one time that he stormed in and started banging on about me having bought Mick a private plane. Someone had told him that I had. Actually, Mick was taking flying lessons. I told him to go and boil his head.'

17

Hard Times

As Entwistle was going through the last, messy throes of his marriage, he also got taken up with the making of a new Who album. The sessions, which went ahead at intervals in London, spanned the midsummer of 1980 through to the end of that year. The band took on a new producer, Bill Szmczky, an American who had worked extensively with both The Eagles and Joe Walsh. However, there was to be nothing else that was fresh about *Face Dances*.

Numbed by booze and drugs, Townshend was almost utterly devoid of inspiration. He submitted only a single song that cut the mustard – 'You Better You Bet' – which ended up firing the album off. His six other songs were variously limp, directionless or else plain awful. Entwistle served up a pair of snub-nosed rockers – 'The Quiet One' and 'You'. Neither of these was any great shakes as a song, but the simple fact that each had a bit of get up and go was enough to make them high points of the whole album.

Elsewhere, Entwistle played furiously on the record, as if by getting busy he could rally the rest of the band and inject life into

237

Townshend's worst songs. What actually happened, though, was that Szmczky suffocated his bass under a thick, turgid layer of brass and synthesisers which left the whole album sounding soulless and vacuum-packed. Speaking the following year to *Rolling Stone* about the album, Entwistle lamented, 'We never got inspired by what we were recording, but we figured it must be on the tape – and it wasn't. Before we recorded, everybody was going around saying that we had to do a real up-tempo, bombastic Who album. So I wrote two up-tempo songs and they ended up being the only songs where Pete laid down some really heavy guitar . . . It's like being in two different bands. Onstage, we're almost heavy metal, and on record it's so toned down. That's a real failing.'

Normally so tight-lipped, this was strong stuff coming from Entwistle and indicative of the depth and intensity of his frustrations at the state of the band. The critical consensus on *Face Dances* was much the same when it came out in March the following year. *Rolling Stone*'s review of the album posited that it was 'winsomely slight at best, bafflingly circumlocutory at worst . . . Entwistle's numbers work because they ignore the rest of the record's content.' Nevertheless, The Who appeared bullet-proofed and *Face Dances* charted high in the UK and North America, rising to Number One in Canada and going platinum in the US. In advance of its release, they undertook an extensive, twenty-six-date tour of the UK that opened at the Granby Halls in Leicester on 25 January, carried on through to the Arts Centre, Poole, on 16 March, and with a three-night stand at Wembley Arena sandwiched in between.

Up on stage, they were laid bare and found wanting. Townshend seemed to be in a daze, his playing dulled by the chemical fog he was under. Daltrey gamely tried to front it out, but Entwistle and Jones, who each maintained a debilitating nocturnal schedule all tour, were also far from their best. All this was in spite of their being prescribed pep-ups. 'In London, the doctor that the guys went to was the same one the Queen saw,' claims Maxene, who was again at Entwistle's side on the tour. 'They got these pills off him that they used to call Smarties. It was a little, round, orange pill that looked like candy. They would take these, be able to drink as much as they wanted and wouldn't have a hangover. It was scary what it allowed them to do. They had mounds of energy, but crazy things would happen whenever they took those pills.'

They were supposed to go on to do dates in Europe, but Townshend had these cancelled. Even in his shambolic state, he knew better than to flog a dead horse. Worse news was to follow. Exactly three weeks after the Poole date, Kit Lambert died in desperate circumstances. In his last years, Lambert had spiralled down into alcoholism and heroin addiction. That night, he had gone to a nightclub, El Sombrero, near to his home in Kensington, and where, according to witnesses, he was beaten up and pushed down a flight of stairs by a drug dealer over an unpaid debt. Lambert sustained severe head injuries in the fall and died sometime later of a cerebral haemorrhage. He was just forty-five years old and with his death a pall, black and inescapable, also seemed to have settled over The Who.

■ ■ ■

As ever for Entwistle, there was the solace of being able to spend his money. That summer, he shelled out for a new home for Maxene and him in Roehampton, an upmarket enclave of south-west London that backed on to Richmond Park. The large, double-fronted house was sited at one end of Priory Lane leading directly on to an entrance to the park. On the same road, there was a private hospital – The Priory – that, among other things, specialised in the treatment of addictions.

Once more, Entwistle had the new house remodelled according to his own particular tastes. To one side of the long, wood-panelled hallway, he had installed his now customary bar. To the other was a big living room that he furnished with expansive leather sofas and a huge TV set. The ranging kitchen he had tiled in orange and fitted with a red Aga oven. Next to it there was a breakfast room. Upstairs, there were three bedrooms. One, he turned into a recording studio. The guest bedroom he had decorated with silver walls and carpets. The en suite bathroom came with a built-in sauna; this he christened the Hollywood Suite. The master bedroom had an adjoining dressing room and also a massive en suite. A spiral staircase led up to the attic, which he had converted to encompass a games room, spare bedroom and a second dressing room for Maxene.

In London, their social lives were a whirl of parties and premières. At weekends, they would be driven up to Quarwood where they would do yet more entertaining. So much was Maxene the life and soul of these events that, among their wide circle of acquaintances, she came to be known as 'Mad Max'. She also made herself Entwistle's guard and protector. According to Christopher, 'You didn't get hangers-on with Max. Everyone that partied with them she would have vetted effectively and that was better for Dad. You got a lot of people hanging around, but they wouldn't have huge amounts to gain from knowing Dad, apart from being his friend. Also, they would be people that gave as well as took.'

Maxene says, 'What happened was that John allowed me to take care of everything and most especially him. I was the one in charge of getting him here and there, doing this and that. I kind of ran things for him because he was like a big kid. His mom was doing the cooking for him at Quarwood when I arrived and he hated that. She would never fail to overcook the vegetables and meat. I had to learn to cook all of these English dishes for him, like roast beef and Yorkshire puddings. John taught me to do bubble and squeak, which he loved. He was a good cook, too.

'John was overweight when I first met him. He wasn't obese, just on the chunky side and he loathed that, because he had no energy. I got him down to a good weight. My weight also fluctuated. I'm tall and big-boned, and I started packing on the pounds when I first got to England without even realising it. The ice-cream's better, the butter's better, we had bottled milk delivered to the house. I got up to almost two hundred pounds and John didn't like that. He preferred me to be skinny.'

Entwistle also treated himself to a new car, a 1980 Rolls-Royce Silver Shadow Shooting Brake, which he had converted to an estate to accommodate their dog pack. The arrangement so well suited their latest addition, a grey Irish Wolfhound, that Entwistle named the giant, bounding beast Fitz Perfectly. He had one more embellishment still to make to the classic car. He took it along to a body-shop and instructed that it be spray-painted the exact same shade of green as a Harrods shopping bag.

During this same period, Bill Curbishley was producing the *McVicar* movie with Daltrey in the title role. Through this venture, he got to know Walter Probin, a fellow con of John McVicar's and who had engineered his notorious escape from Durham Prison in 1968. It so happened that Probin's brother ran a delivery company that did sub-contractual work for Harrods. Probin approached Curbishley on set one day to extend an offer to Entwistle.

'Wally had got to know that John shopped at Harrods all the time,' explains Curbishley. 'He said to me that if John was to give his brother the catalogue numbers of all of the stuff that he wanted, he would be able to get him a sixty per cent discount on every item purchased. So, I dutifully passed this on to John.

'Sometime afterwards, Wally came back to me. He asked me, "Have we upset John?" It turned out that John had got in touch with Wally's brother and, through him, started to buy things such as four-poster beds for Quarwood. Then, without so much as a word, he had stopped and gone back to getting everything direct from Harrods. I phoned up John and asked him if there was a problem. He told me, "I don't like to have their fucking old van coming up my drive at Quarwood." What he meant was that he wanted to be seen to be having a Harrods van making the deliveries to Quarwood. With the amount of money he had been saving, he could have got "Harrods" painted on the side of their van. He could have even bought them a new van, but that was John.'

That May, Entwistle arranged to have Joe Walsh and Joe Vitale fly over to London to resume work on his interrupted solo album at Ramport with Cy Langston engineering the sessions. On weekdays, Entwistle would have Kenny Wyatt pick up Walsh and Vitale from their hotel in the Rolls-Royce and ferry them to meet him at a Wimpy's fast-food restaurant nearby to the studio. 'That was John's favourite place,' says Vitale. 'Every day for a month, we would load up on a bunch of hamburgers and go over to Ramport. I mean, Wimpy burgers were good, but I kind of got tired of them. After that lunch, we would spend hours and hours in the studio and then go hang out in the pub.'

At weekends, Wyatt would chauffeur the three of them and Maxene down to the Cotswolds for rest and relaxation. Joe Walsh sets the scene for those easy, lazy days at Quarwood: 'John wasn't an early riser, but at some point in the course of a day he would show up and always be impeccably dressed and groomed. He had such a fantastically positive attitude, too. I would get such a good feeling from having him come into the room and say, "Good morning!" And even if it was three in the afternoon, it always was, "Good morning!"

'Those were favourite times for me, hanging at Quarwood, playing billiards. Never pool, always billiards. Do you know that John locked every door in that house? He would go around the place with a big pocketful of keys. He would unlock a door, shepherd you into the next room, and then close the door behind you and lock it again. Just to see his guitar collection upstairs, you would have to pass through three different rooms with three doors for him to unlock and lock once more. But, man, that collection was profound. He had Fender guitars from pretty close to every year and in every colour that they came out. A lot of them were still in their cases with the receipts, virtually brand new.'

Walsh was at the same time finishing up producing an album for Ringo Starr that had also had a long gestation, called *Old Wave*. No sooner had the three of them wrapped up at Ramport than they went off to cut a track for that record at Starr's home studio in Ascot. A busy, rolling two-minute instrumental, 'Everybody's In a Hurry but Me' came out of an extended jam session that also featured Eric Clapton. 'John was just *steaming* on bass,' Starr later told *Beatlefan* magazine of the recording. 'I remember saying to Joe, "God, he's busy." And Joe said, "He's even like that on a ballad."'

The album completed over those four weeks at Ramport, *Too Late the Hero* ended up having more life and purpose to it than *Face Dances* and, for the most part, better songs, too. However, as with The Who's record, the production, by Entwistle and Langston, has aged badly. All too symptomatic of the period, it turned out to be an unappealing gloop of synthesisers and effects, and which smothered Walsh's contributions most of all. The abandon of the LA sessions was also nowhere in evidence, the playing uniformly excellent but regimented.

There were a few high points: a stately ballad, 'Lovebird', and a love-letter to Los Angeles, 'I'm Coming Back', upon which Walsh's liquid guitar did manage to make it up to the surface.

And especially, the keening, seven-minute title track. Entwistle sings this, the last song on the record, in a desolate, haunted voice. Whether by Moon's loss, the breakdown of his marriage, the travails of The Who, or all of these things at once, is unspecified, but altogether it is the most revealing, and human, moment that he ever allowed himself on record. Events to follow would add weight and new meaning to the song's stark opening lines: 'Too late the hero; it all comes to zero. And I wish I could stop and start again.'

In the US, *Too Late the Hero* went on to be his highest charting solo album when it was released that November, although it didn't rise higher than 71 on the *Billboard* chart. For the album's front cover, Entwistle once again presented himself in his familiar guise of being strong, upright and unwavering. In Gered Mankowitz's main portrait photograph, he is shown standing tall and indomitable, resplendent in a red, three-piece suit with his Alembic bass. Superimposed on to this are images of Entwistle done up as a roundhead dragoon, a Napoleonic era cavalryman and a medieval knight in full armour.

'The shoot was done in my studio in Hampstead,' says Mankowitz, who had made his name in the sixties photographing The Rolling Stones and Marianne Faithfull. 'The uniforms and weapons all came from John. I think he rather enjoyed posing in the uniforms and waving the swords around. In fact, I don't think I've ever photographed anybody else who had his passion for dressing up as someone else.

'He was very good to work with in as much as he wasn't remotely a prima donna. He was very professional, but also not particularly friendly or endearing. He wasn't enormously communicative. There was an eccentricity to him, something strange about him. Yes, definitely, he was quite odd.'

■ ■ ■

The following summer, The Who set about preparing for another album. Glyn Johns had returned as their producer, but they began the sessions a man down. Having burned through his marriage and hit bottom, Townshend took himself off to a rehab clinic in California. In his absence, Johns suggested that the others start work with Andy Fairweather Low filling in on guitar. With 'Rabbit' Bundrick out of favour, the producer also paired them with another American keyboard player whom he had under contract, Tim Gorman. This five-piece spent three weeks kicking ideas around at Johns' home studio in Surrey, before Townshend flew back to England and work started in earnest.

Not that the *It's Hard* album ever got close to re-galvanising the band. As well as *Face Dances*, Townshend had made two solo records, 1980's *Empty Glasses* and *All the Best Cowboys Have Chinese Eyes*, released that same summer of 1982, and these had gobbled up whatever half-decent songs he had stored up. *It's Hard* found him creatively bankrupt. As on *Face Dances*, Entwistle got three songs on the album, each an identikit driving rocker. Two of these – 'Dangerous' and 'One At a Time' – were makeweights, but the other – 'It's Your Turn' – was the pick of the album. It spoke volumes of *It's Hard* that what stood out was a song that Entwistle might have tossed off in his sleep.

It did give The Who another gold record in the US when it was released that September, but the terms of success had now changed. After the launch of MTV the previous August, artists were at a stroke being marketed as image-driven brands and a proper hit album had started to be defined as nothing less than a multi-platinum blockbuster. In 1982, the embodiments of this were a pop group from Birmingham, England – Duran Duran – whose second album, *Rio*, went double-platinum in the US; a musical polymath from Minneapolis – Prince – who doubled that tally with his fifth, *1999*; and the twenty-five-year-old

Michael Jackson, who that November put out *Thriller* and rewrote the whole rulebook. Next to these albums, *It's Hard* barely even registered.

Even still, The Who's appeal to concert-goers was undiminished. A forty-date North American tour was lined up to start on 22 September in Landover, Maryland, which would see them play to 60,000 people at the Astrodome in Houston, 90,000 at Philadelphia's JFK Stadium, and to 140,000 over two nights at New York City's Shea Stadium. Travelling aboard their own 100-seat Boeing 707 airliner and backed by a 90-strong crew, The Who were predicted to gross $15 million in ticket sales alone. The tour was also being sponsored by a beer company, Schlitz, which netted them another seven-figure windfall.

Upon the announcement of the dates, Daltrey dropped the bombshell that it was to be The Who's farewell tour. Wearied of persuading Townshend out on to the road, Daltrey could also now no longer countenance being in the band with Jones. 'That was a mistake that Roger made,' insists Glyn Johns. 'Kenney is one of the best rock-'n'-roll drummers there is; and I know that from having worked with him from when he was fifteen years old with The Small Faces. He was an excellent choice for The Who, so long as nobody expected him to be Keith Moon. Roger never acclimatised himself to that.'

The tour proved an unqualified success at the box office and the band's performances throughout were slick and professional, a marked improvement on their last time out. Yet for all that, it passed in an awkward, dislocated and end-of-days atmosphere. Daltrey kept up his sniping at Jones. The drummer, meanwhile, like Townshend, had quit drinking for the tour, so that they were not so much a band any more as four independent fiefdoms. With his bearings temporarily righted, Entwistle alone among them carried on as if he were resolved not to go out quietly. Prior to the tour, Maxene had convinced him to stop dyeing his hair and he had let it go grey. The new look suited him, made him appear dignified, but he wasn't about to start acting his age.

'John was like a bloody oasis on that tour,' says Richard Barnes. 'You would make your way up to his room and always there would be a party going on. That was John's lifestyle: loads of booze, lots of coke, chain-smoking, no exercise whatsoever, a great big steak at three in the morning, and then there were some of the dodgy women that he would go off with.'

The curtain was brought down with two shows at the Maple Leaf Gardens arena in Toronto on 16 and 17 December 1982. The original plan had been for The Who to continue to make records together, but then, early in the New Year, Townshend nixed that idea and officially broke the band up. Ramport and Shepperton were sold off. To Entwistle, Townshend's decision was a personal affront. Initially, he was despairing, but soon enough this turned to a seething, burning resentment.

'He just couldn't understand why it was over and he got very angry about it,' says Maxene. 'But then, I think also he had it in the back of his mind that it may not be true that The Who was finished.'

'John was upset because he would have toured and toured,' adds Curbishley. 'That was his life. You have to understand that when you choose this as a profession, you're making lots of sacrifices. You find with a lot of musicians that they have very few, if any childhood friends left, because they went off in a different direction. They have acquaintances, but not what you would call a mucker. That was certainly true of John, and also I think of Pete and Roger. It makes them even more reliant on their fellow musicians. So, when it all stops, there's a big vacuum in their lives to fill. And if you're not careful, that's going to end up damaging you.'

Part III
Too Late the Hero

It's Christmas Eve 1949 – at 81a Southfield Road, five-year-old John Entwistle is about to go to bed. More than forty years later, in notes for his memoirs handwritten out in black biro, he references this as the first Christmas that he can remember. He begins:

> My mother told me Father Christmas would be arriving via the kitchen chimney and would fill my pillowcase during the night.
>
> I was scared. I had spent so many sleepless nights with catarrh noises filling my head and waiting for Great Grandmother to come crashing through the curtains. I didn't want some old geezer in a red suit creeping into my room while I was asleep. I sat up in bed waiting for him with my half-size cricket bat clutched in my hands. I fell asleep just before my grandfather delivered my toys.
>
> I was up and playing with the toys before anyone else that Christmas morning. Lots of relations and friends were coming over after dinner. My Grandmother's sisters, Flo and Edie, with their husbands, Bert and Alf; cousin Joan and her husband Johnny; and Jock and Florence Leslie from downstairs. When dinner was over, Gordon and Grandad fell asleep in their chairs. They had been to the pub before we sat down to eat. You could always tell when Jock and Florrie were on their way up our front stairs. Florrie's bad feet

caused her to moan, 'Ooooh . . .' all the way up, and Jock would add the occasional, 'Shut up, you silly cow.'

Flo and Bert were next to arrive, my favourite aunt and uncle. They were not exactly an attractive couple, what with my Flo's buck teeth, but they had hearts of gold and, being childless, they spent a lot of time and money on their nieces and nephews. Both of them also chain-smoked and had the ability to walk around with two inches of ash on the ends of their cigarettes. No matter what they were doing, the ash never, ever fell off. I had bought Uncle Bert fifty Player's Weights non-filter cigarettes for Christmas and he had smoked them all before dinner.

Everyone congregated in our sacred front room. The party went through several stages. First, chestnuts were cooked on the open fire. Then, more drinks. Next, there were a few hands of cards – twenty-ones, which was a primitive form of blackjack. After that, more drinks. Jock and Florrie were first to leave after a hiccupping version of 'I Belong to Glasgow.' Florrie's 'Oooohs' fading as they staggered arm in arm down the stairs. It was time then for me to do my usual party piece. I performed my arm-gesticulating, down-on-my-knees version of Al Jolson's 'Sonny Boy' with the fireplace as my stage. This was followed by my leading the whole ensemble in a rousing version of 'Down on the Swanee.'

A couple of hours later, I was told it was time for me to go to bed. I poured myself a glass of water from the kitchen and shuffled past the stairs towards my room. At the bottom of the stairs, face down and arms still around each other, were Jock and Florrie. They had never quite made it out of the door. They were still there the next morning.

18

The Rock

Of each of The Who band members, for Entwistle most of all it was as though time had stopped dead. For more than twenty years, he had run his life, measured the entire course of it, around the band. Through The Who – their tours, their recording sessions, their petty bickering and raging arguments, their giddy highs and crushing lows – he had marked out the passage of his days, weeks, months and years. He saw himself, and was seen by others, at his most well defined and at his best through the prism of the band. The Who had allowed him to fix his character, gain his reputation, and to realise his greatest ambitions, wildest fantasies, and things that he hadn't even dared to dream. The Who had made him, and now The Who was gone. Such was the vast, unfathomable scale of the void that opened up to him that year of 1983.

Two years went by. Two years of slow days and long nights. Mostly, he split them between Priory Lane and Quarwood. Kenny Wyatt was retained to do the driving. In due course, he had acquired more cars for Wyatt to drive – a Bentley and a second Rolls-Royce, gold this time, and with a personalised number plate that read FAL 1C. The summer of 1983, he took Maxene and

Christopher out to visit Bill Curbishley at his place in Spain for two weeks' holiday. With Townshend and Daltrey, he had only minimal, tenuous contact, and about business matters, nothing personal. He went along to sports days at Christopher's west London prep school, Colet Court. Those afternoons in summer, Christopher would never fail to spot his father up on the grass bank that encircled the games field. He would be dressed up in his finery, suit and waistcoat, sitting on a blanket with a picnic hamper from Harrods.

At Quarwood, he would shop for antiques in Stow, go off shooting, or else walk the dogs around the grounds. Over time, Fitz Perfectly was joined by other giant beasts, Irish Wolfhounds and Rottweilers. He had also almost filled the place now with his many collections. Armies of toy soldiers crammed glass-fronted cabinets, bone-china animals adorned shelves and tables. In a cage in the kitchen was Doris, a female tarantula gifted to him by Joe Walsh. If he had Christopher for the weekend, he would rent a pile of movies from the local video store and they would binge watch them on a Saturday night and Sunday afternoon. 'At home, he was Joe Normal,' says Christopher. 'The living room at Quarwood had a massive television and loads of comfy sofas. Then there was the bar, which was the evening playground where everybody would sit around and be jolly.

'He used to call me Splonk. He was a very affectionate man. I did a lot of hugging with my dad and he always gave me a kiss on the lips goodnight. That went on right up until I was thirty. To be honest, I worshipped him. We used to have a lot of chats about life in general. He told me, "If someone tries to start a fight with you, put them down as fast and nastily as you possibly can." As I got older, I would obviously also talk to him about girls and he would tell me about some of his experiences. That was an eye-opener.'

Quarwood was where Entwistle and Maxene threw the greatest of their parties. One year, they put on a fancy dress ball for Hallowe'en. Entwistle went as a Southern gentleman from the American Civil War, Maxene as a murdered bride, done up in a charity shop wedding dress, and with a bleeding bullet-hole using stage make-up on her forehead. They arranged to have a huge firework display out on the croquet lawn, but a downpour washed it out. At Christmas, they would host the actor John Hurt and his American wife Donna, who Maxene had first met and befriended at the Rainbow. Hungover on Boxing Day, the two couples would trek out to watch the horse races at nearby Cheltenham.

The Hurts would also be among the guests at their annual New Year's Eve bash where they might be joined by the likes of fellow actor Robert Powell, Steve Winwood, Kenney Jones, Midge Ure and their wives. Those nights unfolded within the confines of The Barracuda Inne where Entwistle would station himself behind the long bar, making up his own cocktails for his guests – one, a mixture of cherry brandy and crème de menthe, he called Traffic Lights; another, Link-Up, made with three shots of Stolichnaya vodka and three of Southern Comfort, something he claimed to have created to commemorate the joint American Apollo–Soviet Soyuz space mission of July 1975.

Royalties came in from The Who, but without the income from touring and record advances, financially these were leaner times. Entwistle, though, preferred not to see this as being a handicap to him maintaining the lifestyle to which he had grown accustomed. He had two recording studios put in at Quarwood – a smaller, private room on the top floor that he used for writing, a relatively modest affair, and a bigger facility on the ground floor that was as well equipped as any professional studio that he christened Hammerhead Studios. He arranged for Cy Langston to oversee the building and kitting out of the main studio and, once that work was complete, hired him to manage the place. After that, Langston was a larger-than-life fixture at Quarwood, along with his assorted girlfriends and wives, one of whom was a trapeze artist who went by her stage name of Dizzy Heights.

'Cy is a strange duck,' says Maxene. 'He was funny, but also he would get angry and jealous of me at times. He didn't like it that I took over from him with John, I guess. I never did understand the dynamic that went on between the two of them; it was pretty complicated. But I didn't want to drive a wedge between them, or make John choose either Cy or me.'

The presence of Gordon and Queenie only added to the tangled web of relationships at Quarwood. According to Maxene, Entwistle's loathing of his stepfather grew to be even more acute and sharp-edged. Increasingly, Queenie also began to interfere in all aspects of the running of the estate, which Entwistle bore with his usual stoicism. Indeed, a casual observer to life at Quarwood, and Priory Lane, would have found him to be content, relaxed and seemingly at peace. As always, one would need to have known him more intimately, and to have looked hard, to detect the empty, black hole inside him and that he was not able to begin filling up.

'When I married my second wife, we spent our honeymoon with John and Maxene at Quarwood,' says John Alcock. 'Already then, something about John started to bother me. On the surface, he was happy enough, but there was an undercurrent going on. He did go to extremes, which was why he had got Quarwood in the first place. John was a perpetual shopper, but he would buy stuff to cheer himself up, almost like the equivalent of an anti-depressant. He was like those housewives who go to the shops every day to buy a trinket to lift their mood. Except John's trinkets ended up costing him a fortune.'

THE OX

'I got bored as well with being chauffeured around by Kenny Wyatt and with having nothing to do,' says Maxene. 'Things got to be particularly awful at Quarwood, because I felt like Gordon and Queenie were spying on me. Queenie was a control freak, but John didn't do anything to stop her.

'In certain aspects, John seemed to me very insecure. He got to be very jealous if another guy so much as talked to me, or paid me the slightest attention. There was one time that he thought a friend of ours was flirting with me. Actually, we were having a normal, everyday conversation, but John came over and said to him, "Oh, I wouldn't do that if I were you, mate – it's that time of month for Max." My God, why would you say something like that? I started to have to mind my Ps and Qs around other people, because I feared that John would embarrass me and also himself.'

■ ■ ■

In the summer of 1985, there was a temporary reprieve from this aimless drift. Bob Geldof was rallying bands and artists to play his Live Aid concert at Wembley Stadium on 13 July and made entreaties to Townshend and Daltrey about reforming The Who for the show. Townshend was open to the idea, but Daltrey didn't want to play with Jones again and dug in his heels. Eventually, Geldof used the plight of starving children in Ethiopia to browbeat Daltrey into acquiescing. When Curbishley then approached Entwistle with the idea, he agreed to it without hesitation.

With 'Rabbit' Bundrick also returned to the line-up, The Who came back together on 11 July for two days of rehearsals. Jones recalled, 'We met up, ate a bacon sandwich, talked all day, then ran through two numbers and went home.'[32] That

[32] Taken from *Let the Good Times Roll: My Life in the Small Faces, the Faces and the Who* by Kenney Jones, Blink (2018)

Saturday afternoon, Kenny Wyatt drove Entwistle and Maxene to Wembley in the gold Rolls, a nip of brandy to hand. The Who took to the stage just before 8.00pm, coming on after Queen and David Bowie, and with the day's light just starting to fade. They were introduced by the actor Jack Nicholson and struck up 'My Generation'. Immediately, the sound feed for the live television transmission cut out. It remained dead all through the next song, 'Pinball Wizard', and was only corrected in time for their third and penultimate number, 'Love Reign O'er Me'.

They were unaware of this technical hitch, but even still, they seemed unsure of themselves and under-rehearsed. There was also something forced and joyless about their performance. Entwistle looked subdued, and dressed it, too, in a tan leather jacket and jeans. Townshend, pale, rail-thin and balding, dutifully windmill-armed his guitar and scissor-kicked, but like an actor now, playing a role. While Daltrey, bare-chested and stone-faced, seemed blank to, and disengaged from, everything and everyone around him, but most especially from Jones, who played just as ably as he always had, but not so as to lift even the closing song, 'Won't Get Fooled Again', from being above perfunctory.

Later on, Entwistle described The Who's Live Aid set as 'a complete disaster'. That night, he went off with Maxene to party at the old Speakeasy club, renamed now Bootleggers, and where they helped themselves to strawberries and champagne. 'John enjoyed the day,' insists Maxene. 'Truly, he did.' Certainly, Entwistle would have relished the attention and being back in the spotlight, but no sooner was Live Aid over than The Who receded once more to memory.

What the brief reunion did do was encourage Entwistle back to work. Immediately afterwards, he told Curbishley of his intention to put a new band together and make a record at

Quarwood. Curbishley hooked him up with a young English guitarist, Andy Barnett, and also a keyboard player, Andy Nye, whom he had signed up to his publishing company, Trinifold Music, and who had just come off a stint writing for Daltrey. Cozy Powell expressed an interest in being the drummer, but didn't come through. That role was filled for a short while by Barriemore Barlow of Jethro Tull, before Entwistle settled on Ringo Starr's son, Zak Starkey. A deal with a subsidiary of Atlantic Records, WEA, was on the table, but until it was signed, Entwistle would have to fund the sessions out of his own pocket.

That autumn, Entwistle assembled his new band, which he planned to call The Rock, at Quarwood and the initial sessions started with Langston engineering. They were to proceed in a haphazard fashion for the next eighteen months. Early in 1986, Entwistle added a singer, Henry Small, a Canadian, to the ranks. Soon after, he decided to dispense with Barnett's services and replaced him with an American, Devin Powers. 'I was given the job of sacking Andy Barnett,' says Andy Nye. 'John was unhappy with Andy, but didn't want to have to do it himself, so he asked me to let him down gently. Andy was devastated, because he'd spent nine months on the project by then.

> I have to say, I found the whole process incredibly frustrating. It was a very slow routine. For that year-and-a-quarter, we would all be at Quarwood from Monday to Friday most weeks and we were trying to pay out our day-to-day bills without actually earning anything. All musicians have a late clock. But John's was phenomenally late. He would be up with Zak and a couple of others till three, four in the morning, so we wouldn't even begin to go to work till midday, or even later. John was a real gentleman, but I just found that exasperating.

Quarwood was so huge that it took me two weeks to be able to move around it without a map. On occasion, John would take me for a walk around the grounds. One day, we were walking round the outside of the house when he suddenly did a double-take. There was an external door, very roughly painted and he said to me, 'I've never seen that before.' He'd had the place almost twenty years by then. There was another afternoon that we were sat at the huge kitchen table and I spotted two fox cubs playing on the lawn outside. I pointed them out to John and, straight away, he stood up and ran from the room. I assumed that he was going to fetch his camera. Next thing, he stomped back through the kitchen with a shotgun and a belt of bullets, like a Mexican bandit in a Western. He went out and tried to shoot the foxes.

Things got very stressful towards the end of that time. The record deal wasn't coming through. The agreement we had with John was that we would pay him for feeding and watering us out of whatever advance we got, but which we expected to be considerable. When that advance carried on being delayed, John started to say to the rest of us, 'Well, look, I'm owed all of this money.' He wasn't being nasty about it, but it was an awkward situation. John had a guy come round to the house who sold him wine for his wine cellar. This guy was delivering five or six bottles every night, and we were drinking them. Off the top of my head, the total bill added up to something like £120,000.

'When we broke up for Christmas 1986, John gave me a really big hug and held on to me. I drove home thinking that was incredibly strange, because John wasn't a demonstrative person at all. After the holiday, I called him up to see when he wanted me back at Quarwood and he said, 'Ah, I think you need to talk to Bill.' That was the end of my involvement with the band. Bill told me that Zak had a problem with me, but John wouldn't do that.

The sessions went on for another four months. Still the deal with WEA didn't materialise, forcing even Entwistle to make economies. Gradually, the deliveries of wine to Quarwood became less frequent and those days The Barracuda Inne wasn't always so fully stocked. Every weekend, though, he would round up the troops and whisk them off to London for a night on the town, plying them with bottles of brandy and champagne at his favourite clubs and always picking up the tab.

'That probably prolonged the album,' reasons Henry Small. 'We would go to these private clubs that would open at midnight and stay there until morning. One time, a girlfriend of Max's was over visiting from Chicago. Zak and I were sat at a table in this club. It was 5.00am and everybody was pretty well down the road. We looked up and there was John, holding this friend of Max's up by her ankles, dancing to "Sledgehammer" by Peter Gabriel and banging her head off the floor on each beat. Whenever I hear that song now, I have that vision and how we howled.'

The project ended in fiasco. The finished album, also titled *The Rock*, sounded as if it had been made almost without Entwistle being fully present. He had written just four songs to the six by Small and Powers. Small also sang all of the lead vocals. The playing was crisp, well-executed, but was tailored to fit the bland, ordered format of American FM radio. Then, at the crunch, WEA pulled out of the deal and Entwistle was left holding the bill. He dissolved the band. Without a record label, the album got mothballed and it was to go unreleased for the next ten years.

■ ■ ■

Notwithstanding his bank balance, the whole affair dealt a blow to Entwistle's confidence and self-esteem. Through the course of it, he had also reached the end of his tether with Langston, who kept the same gentleman's hours that he did but as an employee. Finally, Entwistle deemed that Langston's absences from the studio had become too frequent and dismissed him from his post, but not from his service. Langston relocated to Los Angeles and Entwistle re-employed him to be his personal assistant whenever he was in America.

Bobby Pridden was brought in to take over the reins at Hammerhead Studios. Pridden set about remodelling the studio and also making it available to other artists to rent. On Pridden's watch, the studio business grew steadily with the likes of Steve Winwood and his fellow Traffic alumnus Jim Capaldi, Britpop band Cast and folk singer Martin Simpson among those who passed through the doors. Artists were able to be resident at one of the cottages on the estate; Pridden had the use of another; a third cottage Entwistle eventually had converted into an art studio for his own purposes, while two more were occupied respectively by the Quarwood groundskeeper, Sue, and an elderly lady, Mrs Gibbs, whom Entwistle had inherited with the property on a peppercorn rent. Entwistle enjoyed having other musicians around the place.

'We would walk out of the studio and there would be John, next door in The Barracuda Inne, tinkling with a guitar,' says Pridden. 'He would then go on to hold court in the bar, which the younger artists would think was fantastic. As the night wore on, John's speech would get slower. He would lean over and always he would say, very slowly, " . . . And another thing . . ."'

He got another boost to his ego from attending trade fairs and where he found himself being fawned over and fêted. In America, the biggest of these were put on by NAMM and Entwistle was flown out to one such event in Chicago in June of 1987. At this, Entwistle found himself being introduced to the members of a hard-rock band from New York City, Rat Race Choir, who were Who acolytes. Not lacking in front, their fast-talking drummer, Steve Luongo, instantly pitched Entwistle the idea of him playing a set of Who songs with Rat Race Choir at the jam show that traditionally ended the fair.

Entwistle readily agreed to do a short, four-song set. This was so well received that in July, a representative of Kramer Guitars approached Luongo with an offer for Rat Race Choir together with Entwistle to headline New York radio station K-Rock's annual Blood Drive benefit concert. The show was scheduled for 8 November and at a Greenwich Village club, the Bottom Line. When the time arrived, the Kramer rep arranged for Entwistle to be flown out to New York first class. With his new band-mates, he was put up for four days at Kramer co-founder Dennis Berardi's mansion house in southern New Jersey. There, the musicians rehearsed and were fed by Berardi's private chef.

Luongo's wife, Laurie, was with them that week. She recalls, 'This guy cooked luxury meals, nine courses paired with the right wines. Afterwards, John would switch to drinking Rémy brandy and ginger ale. I started drinking those with him and we both ended up getting wasted. We both cursed like sailors. And we were both having gum problems. At one point, we were stood in front of the bathroom mirror comparing how much our gums were bleeding and talking about gum disease. I liked him a lot. He was very natural, there were no walls up. He didn't bring Max over with him that first time, but he was looking for girls. I said to him, "But you have a girlfriend!" He didn't want to talk about it, but as I got to know him, I learned that he always had to have a girlfriend wherever he went.'

With Entwistle seeming to revel in the atmosphere of the rehearsals, Luongo pressed him once more and this time to allow him to book a run of dates to follow on from the Bottom Line show. Entwistle's response was positive but, according to Luongo, right away an obstacle was put in their path. It had not escaped the attention of Entwistle's former colleagues that he was out playing Who songs with another band. When they arrived at the Bottom Line, Luongo says they were met by Bill Curbishley and his number two, Ann Weldon. Luongo claims Curbishley was carrying with him a letter written to Entwistle from Townshend. The substance of it, he says, was a warning from Townshend to Entwistle that if he carried on in the same vein, The Who would never again play together. Curbishley says he has no recollection of delivering such a letter.

'Bill asked for a few minutes alone with John in the dressing room,' Luongo insists. 'When Bill left, John came out and told me, "Book the tour. I want to play as much as we can." My take on it was that Townshend's slap on the wrist made John all the more obstinate. You know: "You haven't been paying attention to me for however many years, and now you're threatening me?"'

19

Club Ox

Right away, Luongo managed to fix up nine additional shows on the East Coast. The night after the Bottom Line gig, 9 November, Rat Race Choir and Entwistle played the Tower Theatre, Philadelphia. They went on from there to do dates in Washington DC, Asbury Park, Albany, Syracuse, Boston, Salem and the town of Huntington, New York, on the cusp of Long Island Sound, before finishing up back in New York City at the Ritz on 2 December. Their sets were mostly comprised of Who songs and they travelled together by bus. Arriving in Salem on the Thanksgiving Friday of 27 November, they were scheduled to meet up with the promoter of that night's gig who had invited Entwistle and party to dinner at a local restaurant.

'The bus driver couldn't find the appointed restaurant, so we were driving around town looking out for it,' describes Luongo. 'Eventually, we saw a strip mall with one place that had neon lights on the ceiling. We thought that had to be it – where else would be open? We went in and joined a line of people who were waiting to be served. We were given plastic trays and it was then that we noticed that the other people in line weren't so well dressed. Turned out the place was a mission for homeless people.

'Our road crew kind of blended in, but there was John dressed up like a peacock. He was standing in line with his tray, like everyone else. He got up to the food service and all that he asked for was some more cranberry sauce. But I was really embarrassed. I said to him, "John, man, I am *so* sorry about this." All he said was, "That's all right. It isn't my holiday." At times like that, he wouldn't want to be The Ox, or *that* guy, but just the bass player and your friend.'

Entwistle's readiness to muck in, though, only extended so far. He didn't want to sleep on the bus with the others, but in a hotel bed and preferably at a five-star accommodation. Since he also wouldn't want to be on his own at such times, he had Luongo book into a room as well so as to keep him company. Inevitably, this soon drove a wedge between Luongo and his much longer-standing band-mates, and about which Entwistle wasn't the slightest bit troubled. In Luongo, he had found an altogether less volatile, surrogate Moon. The rest of the guys in Rat Race Choir, well, he had assessed now that their musical chops weren't up to much and that they would hold him back.

'John told me, "You've got to get away from these guys as fast as you can,"' says Luongo. 'They were my lifelong friends and now, all of a sudden, I was the evil one to them. They were on the bus and I would be upstairs with John drinking Rémy. You know, I understood it, but the tour wouldn't have happened had it not been that way. These were John's conditions, not mine. But they resented it and it got ugly.

'In any case, we made quite a bit of money from the tour. I believe I put $90,000 in John's pocket at the end of it and he was very pleased. On the last night in New York, I threw a dinner for everyone on the tour. At the restaurant, John ordered up an outrageously priced bottle of wine and this and that – didn't make me flinch. We were partners now and this guy had just helped me to make a lot of dough, so you know – whatever he wants.'

However estranged they had got to be, whatever the bitterness that festered between them, the truth was that what Entwistle desired the most was for The Who to be revived. That would go on being the case, despite their misfire at Live Aid. A second, brief and also unedifying reunion went ahead just a few weeks after he got to back to Priory Lane. On this occasion, the band was nominated to receive an Outstanding Contribution to Music award at the British music industry's annual prize-giving bash, the Brits. As with Live Aid, the four principals, with 'Rabbit' Bundrick to be shunted off to a far side of the stage, agreed to perform a short set at the ceremony, which was also broadcast live on BBC television from the Royal Albert Hall on the night of 8 February 1988.

At rehearsals, Townshend and Daltrey argued with Entwistle about the volume of his bass. They were no more together on the night itself, playing desultory versions of 'Who Are You' and 'My Generation' with scarcely a glance passed between them, like strangers who had been forced upon each other. Aptly, the whole sorry spectacle came to an abrupt and inglorious end on television, when, with the event overrunning its time slot, 'My Generation' was faded out to go into the *Nine O'Clock News* bulletin. The Who would play together again, but not with Kenney Jones. It was, he wrote later, 'a final, and perhaps fitting, end to my Who career'.[33]

If not The Who, Entwistle just wanted to be able to tour again in some capacity. Back he turned to Luongo. Between them, they

---

[33] Taken from *Let the Good Times Roll: My Life in the Small Faces, the Faces and the Who* by Kenney Jones, Blink (2018)

hatched the idea of reviving The Rock band, but with Luongo taking over from Zak Starkey. Entwistle persuaded Henry Small and Devin Powers on board once more and had The Who's one-time sideman, Tim Gorman, join them on keyboards. Next, Luongo talked him into calling this new line-up The John Entwistle Band, reasoning that would make it easier for them to get gigs booked, specifically in America. A twenty-nine-date North American tour was subsequently set up, scheduled to begin on 24 June in the picturesque seaside hamlet of Bay Shore, New York.

In advance of the dates, Entwistle made arrangements for the band to get together for two weeks of rehearsals at Quarwood. He had Steve and Laurie Luongo fly in to London a fortnight earlier so that they could spend additional time together. After a few days at Priory Lane, and with Queenie and Gordon having gone off on holiday to Turkey, Entwistle had Kenny Wyatt drive him, Maxene and the Luongos down to Quarwood. 'I grew up in Westchester County, New York, so I was no stranger to mansions,' says Luongo. 'I mean, the Rockefeller estate was there. But Quarwood was a gorgeous place and John was *so* proud of it.

> Of course, he had all of these antique weapons on display. He had crossed broadswords, duelling pistols and four guns from the American Civil War – a pair of Colt Dragoons, a Navy Colt and a Remington. He ended up giving me those guns as a gift. And he knew everything about them. We would be watching a cowboy movie – because he loved the American West – and he'd go, 'Wrong!' Then, he would rattle off about how they were showing a gun that wasn't invented for another twenty years.
>
> The whole place was like a grown-up funhouse. In the hallway, he had something that he called 'Leather Man' propped up on a round, glass coffee table. Leather Man was a waist-

up, life-size bust of a human being. You could unzip his skin and, when you peeled it back, it would reveal the musculature of a man done in red leather. In one of the downstairs rooms, he had a hand-made, World War Two-themed chess set. The black pieces were Nazis, with figures for Hitler, Goebbels and Goering. The white pieces had Churchill, Montgomery and the Brits. Instead of white squares, it had Union Jack symbols and the black were swastikas. There was stuff like that all over the house and he had televisions in virtually every room, too. There was a massive TV set on the kitchen counter. We were going out one afternoon and I went to turn it off. John told me, 'Don't do that – I never turn them off. They might not come back on.' That TV in the kitchen was going full-on for the next thirteen years that I knew John.

Laurie and I are from the centre of the universe. We were used to something happening every minute of the day and now the nearest town was a mile up the road. John had also sent Kenny back to London. Daytimes, we got bored to tears. One afternoon, the two of us went for a walk around the property and came across a Ford station wagon that was parked up. I ran back to the house and told John that I could drive us into town, but he said, 'No, I can't let you do that. It's my mother's car.' I kept on at him and eventually he did hand over the keys to me . . . but only after he had made Laurie and I promise that we wouldn't let on to Queenie.

We got on well with Max, but she was somewhat guarded and a little distant. She was very protective of John and I admired that. At that time, John was fastidiously organised in his social life. We partied and drank and did whatever, but it was always extremely controlled. There wasn't a sense of excess. We had a great time and laughed our asses off, but John never overdid anything. He was living the life for sure, but in balance.

Anything went up until midnight. But then at midnight, no matter what it was, it stopped. If you wanted to keep talking, you could do that till three in the morning, but the recreational portion of the evening had ended. I remember distinctly that I thought to myself that this guy would never be another rock-'n'-roll tragedy.

Laurie Luongo adds, laughing, 'It was like, "Come on, John, let us do another line of coke!" But no, he wouldn't do it.'

■ ■ ■

A convivial atmosphere pervaded at Quarwood right up until the other members of the newly-named John Entwistle Band rolled up. By Luongo's account, Small and Powers resented his new-found status as Entwistle's business partner and the mood soured as the rehearsals got going. The quiet, passive Gorman kept to himself; Entwistle, though, fully aware of the escalating tensions and back-biting, as usual didn't intervene. 'With Zak gone, it was like to the other guys that I had ousted their drinking buddy and was now telling them what to do,' says Luongo. 'They were being very unpleasant. What John did do was took me into his suite and tell me, "They're just jealous of you – ignore it."'

Luongo describes the tour that ensued as the most miserable of his career. Entwistle had Bobby Pridden come out and do the sound and Cy Langston on hand to cater to all of his other needs. He left Maxene at home, telling her that there simply wasn't the budget for another member of the touring party. 'I was pissed off that I had to stick around at Quarwood,' she says. 'Did I trust him when he was away? No, I didn't, but then again, I was in major denial.'

All that summer, The John Entwistle Band bussed around North America. They wound up and down the East Coast to Boston and Baltimore, crossed over to Cleveland, Detroit and

Chicago, made it out to California by mid-July, and finished up with three dates that August in Seattle, Toronto and Providence Rhode Island. From the outset, says Luongo, there was a toxic air backstage and on the tour bus. That being the case, Entwistle made sure that he was anaesthetised to it. There was no midnight curfew in operation now.

'After shows, we closed down nightclubs and bars,' says Luongo. 'The excesses were present, but also John loved to meet his fans and to tell his stories. He would go back to the hotel lobby and wait for people to turn up, and then he would start talking. You would hear him laughing from across the room. Between the two of us, we would have what he called "elbows time". That was when he would have had a little too much to drink and it meant, "OK, grab me by the elbows and don't let me fall down."'

'John was never inappropriate, never boisterous,' adds Henry Small. 'That was the loveable thing about him. I was brought up to believe that if you want to drink, well, go ahead, but handle yourself with some semblance of grace. On that tour, not once did I see John out of character. And God knows, we certainly drank, did a few drugs and the whole deal.'

Even so, by the end of the tour, Entwistle seemed to be tired, depleted. All the petty squabbling had worn him down, but at forty-six, he was also starting to feel the pace. On top of the booze, drugs and late nights, he smoked almost constantly and existed on a diet of fried food with no vegetables or fruit. His hearing had been near enough ruined from the years of playing at excessive volume. Before the tour started, he had been prescribed medication to help with his high blood pressure and soaring cholesterol.

'I did worry about him, yes, and many times,' admits Small. 'He would look very grey to me sometimes and obviously he didn't do any exercise whatsoever. Then, there was the cocaine. John was always a stalwart, though, and held his own. I knew he was taking something for his heart, but he didn't appear to me to give a shit about his own health. That was depressing for me, because here was a guy who as far as I was concerned was the greatest bass player of his time. I guess it taught me not to make heroes of people.'

'At one point, Henry and I really didn't think John looked well and we tried to talk to him about it,' says Gorman. 'We said to him, "Can't you just try to pull it back?" He told us that he wanted to have the world's longest bachelor party. That was his sense of humour. None of us is an angel and that's the way that I looked at it.'

Entwistle was also starting to be stretched financially. Next to The Who, his own band was more like a cottage industry and one that he had to prop up. Added to that, he had the cost of running two houses and also keeping up with his divorce settlement payments to Alison. Something had to give and, when he got back off the tour, he made the decision to part with the Priory Lane house and move full-time to Quarwood. After that, though, he went right ahead with ploughing yet more money into making improvements at Quarwood.

Principally, he had two of the main rooms made even bigger. The kitchen he had opened out by knocking through into the old servants' quarters. In the master bedroom suite, he had the en suite bathroom and dressing room converted into a single huge bathroom. Christopher's old bedroom was turned into a spacious adjoining dressing room for him and Maxene. All of these rooms were redecorated, so that the Blue Suite was transformed into the Coral Suite. Now that Entwistle was fully resident at Quarwood, he was also properly able to play the role of eminent landowner. If he had to go into Stow, whatever the reason, he would dress his best and make sure to have Kenny Wyatt on hand with one of the Rolls-Royces. At weekends, he would take Maxene up to London. They would fill up a hamper at Harrods' food hall and picnic in their suite at the Dorchester Hotel on Park Lane.

'In every way, John lived like a king,' notes Bobby Pridden, and this was even without The Who to fund him. Yet he also allowed money to be drained away from him. Invariably, builders and other tradesmen would see him as a soft touch and habitually over-charge for their work at Quarwood. In more than one instance, people whom he employed directly also took advantage of what appeared to be his relaxed, or even careless, attitude towards his own business. Maxene claims to have picked up on a series of discrepancies in the Quarwood accounts – bogus expense claims and doctored invoices.

'At college, I got an A+ in accounting class so John would allow me to take care of his affairs,' she says. 'He was never very good at it and the books weren't coming out even-steven. I took this to him and pointed it out but, instead of getting angry with the people who were doing him wrong, he came down on me. I never understood that; I thought I was protecting him and showing him where the problems were, but he didn't want to know.'

'He would give people an inch and they would take a mile,' adds Christopher. 'A lot of things were also done without his knowledge. What he was aware of, he would let build up, but only to a certain degree and then he would have had enough. He described it to me once by saying that he had got used to people pulling his plonker, but when they start to yank on it, that's the end.

'You couldn't actually rip him off, because he knew precisely what he should have. Grandmother once accused him of not knowing what was going on and he said to her, "I could tell you what's in the bank to within a hundred pounds." He never saw the bank statements, but he proceeded to do just that. He kept a mental record and would plus and minus everything in his head.'

According to Curbishley, though, Entwistle's cash flow did reach a crisis point in 1989, having been hastened by a substantial tax bill. Townshend and Daltrey were made aware of the situation. Both men have said since that they were persuaded to commit to the idea of a Who reunion tour in large part in order to help ease Entwistle's burden. It was also the case that each of Townshend's and Daltrey's solo careers had at best only been fitfully successful, and that they, too, would stand to make fortunes from such a tour.

■ ■ ■

Both Townshend and Daltrey agreed to tour, but with conditions – Daltrey point-blank refused to go out again with Kenney Jones and, this time, Townshend and Entwistle conceded the point. Ace session drummer Simon Phillips was recruited instead. Townshend's hearing was also shot and he was handicapped with a persistent tinnitus in both ears. He insisted that he would only be able to play acoustic guitar and that The Who didn't go above a hundred decibels onstage. Since this would also require Entwistle to rein in his playing, Townshend wanted to recruit extra musicians to fill in the gaps in their sound.

In the event, the original members, Phillips and 'Rabbit' Bundrick would be joined onstage by a five-piece brass section, an extra guitarist, Steve 'Boltz' Bolton, an additional percussionist and three backing singers. A fifty-date tour of North America and the UK was announced, to start 21 June in Glen Falls, New York. The vast majority of the shows were in stadiums and arenas. At four more intimate dates – Radio City Music Hall, New York City, on 27 June; the Universal Amphitheatre, Los Angeles, on 24 August; and at the Royal Albert Hall, London, on 31 October and 2 November – The Who were to perform *Tommy* in full for the first time since 1970.

Two American beer companies, Miller and Anheuser-Busch, brewers of Budweiser, paid out $3 million between them to be co-sponsors of the tour, which was predicted to gross $55 million in ticket sales. A further $2 million was to be reaped from merchandising and $2 million more from a pay-per-view TV deal to broadcast the Los Angeles *Tommy* show and at which Elton John, Billy Joel and Phil Collins were among a supporting cast of guest performers.

Entwistle, Townshend and Daltrey were to take an equal split of the net profit from the tour. From Entwistle's perspective, such riches were long overdue. Speaking the following year, he claimed, 'Being in The Who has always been like winning the football pools and not bothering to cash the cheque in. We're an extremely famous, semi-professional band that didn't earn any money. We figured it was about time we cashed the cheque.'[34]

'For John, it was like Christmas all over again after the wilderness years,' says Pridden. 'Before they set off, he made up a tour survival kit and had it sent off to Bill. It had all kinds of things in it – English mustard, HP sauce, tea bags and a doctor's bag. Absolutely, he was happy.'

Rehearsals with the full, expanded line-up went ahead at Nomis Studios in Hammersmith, west London, and back at Shepperton. After warming up in Glen Springs, the tour properly kicked off with two shows at the CNE Stadium, Toronto, in front of a combined audience of nearly 93,000. Nightly, their regular sets ran to well over three hours with the first hour given over to *Tommy*. Leading into a fifteen-minute intermission, Entwistle fronted two of his songs, 'Trick of the Light' and 'Boris the

---

[34] Taken from 1990 television interview for *Rapido*

Spider'. The hits made up the other side of the break, with 'You Better You Bet', 'Behind Blue Eyes' and 'Won't Get Fooled Again' closing out the show.

Most nights were sell-outs. The expanded band sounded muscular and well drilled, but the shows were almost too rehearsed, too clinical, and the surfeit of extra musicians diluted, and made it harder to pick out, Townshend's and Entwistle's contributions. Throughout, Daltrey was ailed with a benign but painful tumour in his stomach. Offstage, and with Daltrey and Townshend keeping their counsel, Entwistle was once again ringleader for whatever passed for after-hours entertainment on the tour.

'Onstage every night, John would put a sticky note on my amp that would say something like, "Club Ox, Twenty-Fourth Floor, tonight, 2.00am",' says Steve Bolton. 'He used to have the penthouse suite in whatever hotel we were staying in and I'd be among those he invited up to his soirées. But it was kind of a secret club and we weren't to tell Pete or Roger.'

'Once again, I got to go out as John's assistant on the tour and had to make sure that he ate properly and didn't drink too much,' continues Maxene. 'John was an alcoholic, I think, but still then not so as you might notice. I, on the other hand, would have blackouts.

'In Toronto, I had a sore throat and Roger prescribed me brandy. I drank all day and, after the show, we went to a nightclub. I ended up inviting everyone in the place back to our suite to carry on the party. I have no recollection of it, but I must also have picked a fight with John. When I woke up the next day, I was covered in scrapes and bruises. The room was in disarray. John told me that I'd come after him and that he'd had to defend himself. He'd pushed over a table and the television set.'

As the tour progressed, Entwistle began to have his bass exponentially turned up onstage. Townshend shrugged this off, but Daltrey was infuriated. At Houston Astrodome on 2 September, the penultimate night of the North American leg, Daltrey vented his frustrations in front of the audience. Over his microphone, he repeatedly instructed Entwistle to turn down. Entwistle finally reacted, taking off his bass, throwing it to the floor and storming off.

'He walked to the back of the stage and just jumped off,' recalls Curbishley. 'The stage must have been 10ft high and John was the most unathletic person you could meet. Plus, he had on his high-heeled Cuban boots. I thought to myself, "Oh my God, he's fucking dead." Or at the very least, I expected that he'd broken both of his legs. I rushed backstage and there was John, stood outside the dressing room, smoking a cigarette. I said to him, "John! *How* did you land?" Casually, he replied, "On my feet."'

Before the UK dates, there had been optimistic talk of carrying the tour on across Europe and into Japan and Australia. That, though, fizzled out and the two Royal Albert Hall shows ended up being the closing nights. Townshend had lost interest by then and Daltrey needed surgery on his stomach. Even Entwistle's enthusiasm had dimmed. 'I don't have *very* good memories of the tour,' he said soon after. 'I don't think the other two had changed at all. Nothing at all had been solved from the day we broke up. We all had completely different musical tastes still. Roger still thought I was too loud. Pete still couldn't hear properly. Fortunately, on the tour we found a way to keep the problems out of the way – most of them anyway.'[35]

The three of them did make one more appearance together in January of 1990. The occasion was The Who's induction into the Rock & Roll Hall of Fame, then in its fifth year, at an event staged at the Waldorf Astoria Hotel in New York City. Entwistle

---

[35] Taken from 1990 television interview for *Rapido*

was nonplussed by the whole affair. 'I asked about fifty people – "What is the Rock & Roll Hall of Fame?"' he said. 'And no one could tell me. I went to the ceremony, but I had no idea what was going on.'[36]

Two months later, Townshend wrote to both Entwistle and Daltrey, telling them he didn't want to continue with the band and would be pursuing other projects instead. Entwistle wasn't unduly bothered. Give or take, he had made around $3 million dollars from the reunion tour. Such as they were, his only immediate worries were what to spend it on and how fast.

[36] Taken from 1990 television interview for *Rapido*

20

Mr Loud

Cash rich once more, Entwistle decided to go into tax exile. This would necessitate him spending ten months out of the next year outside the UK. Even then, he didn't actually mean to save any money. Rather, whatever he saved in not having to pay UK taxes he intended to splurge on other things. He would buy even more cars and guitars, and whatever else took his fancy. In short, he was going to please no one more so than himself.

However, the first thing that he did to lighten his mood was to confront at last the situation that had lingered at Quarwood with his mother and stepfather. In his absence, Gordon had decreed that keeping the indoor swimming pool heated would waste electricity so he had had it shut off. Entwistle came home to find the pool house overrun with plant life from the surrounding woodland. Invasive roots had cracked and ravaged the bottom of the swimming pool beyond repair. Furious, he resolved to evict Gordon and Queenie. In due course, he bought and moved them into a new-build house in Deddington, a small town in Oxfordshire twenty miles to the east of Stow. Over time, he had their old living quarters at Quarwood converted into offices for the studio and estate. Their bedroom became a storage room for his ever-expanding guitar collection, which by that time had grown to around 250 instruments.

He spent the greater part of his year in exile in Los Angeles billeted in a suite of rooms at a hotel on Sunset Strip. Seventeen-year-old Christopher came out for two weeks' holiday and remembers his father and Maxene taking him out on the town every night of his stay. 'I never got over my jet-leg,' says Christopher. 'I went home knackered, but not that I didn't have fun. But then for heaven's sake, I had a gold membership card for Stringfellow's at fifteen.'

Cy Langston was on hand to drive Entwistle around town and run his errands. Entwistle would also expect Langston to fix him up with whatever he might need to get him through a night, and usually a line or two of cocaine. Like The Who, The Eagles had also come to a grinding halt. Joe Walsh says, 'I did meet up with John a couple of times in LA. Neither of us really knew what to do with ourselves, because our bands were our lives. We partied more and more and played and composed less and less, because we could. We were successful and we could afford it, but both of us went into a very subtle, gradual decline.'

Far away from the helter-skelter whirl of Los Angeles, that same year Entwistle also chose to spend a couple of months domiciled on the west coast of Ireland. With Maxene, he made for Connemara, a bucolic corner of County Galway buffeted by winds from off the Atlantic Ocean. There, occupying a prominent position at the head of an exposed sea bay, they rented a grand, albeit tumbledown, old stone house that had once been the residence of the Archbishop of Tuam. Entwistle also took along Bobby Pridden; he had made up his mind to write his memoirs and wanted Pridden to help him with the research and other paperwork. As it happened, work on the proposed book, which he provisionally titled *Don't Give Up Your Day Job*, went ahead erratically and he left Ireland with it nowhere near complete.

'I went and stayed there with them for a weekend,' says Christopher. 'The house was kind of like a castle, but basically full of shit and there were no curtains. You looked out to sea and nothing else. There was a storm one night and I was sat thinking to myself, "Jesus, where am I?" Dad really enjoyed that year away, I think. Why wouldn't he? He was loaded at that particular point and he got to play with what seemed like all the money in the world.'

During the two months that he was allowed back into the UK, Entwistle got involved in yet another project that would go on to lie dormant for years. He was recruited to it by Ron Magness, an American musician-producer whose former band Felix had opened up for The Who in the seventies. Magness was pushing a Canadian singer-songwriter, Chris Tassone, whose main claim to fame was that he bore an uncanny likeness to Ringo Starr while endeavouring to sing like John Lennon. Magness arranged for Tassone to make an album at The Beatles' old stomping ground, Abbey Road. Along with Entwistle, he also convinced Manfred Mann, Georgie Fame and Roxy Music guitarist Phil Manzanera to play on the sessions, which altogether went on for six months.

'It was an honour for me to play with John in particular,' says Mickey Wynne, who also played guitar on the dates. 'Typically, he would whizz through a bass part first take. He rattled through each track like that, one by one, sat up in the control room and the rest of us could only marvel at him.

'The first day John was at Abbey Road, Ron told me to go up and introduce myself. I went over and said, "Hi, John, how are you doing?" There was no response, so I said it again, and again. Finally, I had to roar at him, "HELLO, JOHN, HOW ARE YOU??"

He jumped back and said, "No need to bloody shout!" Of course, I'd been talking into his left ear, which was the deaf one.'

In the event, Entwistle played on nine of the album's eleven tracks, including covers of Lennon and McCartney's 'You Can't Do That' and an American folk standard, 'Stagger Lee'. Magness, though, wasn't able to convince anyone to release the finished record and it was shelved. Three years later, it was snuck out under the title *Looks Like Ringo, Sounds Like John* and credited to Chris Tassone and the Wiseguys Intl., becoming an instant curio.

Back in LA, Entwistle was next co-opted into an all-star jam band that was put together by Steely Dan/Doobie Brothers guitarist Jeff 'Skunk' Baxter. Named The Best, the stellar line-up was completed by Walsh, Keith Emerson and Simon Phillips. They played two dates together in Japan that September, but an American tour that Baxter had planned to follow never went ahead. 'The degree of musicianship in that band was pretty powerful and it was all very free-form,' says Walsh. 'In Japan, the audiences were amazed *and* confused, which was exactly how I felt, too. I didn't know what the fuck that band was, but it was working. We came back with grandiose schemes, but people got busy and went in various directions. That band, to me, was John playing at his very best.'

Los Angeles became Entwistle's second, adopted hometown. In 1990, he forked out for a house at Queen's Court, up in the Hollywood Hills. There, he lived a life of leisure and indulgence. The lifestyle limits that not so long ago he had imposed on himself and others at Quarwood were all but forgotten. On one occasion, Maxene came home from a trip away to find a stretch limousine parked up in front of the house. Inside, the comedian Sam Kinison was passed out on the living room floor. 'John and Sam had stayed up all night, drinking and partying and carrying on,' she explains. 'I went upstairs to find John sat up in bed and laughing. It was definitely a party house and sometimes I didn't want to go there with him. John had a dual personality. He would be one way when he was on his own with me at home, and then someone completely different in front of other people and his fans. I used to call it his "Who" persona.'

Another night, Entwistle was holding court in his usual booth at the Rainbow when a waitress approached him with a drink. 'It's from the lady at the bar,' she told him. The lady in question was Lisa Pritchett-Johnson, Joe Walsh's girlfriend. By then, their relationship had hit the skids and Lisa was living just as fast and loose as Walsh. Late one evening not long after that, bedraggled looking, she pitched up on the doorstep at Queen's Court and following a fight with Walsh. 'John felt sorry for her and took her in,' says Maxene. The talk around town was that Lisa was too much for even a notorious wild man such as Walsh to handle. She was damaged goods, they said, but either Entwistle hadn't heard, or else he chose not to listen.

'I found out later that they had begun their affair right around then,' adds Maxene. 'I don't know why I thought I was uniquely different, because he was having a fling with me when he was with Alison.'

■ ■ ■

As one year rolled into the next, Entwistle and Maxene went back to being resident at Quarwood. Pridden kept the studio business ticking over. Entwistle put his memoirs to one side and eventually forgot about them altogether. If he travelled, it was invariably to go back to Los Angeles to attend the regular trade fairs. He would go alone so as to be able to hook up with Lisa, who by now had split up with Walsh. Their affair had become common knowledge among Entwistle's circle of friends and associates. Nevertheless, he was at that very same time planning to wed Maxene.

Originally, he proposed that they get married at Quarwood with John Hurt acting as their minister. In the summer of 1991, though, he was invited out to Las Vegas to attend the opening of a new Guitar Centre store. Maxene went with him and, on the spur of the moment, he insisted that they should get married there and then. On the morning of Saturday, 21 September 1991, they were pronounced man and wife at the Graceland Wedding Chapel on Las Vegas Boulevard. Apart from the pastor, the only other person present was an Elvis impersonator who serenaded Maxene down the aisle with a chorus of, 'She ain't nothing but a hound dog . . .' That very same wedding night, Entwistle told Steve Luongo that he also entertained Lisa back at their hotel.

'He said that Lisa had just turned up and that they had carried on a bit,' says Luongo. 'Lisa was a gorgeous-looking girl – long legs, beautiful hair and an angel's face. But she could be one of the ugliest human beings on the planet.'

'We were already living separate lives by then,' reveals Maxene. 'I didn't yet know about his affair, but I suspected it. It was a marriage of convenience. I think the only reason that he went through with it was to keep me at bay. It also meant that he could come and go, in and out of America, as he pleased.'

Unsurprisingly, from the start, the marriage was troubled, loveless, and always in the background was Entwistle's other relationship with Lisa. All that really bound Entwistle and Maxene together by now were their own excesses. Less than nine months after their Las Vegas wedding, Maxene says she hit rock bottom. 'I got to a place where I was sick and tired of being sick and tired. Ten o'clock one morning, I found myself in the wine cellar at Quarwood. I cracked open a bottle of the finest wine I could lay my hands on, drank it and nothing happened. I ran upstairs and found John's stash of cocaine, snorted it, and nothing happened.

I rolled up a big spliff of hashish and I couldn't even get stoned. So, I took the first plane I could get back to Los Angeles.

'Nicole Winwood, Steve Winwood's first wife, who had been my friend and neighbour in England, called me up and invited me out to lunch in Beverly Hills. But she asked me to meet her at an address on Fountain and Fairfax. I didn't know it, but that turned out to be my first Alcoholics Anonymous meeting. It was upstairs in a church. Nicole walked me up to the room. There seemed to be a couple of hundred chairs set out, and they were filled with people I knew, and had tailored for in the business. I sat with Nicole. I was rocking back and forward in my chair; I had on these big, dark sunglasses and tears streaming down my face. That was the day I got sober – 24 June 1992. From that day to this, I've never had another drink or drug.'

At Quarwood, things got worse between them. Soon after Maxene returned from Los Angeles, Gordon was diagnosed with lung cancer. He died early the next year, after which Entwistle moved Queenie back to Quarwood, setting her up in one of the cottages on the grounds, the Coach House. Maxene's relationship with Queenie had always been strained, but now, with the two of them being thrown together once again, it descended into an ugly battle of wills. Coincidentally, at the same time, Entwistle gave up even the pretence of being a husband and, as often as he could, he would take himself off to Los Angeles.

'Understandably, there was bitterness on Maxene's part,' says Christopher. 'She would tell me that Dad was doing this and that. Probably he was, but one picks a side, and I chose my Dad's. Max had been Mad Max, but now had become Mild Max – and Dad wasn't ready to stop partying.'

'I was left at Quarwood to run the place and Queenie would be there trying to boss me around,' says Maxene. 'She would also write John in America that I was screwing around, fucking everybody on the Stow-on-the-Wold rugby team, all of this rubbish and lies. Then, she would tell me how it was perfectly OK for John to have a wife and mistress. It was not OK in my book and I let her know that.

'It got so that John was away most of the time, seeing Lisa and whoever else. I very much doubt that she was the only one. Finally, I did start having affairs of my own. I met an Italian guy, an entrepreneur who had a restaurant in London, and I would rendezvous with him. And also a young male model. And I never, ever made my peace with Queenie.'

Early in 1994, Entwistle was able to flee back to work and he had Daltrey to thank for it. With Curbishley all but retired to Spain, Daltrey had taken on a personal manager, Richard Flanzer. To mark Daltrey's fiftieth birthday, Flanzer, an assertive New Yorker, had set up for him a brace of concerts at Carnegie Hall on 23 and 24 February. At these shows, Daltrey would perform The Who's music backed by a full orchestra that was to be arranged and conducted by Michael Kamen. He was also to be joined by such 'special guests' as Lou Reed, Alice Cooper and Eddie Vedder of Pearl Jam. Entwistle accepted an invite from Daltrey to appear at the shows and, when Townshend also agreed to turn up, both nights sold out in a record time for the august venue.

With Entwistle, Daltrey and Townshend staying on cordial terms with each other, the Carnegie shows passed without a hitch and were well received. On opening night, Entwistle made off after the show to a notoriously uproarious Manhattan hot spot, the China Club. A big, noisy hangout on West 47th Street, the China Club hosted a weekly, Wednesday night, open mic jam session at which 600 people would pack into the downstairs bar. On any given Wednesday, Bruce Willis might get up to blow harmonica, or Billy Joel play piano with the house band, which was led by a Brooklyn-born guitarist and Who aficionado ironically named Godfrey Townsend. Looking on from the raised-up, roped-off VIP area, there could be Andre Agassi with Brooke Shields, or Elton John, or Jeff Beck.

That first night, Entwistle showed up with a party that also included Vedder, 'Rabbit' Bundrick, Linda Perry from the band 4 Non Blondes, and Steve Luongo, and sat in with the band for a couple of hours. Whenever after that he happened to be in the city, invariably he would drop by the China Club. Joe Lynn Turner, who had sung with Deep Purple and Rainbow, was another China Club regular at that time. 'Oh boy, did John ever like to let his hair down,' he says. 'Wednesdays, they would close the club down and let certain people stay on and party outrageously. I remember one night being sat elbow to elbow with John, and I left him in that state where you hate yourself and the sun's coming up. I also knew one of the dealers who John got his drugs from; this guy told me that his cocaine was 98 per cent pure. He put out a rail for me once. Man, that shit was strong. It was like Buddy Rich started playing on my heart.'

Since the New York shows were seen to be such a success, Flanzer was able to line up a twenty-date North American tour for Daltrey. This was to run all through that summer, and was billed as 'Roger Daltrey Performs a Tribute to Pete Townshend'. Daltrey recruited Townshend's younger brother, Simon, to play guitar in his band and also Zak Starkey. A local orchestra would back them at each stop. At Daltrey's invitation, Entwistle went along to perform a guest spot in the second half of the concerts, which Daltrey reckoned ended up costing him close to $1 million.

At the same time, Entwistle found himself tied up in a second, ill-starred enterprise that Daltrey was enticed into by Flanzer. A musical production of *Tommy* had been running on Broadway since the previous April. On Daltrey's behalf, Flanzer hired a firm of Madison Avenue lawyers, Gold, Farrell and Marks, to contest the amount of royalties that he was set to earn from this show. Daltrey convinced Entwistle to go in with him on the lawsuit, which they were effectively filing against Townshend and also Chris Stamp.

Their legal bills racked up fast. In a letter dated 2 November 1994, Gold, Farrell and Marks wrote to Entwistle and Daltrey: 'Despite our patience and many good faith accommodations to extend payment times, our accounts have become so overdue in such substantial amounts that we regret that we must stop all further legal services until a large portion of the accounts are paid and you commit to pay all balances on a firm schedule . . . In order for us to resume our services, please wire a minimum of $75,000 dollars to our account.'

'John, I think, believed that he had contributed quite a bit to *Tommy*,' says Bill Curbishley. 'Roger felt that he had at least contributed to the structuring of it, or had changed things in the recording process. Whether one agrees with that or not is another matter, but they didn't end up getting any additional royalties that I know of. And right up to his death, John's publishing went on being controlled by Chris Stamp.'

■ ■ ■

Entwistle's short, miserable marriage ended just as he was preparing to go off on tour with Daltrey. That spring, Maxene had moved her belongings out of Quarwood and returned to Los Angeles to live at Queen's Court. Soon after, at one of her regular AA meetings, she met Thierry Curial de Brevannes, a French nobleman. They had a one-night-stand and Maxene fell pregnant. When she broke the news to Entwistle, he promptly filed for divorce.

'He had moved on already,' insists Maxene. 'And I just didn't want to have to deal with his bullshit and drama any more. From the divorce, I got the LA house, a Toyota Landcruiser and £180,000. That was OK. I just wanted to get on with my own life, too.'

That December, Maxene gave birth to a son, Oliver. Entwistle, she says, sent her a note of congratulation and a bouquet of red roses. Two months prior to that, he had convinced Lisa to leave Los Angeles and go to live with him at Quarwood. She had left behind her a studio apartment in Hollywood and a desperate reputation. 'Cy Langston had told Steve and me all about Lisa,' says Laurie Luongo. 'How she had partied too much for Joe Walsh and that she had a crack problem. To us it was like, "Uh-uh, this sounds like real bad news."'

To begin with at least, Christopher was more positive about his father's latest girlfriend. He observes, 'The first impression I had of Lisa was the one that everyone who didn't know her well got, which was that she was loud, raucous, lots of fun and loving. Right up until I went to work at Quarwood, she treated me as one of the people that was to be kept keen.'

Lisa quickly settled into her role as mistress of Quarwood and, once more, the parade of parties and entertaining started up at the old house. It was not until the next summer that Entwistle left home to go out on the road again. This time, it was as a member of Ringo Starr's All-Star Band. Starr had fixed up a tour that was to begin with eleven dates in Japan that June and continue on through a six-week run around the US. On the eve of the opening night in the Japanese city of Morioka, Starr called a band meeting at their hotel. Seven years sober by this point, Starr issued instructions to his musicians that there was to be no drinking before any of the shows and no drugs whatsoever on the tour.

'Everybody shook hands and we all said OK,' says Randy Bachman, guitarist on the tour. 'The next afternoon, John was in the hotel bar, slamming a few back. I went over and asked him what had happened to our agreement. He said, "Ah, that's just like with your parents. They tell you not to do stuff, and then you go out and do whatever you want."'

'We were also asked not to blow anyone's brains out with our volume. Well, John showed up with 2,000 . . . 3,000-watt Crown amps the size of refrigerators. You could actually see his suit pants waving in the air displacement that came from these things. John was like most quiet schoolboy types – get him alone, give him a drop of something and he would turn into a rock-'n'-roll animal.'

Recalling the tour in the last notes he made for his memoir, Entwistle insisted that he had, in fact, cut his onstage backline in half to placate Starr: 'And still he called me "Mr Loud" – affectionately, I hope,' he wrote, adding: 'I think Ringo and I would have had more in common with each other when he was still drinking. I always seemed to be walking back in to the hotel in the morning when he and his wife Barbara were walking out for breakfast.'

21

Luck of the Draw

Towards the end of 1995, Entwistle phoned Steve Luongo and asked for his help with putting together another version of The John Entwistle Band. Entwistle wanted to go with the same four-piece set-up and to use New York musicians. Luongo suggested a keyboard player, Alan St Jon, who lived in Greenwich Village and had played in Billy Squier's band. Entwistle then remembered Godfrey Townsend from the jam at the China Club. He had liked Townsend's clean, unfussy style of playing, but also his wise-guy humour. The four of them went through a couple of weeks' rehearsals together before he even bothered to ask Townsend for his surname.

'When Godfrey told him, John looked at me like, "He's kidding, right?"' says Luongo. 'Whenever after that John would introduce Godfrey onstage, he would say, "Godfrey Townsend – no relation, no nose, no Ferrari and no 'H'." There was one occasion in front of John when Godfrey referred to Pete Townshend as a genius. John exploded, "A genius? He writes a bunch of crap, lets you do all the work and that's genius?" Godfrey said, "What about *Tommy*?" And John replied, "What a piece of shit! He can't hear you, he can't see you and he can't tell what it's all about, because he doesn't fucking know!"'

On 7 January 1996, they set off on a three-month, thirty-seven-date tour of North America. They played smaller clubs and travelled by bus. Entwistle was still suffering with high blood pressure; on his doctor's instructions, twice daily he had to have Luongo monitor it. Luongo reported the results back to the doctor who would adjust Entwistle's prescriptions accordingly. During the day, he was measured with his drinking, but found other outlets for his excessive impulses – mostly shopping. Always, he bought in bulk. Most days, he would return to the bus cradling armfuls of bags filled with everything from clothes, shoes and cheap sunglasses to toys, maps and condoms. At one stop, he had the bus pull up at a Sheplers outlet specialising in Western wear, went inside and bought a couple of hundred cowboy shirts in every available colour and size.

After the shows, he would cut loose. Then, he would always have a full glass of Rémy in one hand, a cigarette in the other, a line or two to perk him up, and stories to tell to whoever would listen. At such times, Luongo would again be the one to keep a check on him. 'I learned quickly in my relationship with John that he was dependent on me for a lot of the unspoken stuff,' he says. 'That caused a lot of friction, because I had to be band-mate and minder, and a lot of people didn't like it that I got in the way of their access to John.

'One day, we were walking into our hotel and bumped into the wife of a music business executive. She buttonholed him and said, "Oh, John, I've got something for you," and put a bindle [wrap] in his pocket. John was pretty drunk and didn't even notice. The minute we got to his room, I fished the bindle out. It was heroin. We flushed it down the toilet. I didn't really drink and, if I was wired with blow, it only made me more alert and paranoid.'

'John was dysfunctional in a certain sense because of never having had to do many things for himself, and from being a rock star since he was a teenager,' suggests Godfrey Townsend. 'But if you understood that about him, you felt like you wanted to look out for him and take care of him. And he would go out of his way to help you, too.'

All these years, no one could remember Entwistle ever getting truly sloppy, no matter how much booze he might have sunk, or what he had put up his nose. Now, though, there were chinks showing in his armour. Backstage before a gig in Toronto on 17 March, he helped himself to one too many brandies. Onstage that night, his speech was slurred, mumbled. The show was broadcast live on a local radio station. The next morning, they tuned into the same station on the bus to hear the breakfast jocks mocking Entwistle for his incoherence.

'John was laughing as he listened, but he didn't really get what they were saying,' says Luongo. 'That was one of the very few hard-core, serious conversations that we had. I said to him, "You know, man, those guys are laughing *at* you. They're goofing on the fact you were drunk." We didn't speak of it again, but I never heard him slur another word onstage.'

There were, too, lighter, funnier moments on the tour when Entwistle would appear just as delighted to be on the road as he ever was, almost boyish in his enthusiasm. On the bus, he would while away the hours coming up with punning games like 'rock stars into fish'; the merest smirk at the corner of his mouth would telegraph that he was about to pitch in with something such as Pike and Tina Turner. Gleefully, he would think up names to check into hotels with – Tristan Shout and Alan Otherthing being just two examples from that tour. At the start of March, they were able to take a short break in New Mexico and, upon checking into their hotel, went their separate ways. 'Eventually, you start to get on each other's nerves and so, right then it was like, "I'll see you, don't call and we'll catch up in three days,"' explains Luongo.

'I spent my time out by the hotel pool or in the sauna. On the morning of our departure, our regular routine was that I would get the bellman to come and pick up my bags and then we would go together to John's room. To find John's room, you would just have to follow the din. He was so painfully deaf that he would always have his television turned up as loud as it would go.

'That last morning in New Mexico, we got to John's room, knocked on the door and, boy, he was pissed off when he opened up. His room was tiny. He had thirteen suitcases lined up around his single bed. There were room service trays and empty bottles of Rémy strewn over the floor. It was a five-star hotel, but he'd had to climb over his suitcases just to get to the bathroom. Even after three days, he was still raging. There was a little closet with a washing machine and drier and, right next to it, another door. I said to him, "What's in here?" He didn't know, hadn't even looked. So I opened it up.

'Beyond the door, there were seven other rooms. I mean, this was the Presidential Suite. There were flowers that had wilted on the table, chocolates that had melted, and a fruit basket with bananas that had turned. There was crystal this and that . . . ornate chandeliers. I called back, "John, come on in here for a second." He kind of grumbled his way to me and had a look around. Then, he cracked the biggest smile, shrugged his shoulders and said, "Luck of the draw, mate."'

The trouble was that Entwistle didn't make any real money from the tour, nor from the belated release of *The Rock* album. He had finally got a deal sorted out for that with a small, independent Canadian record label, Griffin Music, who put it out that August. By that juncture, its FM rock sound was all but obsolete and it sold minimally. 'John called to tell me it was coming out,' says Henry Small. 'I said to him it would be nice to get some royalties from it. He told me, "Don't worry, I'll take care of it." And that was the last conversation I had with him about that record.'

It wasn't as if Entwistle was ever remotely likely to be made destitute. At a stroke, he could have made millions from liquidating his prized guitar collection, and would have earned as much again, and more, for Quarwood. He wasn't, though, prepared to downsize in any aspect of his life. That would have been a dereliction of his duty as a rock star; a surrender almost. However, Quarwood cost him around £45,000 a month just to upkeep, so he had an ongoing, urgent need for ready cash. At last, this compelled him to take seriously the matter of the estate's porous accounts.

What he required, he concluded, was to have someone he could trust implicitly to oversee Quarwood on his behalf. Once he was back from the tour, he offered this job to his then twenty-five-year-old son. The offer came at an opportune moment for Christopher, whose own software company had not long gone under, and he accepted. That summer, Christopher moved into Quarwood with his fiancée, Leah, to take up the role of estate manager. For the next six years and whenever Entwistle was at home, Christopher essentially found himself also taking care of every other area of his father's life.

'I even fed and walked the dogs for him,' he says. 'Dad didn't want to be bothered with the day-to-day stuff; he let other people do it for him. It meant that I had no time for myself, because I had to do that seven days a week. I couldn't go out. Leah and I didn't go on holiday.

'He used to send me out to the chippy to bring back fish and chips for him. He went up the wall if you ever tried to nick one of his chips, so I would make sure that I did. He would make a growling noise and slap me on the hand. I could always tell if he was genuinely annoyed with me just by the look on his face, a frown. It didn't happen very often. If I had done something he didn't approve of, he would rip me a new one but, otherwise, he would back me to the hilt.'

■ ■ ■

The summer of the following year, Townshend agreed to offers to front seven performances of his other great concept work, one in London's Hyde Park on 29 June in aid of the Prince's Trust and six more at Madison Square Garden that July. He stipulated that these shows not be presented as a Who reunion, so instead they were billed simply as *Quadrophenia*.

Additionally, Townshend described the event in London as a 'celebrity concert performance'. Among those lined up for parts in the Hyde Park production were comic actors Stephen Fry and Ade Edmondson, ageing glam-rocker Gary Glitter, still then widely perceived in Britain as a benign, pantomime buffoon, and the star of the original film, Phil Daniels, cast as narrator. Townshend made an entreaty to Daltrey to appear at the shows. Daltrey thought the whole project 'an overblown ego trip',[37] and bargained to have Entwistle and Zak Starkey also included.

Ludicrously, what transpired in London and New York was that the three surviving original members of The Who got back together to play exclusively Who songs, but not as The Who. Nevertheless, the New York shows in particular were excellent and Entwistle was once again in his element. After each of the Madison Square Garden shows, he could be found holding court in the bar of his midtown Manhattan hotel, the Rihga Royal, on West 54th Street. Cy Langston and Bobby Pridden would be

---

[37] Taken from *Thanks a Lot, Mr Kibblewhite: My Life* by Roger Daltrey, Blink (2018)

at his side and, there, he would regale whatever crowd he had picked up for the night with his tall stories until the sun came up.

He took Lisa along with him to New York. One night, Steve and Laurie Luongo met up with them at the Rihga Royal. The two couples were in an elevator, headed down to the bar from Entwistle's suite. Lisa appeared to be drinking from a tumbler of water. Thirsty, Laurie asked her for a sip. The large glass was, in fact, filled with neat vodka. When Laurie winced, Lisa made a shushing gesture from behind Entwistle's back. Steve Luongo remembers, 'That was right around when everything between them started to get weird.'

With the *Quadrophenia* shows a resounding success, Townshend soon found himself inundated with bids to do more dates. Quickly, he consented to a twenty-five-date North American tour, starting 13 October in Portland. This time around, the shows went on sale flagged as 'Pete Townshend's *Quadrophenia*', but tickets sold sluggishly. Finally, Townshend conceded the point and agreed to let the tour go out as 'The Who's *Quadrophenia*'. After that, the shows sold out and The Who set off again, albeit with another 'big band' line-up that included a brass section. Townshend played acoustic guitar for the most part, backed by his brother, Simon, on electric, and 'Rabbit' Bundrick on keyboards. They played well, powerfully even. Momentarily, one might even forget that Moon wasn't up there with them and that theirs was not any more a precarious tightrope act, but a well-practised and precisely ordered routine.

Offstage, Entwistle, Townshend and Daltrey stayed apart and in their own camps, as separate and different from each other as ever. Sober, Townshend had begun to acquire the air of a dignified elder statesman. Good sense, vanity or some combination of both had kept Daltrey in great physical shape. Alone among them, Entwistle wanted to carry on raging against the dying of the light, but the toll this had on him was becoming ever more apparent to Who observers. Physically, The Ox seemed slighter, frailer, his face more pale and drawn. When they played in Vancouver on 16 and 17 October, Henry Small rendezvoused with Entwistle in his hotel bar before the first night's show.

'This was a couple of hours before we had to leave for the venue,' says Small. 'John drank six goblets of Courvoisier brandy and, by the time we got to the hall, he was quite inebriated. He had trouble putting his pants on in the dressing room. Townshend walked in. He looked at John struggling to get himself dressed, kind of shrugged, huffed, and turned and walked out again. Then, when the curtain came up, John's playing was impeccable.'

To friends and acquaintances, the reason for Entwistle's accelerated decline was all too obvious, since it coincided exactly with Lisa's entry into his life. According to rock photographer Ross Halfin, Lisa was 'a fucking cocaine nightmare and even John would hide from her'. Chris Charlesworth adds, 'I thought Lisa was completely mad. I don't want to be ungracious, but she always looked like a groupie to me. I didn't get to know her at all well, but it was pretty apparent that she shared John's vices. For as long as I had known him, he had liked a drink. And he had a huge capacity for booze. But, clearly, he was killing himself.'

Bill Curbishley takes a slightly different, more nuanced view. 'A lot of things with Lisa have been misconstrued, I think,' he offers. 'Deep down, she was a nice girl – and "nice" in the real sense of the word. But then again, a victim of her own vices, I suppose. In a sense, that exacerbated John's problems. If you're both drinkers, it's going to be harder for either of you to stop drinking. John wasn't about to change his lifestyle, because Lisa *was* that lifestyle. She was like a shadow of him in that respect. I think he felt that gave him a licence to go forward in the same way.'

Three shows in England that December, two at London's cavernous Earl's Court Arena and one in Manchester, rounded off the tour. Then, at the start of 1997, Entwistle got himself involved in another of Ron Magness's projects. This one was a country-rock band called The Pioneers, which again featured Mickey Wynne. With Magness producing and playing keyboards, the band had cut most of an album at Crocodile Studios in Soho. Magness talked Entwistle into overdubbing bass parts to the songs, ballads in the main, all of them competent but unspectacular. Entwistle put his tracks down one afternoon at Quarwood with Pridden engineering. The album, though, would not see the light of day until 2003 when it came out as *The Pioneers with Special Guest John Entwistle*, before quickly vanishing again. Entwistle, at least, seems to have made the most of this fleeting interlude.

'We did a bit of recording with John at Quarwood and then he took us off to the pub with him, Lisa and Bob,' says Wynne. 'After a few drinks, John invited everyone in the pub up to the house for more. All of these people enjoyed themselves at his expense. John wasn't saying much. I looked over at him at one point that night and he just raised his glass of brandy to me and winked. He just loved to be able to entertain other people, I think.'

Directly after that, Entwistle was asked to make a soundtrack album for an animated sci-fi show for children, *Van Pires*, that had been commissioned by the Fox TV network in the US. For this, he reconvened The John Entwistle Band and they set to work at Quarwood that spring. Entwistle had not long returned with Lisa from a holiday to the Mexican resort of Cabo and looked tanned and healthy, and the sessions got off to a laid-back, productive start. Days began with a late breakfast around the giant Quarwood kitchen table. After that, the musicians would record with Pridden through to early evening and then unwind together over dinner.

In short order, they completed all but one of the fourteen songs required. Even the last song, 'Bogeyman', only required a drum track. One afternoon, Entwistle came downstairs clutching a two-inch tape reel. He claimed that it had dropped at his feet from off a shelf on the second floor and with no apparent cause. The tape featured a recording of a drum track that Entwistle had got Moon to put down for one of his solo albums, but never got around to using. It just so happened to fit 'Bogeyman' perfectly.

'John always said that the top floor at Quarwood was haunted,' says Laurie Luongo, who had travelled over with her husband. 'He told me that he had once seen a dog, a Labrador, run off down a hallway up there. When he had gone to give chase, it vanished. He also told Steve and me how Max and he would play with a Ouija board. One time, they had asked it if anyone had been killed in the house. The board answered "yes". They found out that, during the First World War, Quarwood had been used to house convalescing soldiers and a nurse had been stabbed to death by one of her patients. Sure enough, the minute I walked up on to the second floor, I sensed that there was a presence there.'

In any event, as the sessions progressed, often as not it would be Lisa who was the most jarring presence in the house. Afternoon or night, she was loud, attention-seeking and seemingly inexhaustible. Late one evening, Steve and Laurie Luongo were having a nightcap with Entwistle and Lisa in one of the lounges. At a certain point, Lisa insisted upon putting on a video of Michael Flatley's *Lord of the Dance*. Stationing herself in front of the television, she proceeded to dance wildly along to it, seemingly oblivious to the others.

'It was insane,' recalls Steve Luongo. 'Lisa had on these tight pants with the Monopoly board printed all over them and was kicking her legs up over head. She was so jacked up that I feared she was going to have a heart-attack, right there in front of us.

'In general, Laurie and I came to feel that there had been an absolute, tectonic shift in the house. Max had run a more protective household, but now it was New Year's Eve every day. Everything was excessive with Lisa. She was fun, pretty and she appeared to make John happy, but there were all these other things going on. There had got to be a lot of people in John's life whose motives you would question, and who shouldn't have been allowed around him.'

'Basically, Lisa made friends with every cunt in Gloucestershire,' expands Christopher. 'These people would just come to Quarwood for the parties. Things were made a hell of a lot worse by the fact that they used to like joining her in imbibing as much of everything as they could.'

It was also almost as though the bad vibes had filtered through to the record. The loud, quasi hard-rock music that Entwistle and the band recorded during this period was singularly mirthless and unmemorable. Furthermore, it was doomed from the moment the TV show was cancelled after just twelve episodes. Held back for three years, when *Music for Van Pires* did at last slip out in 2000, it was into a vacuum and to be met with indifference.

That April of 1997, The Who took off on another tour, playing thirty-six shows in arenas across Europe and North America. This one seems to have passed without drama or incident, and likewise Christopher's Cotswolds wedding, which took place seven weeks after the completion of the tour on 4 October. The occasion was the first that Entwistle had seen Alison and Mick Bratby together since the break-up of their marriage. At the reception party afterwards, he had a drink with Bratby at the bar. Bratby thought Entwistle seemed a bit on edge, but that they had got on well enough. When the free bar ran out, Entwistle handed over his credit card and bought everyone's drinks for the rest of that night.

'How John felt about Alison and me being together, I really didn't get to know,' says Bratby. 'When we were having our drink, he told me, "Look after her," but that was all. And that was the last time that I saw him.'

'Lisa was shaking like a leaf, too, because she was frightened of meeting me,' notes Alison. 'I wasn't going to bite her head off. She wasn't the one who had caused us to break up. John also wouldn't dance at the wedding, which for him was unusual. But then, he seemed to me to be drugged up a little bit.'

Entwistle didn't go back to work in earnest until the early summer of the next year, and on this occasion it was with his own band once more. That May, he summoned The John Entwistle Band to Quarwood for four weeks' rehearsals with Luongo having fixed them up an extensive American tour. Alan St Jon had moved on to other work by then, so Luongo had also brought in a replacement keyboard player, Gordon Cotton, another New Yorker.

The mood at Quarwood was altogether heavier, more oppressive. Most days, it would be late afternoon before Entwistle appeared from his bedroom suite. When Lisa wasn't off up to London, she was occupied with the business of getting them cocaine. According to Luongo, 'Everyone who would turn up at the house had something to do with drugs. Either you were the guy who had the drugs, or the girlfriend of the guy who had the drugs, or an old friend of John's who had got drugs from his dealer.'

'Lisa had her issues for sure, but John was enabling about that, too,' insists Townsend. 'It seemed to me that Lisa wanted to get help and to not be the way that she was, but she wasn't strong enough to make that happen. I would try and sit and talk with her about it. And John did say to me at one point that if Lisa would get help, then he would also. To me, that seemed like he was putting it all on her. He could have been the one to have picked up that torch and led the way, too.'

In total that year, from mid-June to mid-November, The John Entwistle Band played forty-two shows around the US. To begin with, Entwistle left Lisa behind at Quarwood. Approaching fifty-four, he seemed to want to act now with all the abandon of his youth and without fear of any kind of consequence. He helped himself to more of everything – booze, drugs, sex. Luongo took along a hand-held video camera to document the carousing and like a naughty schoolboy, Entwistle would badger him each day to be shown whatever had been captured of the previous night's indulgences.

'It might be that I would come walking down a hotel corridor and say, "Ah, let's see what's going on in John's room,"' explains Luongo. 'I would open the door and there would be half-naked girls, bottles of booze and whatever else. I was John's licence to get as drunk or jovial as he wanted, because he knew that I would always watch his back.

'Whenever we could, we would get a "green room" in between our two suites and have a party. One night, it got to the end of the party and there were just four or five people left in the room, and John wasn't there any more. The others started to filter out, but there was this one guy who was sat alone on the couch, holding a bass guitar. He had waited all night for John to sign it for him. He went on sitting there until, all of a sudden, the door to John's suite opened. This girl came out first and then John, with his hair all messed up and no socks on. It was obvious what had been going on between them, and it turned out that the girl was this poor guy's girlfriend.

'She looked at the guy sat on the couch and just ran out of the room. John was still stood there with his hair stuck up like a rooster.

He went over and sat down next to this guy. John said to him, "Sorry about that, man. Do you still want me to sign the bass?" And the guy said, "Yeah." So, John signed it and the guy left.'

As the tour wound on, Lisa went on urging Entwistle to let her come out and join them. He relented just as soon as they had begun a second round of dates at the start of that October. Lisa arrived in time to see them play a show in Frazier, Pennsylvania, on 4 October. The tour party spent that night at a tavern on the outskirts of the blue-collar town, just off the Interstate. With a show to do in Chattanooga, Tennessee, two days later, they faced a drive of 700 miles. Luongo made arrangements for them to leave by noon the next day.

At the appointed hour, everyone was on the bus but for Entwistle and Lisa. After fifteen more minutes, Entwistle alone appeared and looking agitated. Once he got on the bus, he told Luongo they should depart immediately without waiting for Lisa. Next morning, Luongo took a call from the night manager of the tavern in Frazier. He informed Luongo that he would be sending him a bill for $1,000 to cover damages and cleaning. The girl they had left behind, he said, had wrecked the furniture in her room, and had smeared excrement over the bed and walls.

'It blew my mind,' says Luongo. 'I had to have the guy repeat the story for me. He told me, "The way I see it, she stood up on the bed, squatted down in the middle of it, and then rubbed her shit all over the sheets and walls. I know what shit looks like and smells like, and that's what she did." The truth of the matter is, maybe it was barbeque sauce and this guy was trying to milk John Entwistle for money. But if you ask me if it was true or not, I would tell you that either one of those things could just as well have happened.

'I talked to John about it in some depth. I said to him, "Look, man, we've got to get her into rehab or she's going to die." It hadn't really taken John down yet. He got Laurie to check out some places for him, but it never panned out.'

'That was their deal,' says Townsend. 'John would always be very excited that Lisa was coming out to meet us on the road. Then, she would come out and they would destroy a room with their fighting, or he would leave her somewhere or other. It was always because of the same things – drugs and alcohol.'

Cooped up back at Quarwood, the cycles of their relationship got to be even more frenetic and volatile. One day to the next, the two of them would wake hungover, party it off, fight, flame out and then repeat, over and again. By this point, Christopher had moved with Leah into one of the cottages on the grounds. The chaos that his father's life had become went on all around them. Twice, he intercepted complete strangers wandering around upstairs in the main house. Both of them were people Lisa had invited back from the local pub and then forgotten about. Whenever he opened up the books, he couldn't fail to see just how dangerously the scale of Entwistle's and Lisa's excesses had shot up. 'A lot of cash was being taken out of machines with his credit cards,' he reveals. 'I saw the statements every month and it was the maximum amount every day, £500.

'Dad wasn't taking the money out, because he wouldn't have been up, or else he wasn't around at the time. His accountant told him that he was spending £25,000 a month on stuff that didn't have any appreciable value. A lot of that went up his nose. I know he wasn't an angel before and did everything to excess, but Lisa made him so much worse. I did ask him about it, and he told me it was never fun to be the only sober one at a party, so he would join in. Whenever Lisa went away, he would have the occasional snort, but that would be it. He wasn't putting half of Colombia up his nose, which is what she did. Those times, we would go out together and actually do stuff.

'There were other times when he got to be very morose about things, and especially about Lisa. They argued all the time, but you couldn't say anything against her to him. You weren't allowed to. To a great extent, that ended up bringing about the end of my own marriage. Leah just didn't understand why I couldn't and wouldn't say certain things to my dad. If I did say a bad word about Lisa when she was back in his good books, he wouldn't forget that. I had to shut my mouth.

'Lisa had him in a dark place in his head. She would be all sweetness and light to my face, but I was aware of the fact that she was back-stabbing me to Dad. She was desperate to get me out of the picture, because I knew the extent of what was going on, even though I could do nothing about it. Those latter years were the most horrible of my life. It's sad, but of that whole time, I can't think of very many high points. I got to be with Dad at least. When he got up, I would go over and sit with him in the kitchen, and we'd chat. He would have his cup of tea and chocolate biscuits, and be doing his crossword. Otherwise, life around Quarwood was not fun. It was Lisa that truly fucked him up, and I hate her for what she did to him.'

22

Last Orders

In the spring of 1999, The John Entwistle Band went back out on the road. Beginning at a Marriott hotel complex in Atlanta, Georgia, on 22 May, they toured through until the third week of August, trawling up and down the East Coast of the US. For the greater part, these were club shows, inglorious and financially unrewarding. One date on their itinerary, though, stood out. On 10 July, Entwistle was invited to appear at the Woodstock '99 festival, staged over three days on a disused airbase in upstate New York to mark the thirtieth anniversary of the original. Since the bill was largely comprised of contemporary, alternative-rock acts such as the Red Hot Chili Peppers, Rage Against the Machine and Limp Bizkit, Entwistle's presence allowed the organisers to claim a direct link between their show and the fabled one of 1969.

'That was a last moment thing,' says Gordon Cotton. 'When we pulled up to the site, all that John said was, "What the fuck am I doing back here?"'

Three decades and a battery of corporate sponsors separated Woodstock '99 from its parent. Yet, as an event, the modern iteration proved to be every bit as gruelling and ill-equipped.

That weekend in New York was a boiling hot one, the daytime temperatures rising to 100°F. The site had been cleared of trees so that there was no shade to be found anywhere. Drink and food prices at the concession stands were exorbitant. A mood of frustration and anger soon prevailed among the 400,000-strong festival audience. This began to bubble up during Limp Bizkit's Saturday night set. There were skirmishes in the crowd and sections of the plywood perimeter fencing were also ripped down.

On Sunday afternoon, Entwistle and his band were the second act on the site's third stage. Under a blazing sun, they played to an appreciative, but distracted, audience numbering a few thousand. Later that same night, Entwistle had also been asked to make a guest appearance with the headlining Red Hot Chili Peppers. However, by then Woodstock '99 had slipped from out of anyone's control. As the Peppers played, fans tore down more tracts of fencing and also vendor stands, using them as kindling to start huge bonfires. With the site aflame, four sexual assaults were reported. A force of New York State Troopers eventually arrived to quell the carnage. Steve Luongo remembers, 'When I got home and turned on MTV, I was expecting to see "John Entwistle's triumphant return". And all I saw instead were fires and mayhem.'

The whole tour also did nothing to alleviate Entwistle's cash-flow issues, which were once again becoming serious. The situation got to be so precarious that Bobby Pridden put in a call to Daltrey, alerting him to the fact that Entwistle would need to be bailed out. Daltrey in turn went to see Townshend and to float the idea of doing a Who tour to assist Entwistle. Townshend prevaricated at first, but was persuaded to go out again the next summer when they would do thirty-eight dates around the US and UK. On the matter of Townshend's initial reticence, Daltrey later wrote: 'Pete was an addict himself – he knew the risks. He knew that if we helped John out, we risked becoming his enablers. John was an alcoholic and he had a good nose for hoovering up whatever was left of the party. It had all caught up with him.'[38]

According to Laurie Luongo, Entwistle by now had reservations of his own about touring with The Who. 'I started to notice that John would be very different around The Who,' she says. 'He had got to feel uncomfortable about being with them, I think. They would have their own dressing rooms. They all flew separately. He was very uptight around them. He likened it to being in jail. He would say to us, "I have to go back to Who jail."'

Ten days prior to setting off with The Who, Entwistle ended up doing a very different kind of show. Going through the Quarwood mail one morning that May, Christopher had happened across a letter from a John de Cani, who drummed with a local covers band, The Stowaways. Tongue firmly in cheek, de Cani conveyed that his band had a charity gig coming up at the British Legion club in Stow, but were without a bass player and would Entwistle be interested in filling in? Christopher dutifully read the letter out to his father.

'He went "Urgh" to begin with,' recalls Christopher. 'But I managed to convince him that it would be a fun thing to do, so he had me call up this guy and invite him round to the house. Naturally, John de Cani was flabbergasted. In fact, he thought I was one of his mates taking the piss. He didn't believe it until the moment that he drove up to the house and Dad went out to welcome him.'

The show went ahead on the evening of Saturday, 27 May 2000 in front of a couple of hundred locals and a crew from a

---

[38] Taken from *Thanks a Lot, Mr Kibblewhite: My Life* by Roger Daltrey, Blink (2018)

regional television news show, *Central News*. Armed with his trusty Alembic bass and sporting a pair of blue suede shoes, Entwistle took up his customary spot stage-right and from where he was the centre of all attention. 'He was up there pissing about and showing off, which he loved to do,' says Christopher. 'That night, he also had everyone tell him what a wonderful person he was and he always loved to hear that, too.'

On 6 June, The Who kicked off their US tour at a New York City arena, the Jacob K Javits Convention Centre, located on the Manhattan bank of the Hudson River. Two months later, they had crossed over to the West Coast and, on 14 August, played the Hollywood Bowl. At Entwistle's invitation, Maxene went along to the LA show. 'I was devastated at how old, haggard and unhealthy he looked,' she says. 'John always was like one of the Lost Boys in *Peter Pan*. He never wanted to grow up. But it's one thing to be young at heart, and quite another to carry on living as if you're still nineteen when you're in your mid-fifties. It just doesn't work.

'At one point during the show, Roger handed the mic over to John and he announced, "I want to dedicate this next song to my second wife, who's out there in the audience." The song was "My Wife" and I all but fell out of my seat. After the show, I went over and gave John a hug. I whispered in his ear, "You never, ever honoured me like that in all of our fourteen years together." Well, John squeezed me so tight that it took my breath away, and he told me, "I'm so proud of you. I wish I could do what you've done." Right then, I knew that his days were numbered.'

'There was a decline in John and you can't beat around the bush about that,' says Bill Curbishley. 'He drank vast amounts, plus he was doing cocaine and whatever else. He was all "up". He had started to put on a bit of weight, too. Everything combined to exacerbate the problem that he had with his heart, but which he had always told us was quite trivial. So, even then, I didn't have any fear for him.'

That October, The Who returned to New York to do a four-night engagement at Madison Square Garden. Entwistle flew Lisa out to join him for the shows. Under any circumstances, New York's night-time temptations, together with Lisa, would have been a potent cocktail for him to take. By this stage in their relationship, it became a shove into a new and hellish frontier.

After the first night's show, the two of them made off to the China Club. Lisa barrelled around the place, looking to score drugs. At a certain point, a stranger invited her along to another club where she was told she would be able to pick up cocaine of premium quality. Without saying a word to Entwistle, Lisa high-tailed it from the China Club and was gone for the next two days. At their Manhattan hotel, Entwistle was left to stew and grew increasingly frantic.

When Lisa did pitch back up, she was in a wretched state, which only intensified Entwistle's fury. The final night of their stay, he invited the Luongos up to their hotel suite after the Garden show. They arrived to find a dreadful scene unfolding. Lisa was holed up in the bedroom, weeping, while Entwistle brooded in the lounge. Lisa beckoned Laurie to join her with the offer of a line of cocaine.

'We did the coke and then, all of a sudden, Lisa completely flipped out,' describes Laurie. 'She took off her shirt – she didn't have a bra on – and then ran, full force, at the window, shouting, "I want to die!" We were on the forty-something floor. She hit the window sideways-on and cannonballed off. She only weighed, like, ninety pounds. She did this again and again, four times in all, and I just about freaked. I ran into the other room and shouted out to John, "You need to come in here right now! Lisa's trying to throw herself out of the window!" He looked up at me and said, "Let her."'

Entwistle did, though, get up and go into the bedroom. When he re-emerged after a time, it was with a prone Lisa hanging off his leg. With each step that Entwistle took, he dragged Lisa across the floor on her bare stomach. Laurie says, 'Finally, he turned to Steve and said, "Get this cunt off me!" When we did manage to do just that, they went off and got Lisa another room of her own in the hotel.'

'In that last phase with John, Lisa was a train wreck,' observes Joe Walsh. 'I know that both of them had got themselves into a pattern of anarchy and chaos. I loved Lisa a lot, but she totally lost her path and her perspective. In retrospect, John must have had the occasional moments of clarity. By then, though, I think that his whole situation must have turned into a big, scary monster that he couldn't bring himself to confront. Even so, if John had really wanted to stop, then he would have done.'

■ ■ ■

Altogether, Entwistle had trapped himself in a vicious circle. There was no difference any more whether he was holed up at Quarwood, or off on tour – he would debilitate himself just the same one way or the other. When The Who played the penultimate date of this latest reunion at Wembley Arena in mid-November of 2000, he appeared to be in a desolate state. Like Maxene at the Hollywood Bowl, Chris Charlesworth was taken aback when he encountered him backstage at Wembley. By that point, Charlesworth had not seen Entwistle for the better part of four years.

'There was a big hospitality area that was full of people I didn't recognise and John was sort of standing off to one side on his own,' Charlesworth remembers. 'He greeted me like an old friend, but he looked sad to me. He was clearly a bit pissed, too.

He had a big glass of brandy and was a little glassy-eyed. He just didn't look a well man at all.'

Sequestered at Quarwood for the next six months, Entwistle locked himself up with Lisa once again with money to burn through. When he grew to be spiritless and unsettled, as ever he would, he put in a call to Steve Luongo and had him set up yet another gruelling club tour of America for The John Entwistle Band. This one was to run from mid-May to mid-July and would take them to places such as Poughkeepsie, New York, Kelseyville, California, and Kettering, Ohio. Like their leader, the band also was running in ever-decreasing circles.

According to Godfrey Townsend, such was Entwistle's weakened state that his doctor cautioned him against doing the tour. Townsend says he was asked not to smoke on the tour bus, so that Entwistle might be encouraged to refrain. Before they set off on the road, Luongo also tried to stop Entwistle from having access to cocaine. 'I called up all of his connections that I knew of, including his assistant with The Who, and said to each of them, "Look, I would really like to shut things down and for him not to be able to reach out to you,"' he explains. 'John always had someone do things for him, so he didn't know anybody to call. He couldn't get stuff on his own, so he stopped trying and, for that one tour, he embraced sobriety.'

This is not a view shared by Townsend. 'In his natural habitat, John smoked two packets of Winston 100s a day and drank a bottle of Rémy Martin every night,' he says. 'On top of that, he would do whatever people brought to him. The same people that had told me not to smoke around John would also bring cocaine to him.

'He wouldn't eat well either. At one point on the tour, we were sitting down to dinner somewhere and the menu got passed round. I was going to get a veggie burger. I turned to John and said, "Why don't you try one of these?" He said OK, but then he added, "Don't let it go to your head." You couldn't stop him from doing anything and, whenever we were out on the road, he would mostly push things to the limit. My wife at the time would see pictures of us and go, "Oh my God, John looks white." He always had that pasty look.'

At the end of the tour, Entwistle heard from Bobby Pridden that Townshend was making plans for a new Who album, destined to be their first in twenty years. Via Pridden, Townshend asked Entwistle to submit up to seven new songs for consideration for this proposed record, out of which he meant to pick four. That Townshend chose not to speak directly to Entwistle about any of this was indicative of just how distant from each other the two men had become. Entwistle, though, was temporarily fired up again. Immediately, he summoned Luongo over to Quarwood. Pridden set them up in the top-floor demo studio and they went to work together writing new material.

Entwistle's burst of enthusiasm soon abated. No longer able to tolerate being around Lisa in the main house, Luongo was put up in one of the Quarwood cottages. One morning, Entwistle called down and asked if he might come over and join him for breakfast. 'It was early for John, 9.30, 10.00am, and so I was surprised,' says Luongo. 'That morning was the most morose and vulnerable that I ever saw John. And it was when he was stone-cold sober.

> I expected him to walk in and straight away to start laughing at the sight of me cooking away in the kitchen. But when he came through the door, he had the most mournful expression on his face. He looked sad, lost, almost in tears. Even at home, I had never known John not to be dressed up like a rock star. Yet he had on an old pair of beige Wranglers and sneakers. Until then, I

hadn't known that he even owned a pair of sneakers. He told me he wasn't really hungry, so I knew that he had something else on his mind. Sure enough, he began to talk about Lisa. He came to me looking for advice. He even asked me, 'How do I get out of this? What should I do?'

Lisa was out of control by that stage. She resented anybody else's friendship with John and things had got to be toxic up at the house. Last time that I had stayed up there, she had gone into a rage and thrown a phone at my head. I just couldn't bear to be near her any longer and John understood that – it was kind of an unspoken agreement between us. I think John was desperate to figure out a way to get out of the life that he was leading with her. Many times, he had told me that he envied me my happy marriage. And it was obvious to both Laurie and me that he had loved Alison deeply. Both of us came to believe that when that relationship ended, it had truly screwed him up.

That morning, I said to him, 'Maybe you don't need a girl that pretty. Maybe you don't need to be the guy from The Who. Maybe you should go out and meet somebody who knows you as just plain old John.' That, though, was something that he just didn't want, or wasn't able to do. That was another thing about John – he was all about collecting trophies. One night, he would tell Lisa to shape up or ship out. By the next, she would have played on his insecurities and things would go right back to being where they were. He was so used to having other people carry out his dirty work for him, me included, that he didn't know how to stand his ground.

Shortly after the sessions at Quarwood wrapped up, Townshend cooled on the idea of making a new Who album. The handful of songs that Entwistle wrote with Luongo that late summer went unrecorded and forgotten about.

■ ■ ■

One bright, clear September day when they were still working at Quarwood, two commercial airlines were piloted into the twin towers of the World Trade Center in New York. As they started to digest the events of that 11 September afternoon, Luongo urged that they should do something positive. The month following, The John Entwistle Band happened to have another handful of shows lined up in the New York area, including one at BB King's Blues Club in midtown Manhattan on 21 October. Luongo suggested that they add a second night at the club and make it a benefit concert.

Entwistle agreed at once and Luongo went ahead and made the arrangements for an extra show to go ahead on the night of 20 October. Almost as soon as he had, Entwistle got a call from Townshend. Townshend had just got off the phone with Paul McCartney, who was also in the process of organising a benefit show for 20 October. It was to be called the Concert for New York and would be staged at Madison Square Garden. For his event, McCartney had already lined up David Bowie, Elton John, Mick Jagger and Keith Richards, Janet Jackson and Jay-Z, and he wanted Townshend to commit The Who to perform.

'I heard John say to Pete, "Yeah . . . Yeah . . . No, can't do it – we're playing,"' recalls Luongo. 'Then, he hung up the phone. When he told me what the call from Pete was about, I said to him, "Are you nuts?" I told him that this was a lot bigger than us and that he couldn't be the guy to prevent The Who from playing. So John called Pete right back and agreed to do both shows.

'He did, though, put in all kinds of stipulations. The Who's rehearsals had to be made to fit around our band's schedule; they would have to go on early on the night, so that we could make our gig. After The Who's set, John also insisted that he and I be able to hop into a limousine and be driven the ten blocks uptown to BB King's. Now, you could say John was a cunt to Pete . . . or that he was a man who didn't want to break his word to his fans. I'd say he was a bit of both.'

The John Entwistle Band's show that 20 October ended up raising $10,000, which they donated to the Putnam Valley Volunteer Fire Department. Earlier that same evening, The Who blazed through their four-song set at the Garden, opening up with 'Who Are You' and closing with a rousing, euphoric 'Won't Get Fooled Again'. By common consensus, they were the highlight of the whole Concert for New York show. It was the first truly great performance that they had given in almost twenty years at least.

From New York, Entwistle, Luongo and Godfrey Townsend flew on to Japan. Entwistle had agreed to perform at a series of Beatles' tribute concerts billed as 'A Walk Down Abbey Road'. The shows were the brainchild of Alan Parsons, engineer on both the *Abbey Road* and *Let It Be* albums. For his show band, Parsons had also recruited Todd Rundgren and Heart singer Ann Wilson. Entwistle had been lured by an offer from Parsons of $10,000 a show. Parsons told Entwistle that he had tried to get Mick Fleetwood to drum, but without success. Entwistle suggested Luongo instead, and even brokered him the same $10,000 terms. When Parsons then found himself short of a guitarist, Entwistle had chipped in once more with Townsend but, on this occasion, the fee was reduced significantly.

The shows went well and Entwistle, who had travelled without Lisa, appeared to be in better spirits. One night in Tokyo, he joined Rundgren and Luongo in walking the two miles from their hotel to a strip club. At the end of their night out, Rundgren also wanted to walk back. Reluctantly, Entwistle agreed. Soon after they departed, he spotted a delicatessen open late. He went inside and bought a cream cake for himself. When they set off again, it began to drizzle.

'Todd was a fast walker, whereas John was wearing his Cuban heels,' recalls Luongo. 'I was trying to keep the two ends of the train together, speeding to catch Todd up and then dropping back to check on John. Also, John was always concerned about his hair, so he was bitching and moaning the whole way. Finally, we made it back to the hotel. It was a luxurious place with an all-marble hallway, so quiet you could hear your own breathing echo in the halls.

'We were stood waiting for the elevator. John was holding his cake in a box. As the elevator arrived, I turned to him and said, "So, let's hear some of that bitching and moaning now." With that, he did a windmill with the cake box, let go of it, and it smashed up against the top of the elevator. It sounded like a bomb going off. The desk clerk near enough passed out and Todd went bug-eyed. The three of us got in the elevator and went up to our rooms without another word. Next morning, I asked John, "How was the cake?" Smiling now, he said, "A bit condensed." Tokyo was the last show that we did together. If I had known that at the time, I would have made sure to remember it better.'

Back in England that November, Entwistle had set up to have a selection of his caricature pictures exhibited at a London gallery, the Cut, which had just then opened on a side street a stone's throw from Waterloo train station. The gallery owner, Terry Rawlings, arranged a launch party for the exhibition that Entwistle attended. 'Dougal' Butler and Richard Barnes also went along to this soirée.

'John turned up and he was all grey,' remembers Barnes. 'He had grey hair, grey skin and he had on a grey suit. I even said to him, "Weren't you on the cover of last month's *Embalming Monthly*?" He proceeded to polish off almost an entire bottle of Rémy to himself. I'm no stranger to people drinking, but that is a fuck of a lot of booze.'

Butler recalls, 'Richard came over to me and said, "Fuck me, Doug, what is John like?" Speaking for myself, I couldn't have been more shocked. John was nothing like the man I had known. I mean, I never even saw Moon get himself into a state that was that bad. As soon as I was on my train home to Twickenham, I got on my phone and rang Alison. I told her that I had just seen John at this exhibition and that he had ended up being near-comatose. I said to her, "Alison, I've got the exact same feeling in my blood and water as I had with Moon. He'll be gone within months if somebody doesn't do something."'

Next day, Alison rang her ex-husband. She told him that she needed to have a talk with him and they arranged to have lunch. Before the agreed date, Entwistle called back and cancelled. It was the last time that the two of them spoke.

23

Exit Stage Right

Entwistle was going to be busy in 2002. The Who had lined up a tour of North America that was scheduled to start in Las Vegas at the end of that June and finish up in Toronto on 28 September. Prior to that, they had arranged to do five shows in England during January and February, among them two at the Royal Albert Hall to iron out their creases. After these commitments and with The Pioneers' album due to get a belated release, Entwistle had also agreed to perform a handful of live dates with that band.

His first obligation of the year was to attend the NAMM International Music Market in Los Angeles from 17 January. He performed a guest spot at the event and, later that same evening, went out to dinner with a group of friends that included Joe Walsh and John Alcock. Like Walsh, Alcock also thought that Entwistle's hearing had become much worse. Indeed, at home at Quarwood, Entwistle had taken to wearing a hearing aid. However, often as not, he would leave this out whenever he was on show.

'I figured that he had all but gone deaf,' says Alcock. 'He talked very quietly, as if he were aware of the fact that he was prone to speak too loudly. I told him that he really needed to get his hearing sorted out, but he just fobbed me off, as he always would do whenever you expressed any concern to him about his wellbeing. He didn't like people nagging at him – it would annoy him. He had put on a bit of weight, too, but he didn't strike me as being in bad condition.'

The first Who shows of the year went ahead at Portsmouth Guildhall on 27 and 28 January. They next played at Watford Coliseum on 31 January and then the Royal Albert Hall on 7 and 8 February. The second night at the London venue, Entwistle was resplendent onstage in a pair of black pants and his Cuban heel boots. He took his solo during '5:15', winding up with apparent nonchalance from a series of tremoring, rumbling runs to unleash a blizzard of rapid-fire, finger-picked notes. It was an extraordinary display, a fact acknowledged by Townshend, who made a low bow towards him when he returned to the stage. Even under the stage lights it was apparent how pale Entwistle was, but to the vast majority of the audience that night, he must have still seemed to be at the zenith of his powers. That was his conjuror's trick. Throughout the rest of that show, a practised Who watcher would have spotted how Entwistle kept a close eye on whatever Townshend played.

'John only did that at the latter Who shows,' says Ross Halfin. 'Originally, he had always looked out to the audience. He was checking to see where Townshend's hands were, what chords he was playing. I suppose that was because he was so deaf that he couldn't hear what Pete was playing. And whenever Townshend was annoyed with John, he would turn his back on him.

'Then again, I remember going along to Pete's boat house to shoot them in rehearsals. When I arrived, John was off by himself in the rehearsal room. He was sat on an amp cabinet, staring down at the floor. Townshend said to me, "I'm going in there to sit with John. He looks like he needs some company." If he was in a bar, John would be great fun. Away from that, I found him to be quite a sad character.'

During the second week of that June, they began a further round of rehearsals for the North American tour. Recovering from 'flu, Entwistle turned up to these sessions looking fatigued and ashen. He asked for a plastic chair, so that he could sit down between songs. Entwistle also complained to Bobby Pridden of pains in his left arm and shoulder, but put these down to the fact that he had not picked up his bass in a couple of months. Townshend claimed later that he thought Entwistle had seemed physically ill. He said that he told his brother Simon, who was back-up guitarist for the tour, that he was worried such a long and arduous engagement would be too much for Entwistle to endure.

'John wasn't going to talk about it,' Townshend continued. 'You wouldn't get a sense from him of what was going on. It was not so much that he internalised it, or denied it. As far as he was concerned, what would be would be.'[39]

'I don't know whether Pete came to that conclusion in retrospect, or if he really thought it at the time,' considers Curbishley. 'Personally, I didn't really think there was anything wrong with John physically. I put John's sitting down to his being bored and wanting to stay out of things. Nobody ever said to me, "We should really take care of John and watch over him." Part of that was John's persona as well. He was like a rock in a sense. He was also just not the sort of person who enjoyed being off the road, so what else was he going to do?'

For insurance purposes, Entwistle had to undergo a medical

---

[39] Taken from the documentary film *An Ox's Tale: the John Entwistle Story* directed by Glenn Aveni and Steve Luongo, Act 1 Entertainment (2006)

before the tour commenced. His high levels of blood pressure and cholesterol were noted at this procedure, but since there didn't appear to be any other significant issues, the upshot was that he was given an otherwise clean bill of health. However, the band's insurers had not required him to have a detailed physical examination. Were he to have had just a routine electro-cardiogram scan, it would have picked up that three of the arteries to his heart were severely blocked – one fully and another by three-quarters.

Christopher accompanied him to the medical. 'In reality, he required a triple bypass, but we had no idea about the extent of his heart problem and nor did he,' he says. 'Dad getting the 'flu was a surprise. He was very rarely ill. Yes, he did look tired. But that was because half the time he was on cocaine, which never makes you look good.'

On the morning of Tuesday, 25 June, Christopher drove his father to Heathrow Airport to catch his flight to Las Vegas. They left Lisa behind at Quarwood. Entwistle was flying out a couple of days early so as to be able to oversee another exhibition of his drawings, this one being mounted at the Hard Rock Hotel and Casino, where The Who were also set to open their tour on 28 June. In the car outside the airport, Entwistle kissed Christopher goodbye and, at the terminal doors, turned to wave him off. Christopher didn't doubt that he would speak to his father some time the next day. Entwistle's absent-mindedness was a running joke between them. Inevitably, he would have forgotten to pack something or other and would call home to have Christopher send it on.

■ ■ ■

Bill Curbishley arrived in Las Vegas the next evening. Checking in to the Hard Rock Hotel, he found Entwistle stationed in the bar with Cy Langston. He seemed to Curbishley to be in good spirits. Curbishley told Entwistle that he was heading up to his room to unpack and shower, but that he would be back down soon to join the two of them for a drink. As it happened, weary from his long flight, Curbishley went up to his room and promptly fell asleep.

Sometime later that night, Entwistle hooked up with Alison Rowse. Petite and dark-haired, the thirty-two-year-old Rowse danced at a local strip club, the Déjà Vu, where she went under the stage name of Sianna. Entwistle had first met her at the Déjà Vu on a previous visit to Vegas and they had wound up having sex. Now, Entwistle and Rowse went on drinking in the hotel bar until the early hours of the next morning. Entwistle also did a small amount of cocaine. At around 3.00am, the two of them went up to Entwistle's suite in room 658. According to Rowse, before they went to bed together, Entwistle took out his hearing aid and put it on the bedside table, and then folded his trousers carefully, precisely, over the back of a chair. 'He was charming and kind, a real gentleman,' she said.[40]

Rowse awoke at 10.00am. Beside her in bed, she found that Entwistle was cold to the touch and unresponsive. She later reported that she had felt him stir at 6.00am and turn on to his left side. At some point during the next four hours, Entwistle's heart had given out and he had died in his sleep. He was fifty-seven. Curbishley was out playing golf with his younger brother, Alan, when The Who's tour manager, Rex King, called him with the news. After hanging up on King, Curbishley immediately phoned Townshend who was in Los Angeles. Stunned, Townshend offered to ring Daltrey and also called Maxene.

---

[40] Quoted from article in the *Independent* newspaper, published 22 September 2002

'I'd had a premonition that he was gone, so I was not at all surprised,' says Maxene. 'But it was a pretty sobering conversation. Pete, and later on Roger, both said that they would pay for my air fare if I wanted to go to the funeral. I explained to them that I had already made my peace with John.'

It was Cy Langston who called Christopher. Instantly, Christopher assumed that Langston was phoning about his father missing an item of luggage. Langston corrected him, saying, 'No, Chris, no mate. I'm really sorry. He's gone.' Once he got off the phone with Langston, Christopher went down to Queenie's cottage to tell her that her son was dead. Then the two of them informed Lisa. Christopher next called his mother. Alison screamed and dropped the phone, leaving Mick Bratby to finish up the conversation with Christopher. It was 11.00pm that night before Christopher was able to contact Entwistle's stepbrother, Bernard. The next morning, Bernard went to see Entwistle's father Bert at the nursing home that he had been moved into in Newport.

'Bert was bedridden and in the advanced stages of dementia,' explains Bernard. 'Quietly, two or three times, I said to him, "Dad, it's about John. He's gone." I didn't tell him the whole scenario, just that John had died. He asked me where it had happened. Then, a single tear ran down from the corner of his eye.'

The report of the Clark County Coroner's office concluded that Entwistle had 'died from heart failure triggered by cocaine'. A subsequent inquest by the Cotswold coroner, Lester Maddrell, clarified that Entwistle had not taken a lethal amount of cocaine, but rather that he had died from the effects of the drug 'superimposed upon ischemic heart disease'. In Britain, the tabloid and broadsheet press were fixated equally upon the more lurid details of Entwistle's passing. Generally, Entwistle's was reported as the archetypal sex, drugs and rock-'n'-roll death. Writing later, even Daltrey surmised: 'John would have liked the way he went . . . If they'd put a glass case around his bed with him still in it, he would have been delighted. He would have thought, "This is exactly where I deserve to be."'[41]

Already grief-stricken, Christopher was appalled at how his father's death was covered. 'It was all so distorted,' he says. 'He had trace amounts of cocaine in his system. As in, he had done a line. It didn't kill him. It may well have sped up the heart problem, but he would have died anyway, unfortunately. I'm sure that it was Cy who would have got hold of the cocaine for Dad. I don't blame him for that. Dad was no angel, and he would have expected Cy to do it. That was part of Cy's job.

'Dad partied with some friends, did a line of coke, had sex with someone he knew, an exotic dancer, and never woke up. You know what? It wasn't the worst way to go. It could have been a prolonged illness. The examiner who did the autopsy told me that he wouldn't have felt a thing, which was one of the things that I appreciated most. Even still, Dad's preferred ending would have been to have passed at Quarwood at a hundred-and-twenty years old and surrounded by a bevy of beauties.'

Four days after Entwistle's death, The Who performed the rescheduled opening night of their tour at the Hollywood Bowl. Pino Palladino, who had played in Townshend's solo band, stood in on bass guitar. Curbishley had initially flown the band's crew back to London from Las Vegas, meaning to cancel the tour. However, the traces of cocaine that were confirmed in Entwistle's autopsy report made it likely that the band's tour insurance would be voided. Together, Curbishley, Townshend and Daltrey decided that they had been left with no option but to go ahead

---

[41] Taken from *Thanks a Lot, Mr Kibblewhite: My Life* by Roger Daltrey, Blink (2018)

with the tour. Addressing a sell-out crowd at the Hollywood Bowl at one point that night, Townshend said, 'This is difficult. Pino came and rescued us. Even without that huge harmonic noise that usually comes from that side of the stage, it's sounding pretty good to me.'

'It was a great show considering,' affirms Bobby Pridden. 'But my memories of it are awful. It was very strange looking across the stage and seeing someone else stood there.'

Nine days after the Hollywood Bowl show, The Who's principals returned to England to attend Entwistle's funeral in Stow. Langston had made the arrangements to have Entwistle's body flown home. In Vegas, he had bought for him an ostentatious coffin. At Entwistle's feet inside the casket, Langston had placed a pair of his Cuban-heeled boots. This coffin was so wide that, back in Stow, they had to take the undertakers' doors off at the hinges in order for it to be squeezed inside the building. 'The undertaker subsequently called me up embarrassed about the whole business with the coffin, because it got reported in the local paper,' says Christopher. 'I told him Dad would have loved it. A coffin so big you had to take doors off the hinges? That would have made him laugh his head off.'

The morning of the funeral, wreaths in the shape of bass guitars and spiders were laid out all across the croquet lawn at Quarwood. The funeral service was held at a packed St Edward's Church in the town. Lisa was so hysterical that she had to be helped into the church. According to Laurie Luongo, 'Afterwards, we all went to John's local for drinks and food. Lisa got really, really drunk and started a scene. Sue, the Quarwood groundskeeper, had to have her brother drive her back to the house. When Lisa got out of the car at Quarwood, she started to scream, "This is *my* house! This is *my* bloody house!" She was just delusional.'

That same day, Entwistle's body was cremated at a private family service. Christopher scattered his father's ashes over the grounds at Quarwood – some out by the fish pond and the rest under the shade of the monkey puzzle tree that they had almost planted together. That escapade had happened just a few weeks earlier, but was also now a lifetime ago.

Epilogue

Encore

It is a Sunday, mid-afternoon, in July 2018. All of Britain is basking in a heatwave and, in the Cotswolds, the sun is high and fierce in a sky of uninterrupted blue. In the back garden of their house, Alison Entwistle and Mick Bratby are hosting a small get-together. Bratby is manning the barbeque, steaks sizzling, Alison nipping in and out of the kitchen with trays laden with salads, sandwiches and drinks. Sitting around a wrought-iron garden table out on the patio, under the shade of a parasol, are Alison's son, Christopher, Peter 'Dougal' Butler and John 'Wiggy' Wolff. All of them, of course, are bound together by the man they are today remembering, Alison's first love and Christopher's father.

Sixteen years gone, John Entwistle's presence is almost tangible here, at one end of this tucked-away, tree-lined nook in another chocolate-box Cotswolds town, and today of all days. Quarwood is just a twenty-minute drive to the east. At the front gates to the house are stationed two life-size bronze busts of Entwistle's and Alison's beloved Irish deerhounds, Jason and Hamish. Inside the house, Alison has arranged collections of furniture and ornaments once brought to Quarwood by a Harrods van of distinctive green. Unmistakable, Entwistle looms from out of the framed family portraits hung on walls and displayed on tables and cabinets.

Out on the patio, the conversation skitters back and forth through the years, the reminiscences tumbling on top of each other. 'Dougal' Butler tells of late-night runs to the Speakeasy in 1967, 1968, Entwistle squashed up in the passenger seat of Butler's Mini Cooper and out for a proper good time. For him to stick around and then drive home whichever girl Entwistle happened to charm that night, Butler would be on the promise of a free drink, maybe two, and a chicken-and-chips-in-a-basket meal.

'Wiggy' Wolff recalls piloting Entwistle and Keith Moon back to London from a trip up north in their Bentley. They pulled off the M1 into a Blue Boar services where, just as soon as you like, sniggers Wolff, Entwistle and Moon 'had picked up two chicks. One pair of them settled in the front seat and the other pair in the back. As knickers were rabidly got off, there was a great scream and a shout . . . "Fucking hell – she's got a wooden leg!" One of the girls had indeed got a false leg. John sat bolt upright and demanded, "Let's get out of here!" With that, the girls were thrown out on to the tarmac of the Blue Boar parking lot and I went speeding off down the motorway.'

The last time that the five of them were together in the same place was on Thursday, 24 October 2002. That was for the occasion of Entwistle's memorial service at the church of St Martin's in the Field on Trafalgar Square. Bill Curbishley, John Hurt and Steve Luongo gave the eulogies that day. Roger Daltrey sang 'Boris the Spider', accompanied by Simon Townshend on guitar. Christopher had 'Too Late the Hero' played out to the congregation. Pete Townshend didn't show up. Afterwards, there was a reception at a hotel round the corner from the church. Once again, Lisa got drunk and caused a scene.

In the immediate aftermath of Entwistle's death, Lisa had gone on living her car-crash life at Quarwood. Sometimes, it bordered on farce. In February 2003, the now-defunct Sunday tabloid, the *News of the World*, ran a splash story claiming that Lisa was conducting an affair with a local vicar, the Reverend Colin Wilson. Not four months earlier, Wilson had officiated at Entwistle's funeral. 'That was probably the only story to appear in the *News of the World* that was absolutely, 100 per cent true,' insists Christopher.[42]

Most of the time, Lisa was just a mess. For a while, she continued to throw parties up at the house for her freeloading 'Gloucester set' of friends and hangers-on, and anyone else who could keep up with her. Christopher put a stop to such goings on when things started to go missing from the house – heirlooms and valuables. Entwistle's Will had split his estate equally between his son, his mother and Lisa, but Christopher was asked to oversee everything in Gloucestershire by John Cohen, a senior partner at Entwistle's solicitors, Clinton's, who were acting as his executors.

'Grandmother and I didn't trust Lisa,' Christopher says. 'So unbeknown to her, we had a security company come in and install cameras outside at Quarwood. They were focussed on the car port at the back of the house. Lisa and her friends would fill up the boot of her car with all kinds of stuff and we would watch them doing it. I also had keys to the car, so afterwards, I'd go down and put it all back. Dad left her a third of everything and we made sure she got just that.'

Eventually, Christopher had Lisa move out of the house and into one of the cottages on the grounds. By that point in 2004, Christopher had been forced to put Quarwood up for sale. His

---

[42] Colin Wilson denies having had an affair. He was, however, subsequently asked to resign his position as the local parish priest.

father's one-time employers, the Inland Revenue, had imposed prohibitive death duties on his estate. As a public figure, the Revenue decreed that everything that Entwistle had ever owned – Quarwood, his cars, his guitar collection and even his boots – had a value attached and that the British government was entitled to claim 40 per cent of that total amount. If what was assessed had not been paid within six months, interest also started to be charged on the lump sum. Quarwood was put on the market for £3.5 million and sold to a property developer. All of Entwistle's guitars had to go, too.

'Basically, we had to sell everything in six months,' says Christopher. 'To do that, we had to literally take Quarwood apart, because Dad had filled up every room in the place. That was a horrible experience. At one stage, the Revenue even wanted £100,000 for Dad's personalised car number plate. In the end, I talked them down to £25,000.'

Queenie Entwistle threw the last great party at Quarwood. A sad-happy occasion, it was a closing down bash for family and friends. The guests set about the last remnants of Entwistle's booze and then The Barracuda Inne was shuttered for good. Queenie was allowed to stay on in her Quarwood cottage. Christopher was a frequent visitor and, a couple of times a month, Alison and Bratby would drop by to take her out to lunch. Queenie slipped peacefully away on 4 March 2011 at eighty-eight having outlived her only son by nine years.

Following the Quarwood sale, Lisa moved back to Memphis. There, at a family member's house, she was found dead in bed on the evening of 6 March 2005. Lisa was forty-three and had overdosed on cocaine. Her relationship with the Entwistle family had stayed poisoned right up to the last. 'All of her friends told her that she could get more out of Dad's settlement, so she got lawyers involved,' explains Christopher. 'But no, she couldn't.

'There was one time that Lisa came to me about a ring that she wanted. She said that Dad had given it to her. Dad had gotten it inscribed with a symbol and I asked Lisa what it meant. She said that it was an eight and that it was Dad's lucky number. I pointed out to her that it was actually an eight on its side, which is an infinity symbol. It was Dad's engagement ring from Mother. He would never have given it to her, but that was the kind of person she was.'

■ ■ ■

Around the garden table on this sweltering July day, the talk goes on until the sun cools and then sets off to the west. At one point, Alison brings out her photo albums where are kept pictures of summers long past. One snapshot, bleached and faded now, captured Entwistle, Alison and the young Christopher standing together out on the lawn at Quarwood. It was taken on the afternoon of a summer fête in Stow and they are all done up in fancy dress.

Alison, kitted out as a Native American squaw, and Christopher, wearing a feathered head-dress and armed with a wooden rifle, both seem to have been happy to make do. Entwistle, though, completely inhabits his part as a gunslinger in a black Stetson, black frock coat, pinstripe trousers and pistol holster. He does not look up into the camera, but down and away from it, as if his eyes might give him away. Or else, it is that he is not really there at all, but gone off somewhere else altogether, to a place inside his own head.

Townshend and Daltrey have kept The Who going without him all these years. Both Alison and Christopher have lost touch with each of them, and stayed at a distance from the band as it is now. Not because they begrudge The Who's continued existence, but that to see the band separate from the man they loved would be too wrenching, too raw. Time has allowed the pain of their shared grief to recede to a dull ache, but not so that it will ever be gone. Alison still has her fly necklace in its box, the silver and emeralds perfectly preserved. Christopher has filled a downstairs room at his own home with his father's memorabilia. At Quarwood, they left behind a plaque, set into a stone wall out by the lawn, in loving memory to John Alec Entwistle, husband and father and, by the by, the last of the great rock stars.

'To me, he was just John,' says Alison. 'He was very generous, warm-hearted, a bit reckless, very, very talented and undervalued, I think. He was my boyfriend, my fiancé and then my husband. Then, he was horrible. But, you know, you forgive all of that. Death is quite a closure. He was a very silly boy, but I loved him for years and years, and I didn't stop loving him.'

The next morning, tucked away in one of the notebooks that Entwistle used to jot down his memoirs, I find another scrap of paper. On it, he had scribbled out lyrics for a song that he would never get around to recording. His handwriting seems hurried, impatient, as if he had to get the words down on paper before he forgot them. He had called the song 'She Ain't My Kinda Girl (Big Girls Always Make Me Cry)' and he wrote out just one verse. It reads:

'I woke up here this morning, 'n' I don't know where I am.
There's a cigarette hole burned thru the bed, 'bout as big as
    my hand.
This room's still spinnin' out of time with the world.
'N' by the size of that dress in the wardrobe, she ain't my
    kind of girl.
Big girls always make me cry; too big to get my arms around.
Not too pleasing on my eyes.
My head's too small for that big fat thumb, to push me down
    to size.'

Acknowledgements

This book simply would not have been possible without the following and I thank them, one and all, deeply and sincerely:

Representatives on Earth, Matthew Hamilton and Matthew Ellbonk; two fine gentlemen of publishing, Andreas Campomar and Ben Schafer; my ever-diligent editors, Claire Chesser and Jon Davies; those who went above and beyond, extending me help, counsel and their hospitality – Bernard Axtell, Mike Brown, Ian Gillingham, Peter 'Dougal' Butler, Steve Luongo, Neil Storey, Ross Halfin, 'Irish' Jack Lyons, Mark Blake and Chris Charlesworth; those others kind enough to share with me their time and memories – Bill Curbishley, Maxene Harlow, Glyn Johns, Richard Cole, Keith Altham, Joe Walsh, Shel Talmy, Jon Astley, Joe Vitale, Steve 'Boltz' Bolton, John Alcock, Al Kooper, Rod Argent, Dave Davies, Vernon Brewer, Alan Edwards, Randy Bachman, Gered Mankowitz, Bob Pridden, Andy Fairweather Low, Andy Nye, Tim Gorman, John 'Wiggy' Wolff, Gordon Cotton, Godfrey Townsend, Peter Noone, Joe Lynn-Turner, Laurie Luongo, Tony Klinger, Henry Small, Mickey Wynne, Doreen Chanter and Richard Barnes; to Sian Llewellyn at *Classic*

Rock for allowing me the starting point; and Robert Rosenberg at Trinifold for providing me with a map; for inspiration, sustenance and welcome distraction – Fiscavaig Bay, the Taigh Ailean Hotel, the Glenview Pie Café and Shilasdair Yarns, the Bog Myrtle Bookshop and Café, the Skye Bakery, the Black and Red Cuillin, North-West Skye FC, Carbost FC and the Thursday Night Elite; as always, the Rees clan; and most especially, for putting up with me, propping me up and their unfailing encouragement, and with all the love in the world – Denise, Tom and Charlie.

To Chris Entwistle, Alison Entwistle and Mick Bratby, a thousand thanks aren't enough, and the rest is more than I can say, but I hope that I've done justice to The Ox.

And the last, loudest words belong to John Alec Entwistle – for the gold mine of his own words and for the story that I was gifted to tell.

Selected Bibliography

Before I Get Old: the Story of The Who by Dave Marsh, Plexus (1983)

The Who: Maximum R&B by Richard Barnes, Plexus (2000)

Who I Am by Pete Townshend, Harper (2012)

Dear Boy: the Life of Keith Moon by Tony Fletcher, Omnibus (2005)

Thanks a Lot, Mr Kibblewhite: My Life by Roger Daltrey, Blink (2018)

Pretend You're in a War: The Who and the Sixties by Mark Blake, Aurum Press (2014)

Anyway, Anyhow, Anywhere: the Complete Chronicle of The Who 1958–1978 by Andy Neill and Matt Kent, Virgin Books (2005)

Twilight of the Gods: My Adventures with The Who by Tony Klinger, John Blake (2009)

The Kids Are Alright booklet notes by Brian Cady, Pioneer Home Video (2003)

Let the Good Times Roll: My Life in the Small Faces, the Faces and The Who by Kenney Jones, Blink (2018)

Sound Man: A Life Recording Hits with the Rolling Stones, the Who, Led Zeppelin, the Eagles, Eric Clapton, the Faces . . . by Glyn Johns, Plume (2014)

Waiting for the Sun: A Rock 'n' Roll History of Los Angeles by Barney Hoskyns, Backbeat (2009)

Mod: from Bepop to Britpop, Britain's Biggest Youth Movement by Richard Weight, Vintage (2015)

White Heat: A History of Britain in the Swinging Sixties by Dominic Sandbrook, Abacus (2008)

Seasons in the Sun: the Battle for Britain 1974–1979 by Dominic Sandbrook, Penguin (2013)

1960s Britain by Susan Collins, Shire (2014)

1970s Britain by Jack Shepherd and John Shepherd, Shire (2016)

The archives of *Rolling Stone*, *NME*, *Melody Maker*, *Q* and *Mojo*, and the ever-wondrous portal that is *rocksbackpages.com*

The Entwistle family archive

The Kids Are Alright directed by Jeff Stein, New World Pictures (1979)

Amazing Journey: the Story of The Who directed by Murray Lerner, Spitfire Pictures (2007)

An Ox's Tale: the John Entwistle Story directed by Glenn Aveni and Steve Luongo, Act 1 Entertainment (2006)

Index

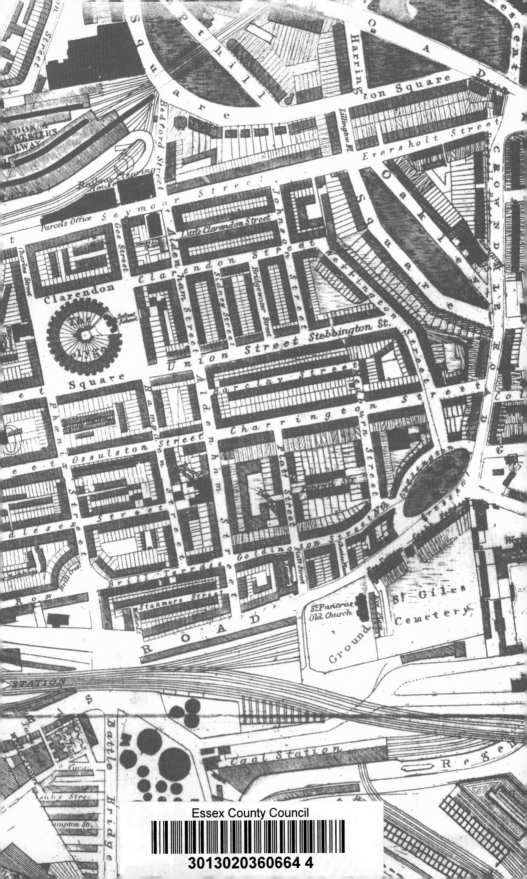

The Streets